D0231475

C800512979

ALESHA

ALESHA

Sean Smith

**SIMON &
SCHUSTER**

London · New York · Sydney · Toronto · New Delhi

A CBS COMPANY

First published in Great Britain by Simon & Schuster UK Ltd, 2012
A CBS COMPANY

1 3 5 7 9 10 8 6 4 2

Simon & Schuster UK Ltd
1st Floor
222 Gray's Inn Road
London WC1X 8HB

www.simonandschuster.co.uk

Simon & Schuster Australia, Sydney
Simon & Schuster India, New Delhi

A CIP catalogue for this book is available from the British Library.

ISBN: 978-1-47110-217-2 (Hardback)

Typeset by M Rules
Printed and bound by CPI Group (UK) Ltd, Croydon, CR0 4YY

To the Cardiff Nans, Margaret and Pat –

Putting a smile on the face of life

CONTENTS

PART FOUR: NATIONAL TREASURE

PART ONE

Alesha Harris

CHAPTER ONE

Daddy's Girl

Reality television is obsessed with 'the journey', the path that a contestant takes from an unpromising beginning to a glorious triumph. When the sixth series of *Britain's Got Talent* reached an unforgettable climax in May 2012, the most heart-warming and inspiring journey hadn't been undertaken by any of the eleven final acts but by the beautiful judge with the most famous laugh in the country, Alesha Dixon.

At the end of a programme watched by twelve million people, a delighted Simon Cowell turned to his panel of judges, Alesha, Amanda Holden and David Walliams, and said, 'A huge thank you to these guys. This has been my favourite year.'

All those viewers who tuned in to watch Ashleigh and Pudsey, her extraordinary dog, win the contest and heard Simon's comments would have had little idea of the obstacles and setbacks the happy and smiling Alesha had overcome to reach this position at the high table of British television. She had emerged from a world of poverty, violence and adultery that would have astonished a scriptwriter on *EastEnders*.

When Pudsey had finished what would be his winning routine, Alesha announced, 'I can't cope. This moment is too much.' She could have been talking about her own life, from her unpromising beginnings in Welwyn Garden City, where she was the poor kid in school, through her disastrous marriage to a black rapper, to the days when she was dubbed the most hated woman in the UK.

Yet she had survived and now here she was, starring on a block-buster TV show that, growing up, she could never have imagined appearing on, let alone judging. She didn't go to stage school or have lessons to prepare her for a life in entertainment. She wasn't in a Disney show or, closer to home, a series like *Byker Grove*, in which Ant and Dec, the hosts of *Britain's Got Talent*, launched their careers as teenagers.

Instead, she had to stop the few dance lessons she did take because her beloved mother, Beverley, could no longer afford them. When Alesha's group, Mis-Teeq, released their first album, *Lickin' On Both Sides*, in 2001, she dedicated it to her mum, declaring, 'I love you end-lessly.' She also revealed that she had watched Beverley struggle but her mother was now probably 'the most content, peaceful human being' and had taught Alesha the 'meaning of happiness'.

Mother and daughter hadn't always been happy. After Alesha's father left home, Beverley suffered an appalling experience as the victim of domestic abuse at the hands of a violent boyfriend. It would prove to be a defining event in her daughter's life. Alesha may have appeared happy on the outside but, as she would later admit, inside she was crying.

Alesha Anjanette Dixon was born on 7 October 1978 in Queen Elizabeth II Hospital, Welwyn Garden City. Her Jamaican-born father, Melvin Dixon, was a refrigeration engineer and her mother, Beverley Harris, worked as a hairdresser. Beverley already had a son called Mark from a previous relationship; he would be his younger sister's friend and protector as they grew up.

The new family of four settled into a council house in the Knightsfield area of the town, ten minutes from the town centre on the bus. Alesha's home was a terraced house in Sewells, a small and quiet cul-de-sac with just sixteen properties in it, and one of a network of neat and tidy streets that make the area popular with young families. It has the feel of a safe and friendly neighbourhood and was nothing like the high-rise sink estates of London, where so many of her future friends were brought up. Sewells was a class above.

The house was small and simply furnished with only two bedrooms, but the second bedroom was split into two to give Alesha some privacy as she grew up. Downstairs there was a lounge, kitchen and and a separate dining area that doubled as a playroom for the children. This was a pleasant place to live and, unsurprisingly, in later years – after her family had moved on – the house was taken into the private sector under the Right to Buy scheme. In 2007 it was sold for £200,000.

Alesha likes to joke that Welwyn Garden City is a town famous solely for the Shredded Wheat factory and as the birthplace of the golfer Nick Faldo, but she remains proud of her home town. Despite all her subsequent success, she still lives within a mile or two of where she was born and brought up. Alesha feels secure here in a strongly working-class community. She is almost bound to bump into someone she grew up with when she goes out to do the shopping or grabs an Indian take-away from the Bipash Tandoori, as she has always done. Best of all, from her point of view, she is just four miles away from her mother, Beverley.

Welwyn Garden City is perfect for families, particularly those with young children, who can enjoy the many green spaces and the little parades of shops that never seem to be more than a five-minute walk away. This was the point of the town.

Garden cities were the brainchild of one man, a social reformer called Sir Ebenezer Howard. He was appalled by the overcrowded slum conditions of Victorian London and decided to do something about it. He wanted to marry town and country together to create a new kind of life or 'civilization' as he grandly called it. He put his ideas into print in a book entitled *Tomorrow: A Peaceful Path to Real Reform*, which was published in 1898. By the time the book was reprinted four years later as *Garden Cities of Tomorrow*, his ideas for modern communities had been well received both at home and abroad. Howard founded a private company to begin work on the first garden city on a site at Letchworth in Hertfordshire in 1903.

He didn't want Letchworth to be seen as a one-off experiment and spotted an ideal piece of rural land for his next project while gazing out of the window of a train. He formed another company and bought the land at auction. Work began on Welwyn Garden City in the 1920s. From nothing, the town's population has grown to more than 50,000. Many of the residents moved up from North London and the East End so that, in effect, the town became a new London borough. People who don't know Alesha's origins often assume she is a Londoner, as she sounds as if she has just stepped on to the set of *EastEnders* and is going for a drink in the Queen Vic.

Welwyn Garden City proved a popular location for industry, most notably the Shredded Wheat factory, which opened its Broadwater Road site in 1926. Sadly, the factory closed in 2008 but it is now a listed building and remains an iconic landmark. The attraction of the town for many American-owned companies was a workforce that was on their doorstep and could literally walk to work. Over the years the pleasant environment of Welwyn Garden City has been the inspiration for New Towns throughout the world.

The town may be pleasant and self-contained but local historian Tony Rook observed, 'Culturally the place is arid, and has never pro-duced a concert hall, viable art gallery, museum, or professional theatre.' You could add a cutting-edge dance school to that list.

Alesha's dad, Melvin, was a popular figure locally – one of the boys with an eye for the girls. At weekends, he was a rugged mid-fielder playing for the Hollybush Globetrotters in the town's Sunday soccer league. One of his old teammates from those days in the eighties observed that Melvin had a twinkle in his eye and the ladies liked him, 'He had nothing to be embarrassed about in the showers.'

The team coach, Pete Simpson, recalled, 'Melvin was a very good player. He was always jovial, with a smile on his face, even though he was a tough player. He would laugh at you if you were the "victim" of one of his tackles.'

All the matches were held at the local King George V Playing Fields. Families would come down to watch and then everyone would gather back at the Hollybush, a big old-fashioned boozer, for a well-earned pint before drifting home for Sunday lunch. Such occasions helped to promote the community spirit and family bonds that make Welwyn Garden City the town it is. Alesha is not alone in staying there when she had the means to move on.

Her parents weren't getting on though, and the atmosphere at home deteriorated to such an extent that they split up when Alesha was four. She admits, 'I don't have much memory of them together and given they are so different in character, I can't really imagine them together either.'

Melvin moved to a house in Cowper Road, two and a half miles away and close enough for him to pop in regularly to see his little girl. He joined another football team, the Welwyn Arsenal, based at the Oak Tavern, which would become his new pub and the one that remains his family's local.

He began another relationship and went on to have three more children – two boys, Jerome and Callum, and a girl, Leyanne. As a result, Alesha grew up with a warren of siblings and cousins, aunts and uncles. Melvin's new partner, Catherine Gamble, was part of a well-known Welwyn family and Alesha had so many relations she could barely walk to the end of the road without bumping into a member of her extended family. One of them observed wryly, 'I can't get a handle on who's who in the family and I'm one of them.'

Alesha admits that she too finds it difficult to keep track and, as a little girl, used to draw a family tree to explain to people who asked how she was related to everyone, which she always found a little embarrassing. For a while she hated her 'dysfunctional' family. Secretly she longed for a normal, old-fashioned arrangement, the kind enjoyed by some of her closest friends and 'what I call the 2.4 family.'

Alesha was badly affected by her parents' split, acknowledging that it knocked her confidence. She was the sad little girl in tears, watching for her dad by the window. She adds, however, 'Despite not having him in my life on a day-to-day basis, I always felt a bit lucky (strange as it sounds), as I knew who and where my father was, even if he wasn't living with me.'

At first, her father was involved in Alesha's life but, understandably, she saw less of him as his new family grew. She observed, 'I didn't have much contact with my dad at all when I was little. My mum brought us up.' It was Beverley who, at night, would read her a story, so that even before she first went to school she was enjoying the Peter and Jane books. This early literacy series for children gave Alesha a love of books. She didn't spend her waking moments in front of the TV and these were the days before most households had a computer – not that the Harris family, as they were known, could have afforded one.

Melvin did once tell his daughter that he thought she should be an accountant when she grew up, which prompted her to go to school when she was five and announce it to be her ambition, even though she hated maths. Perhaps she was just trying to please her absent father. She observed, 'I was very much a daddy's girl, but going to visit Daddy and his new family was difficult.'

When she did spend time with him, he would naturally ask her how she was getting on in class: 'If I had top marks, he wouldn't say, "Well done", he'd say, "Oh, but you didn't get 100 per cent." He was a perfectionist.'

Even though she was close to all her siblings, she reveals, 'I was the only child from my parents' relationship so I've always felt quite on my own.' That feeling gave her a strongly independent streak:

'My mum says that I was the kind of child that if I couldn't tie my shoelaces and she offered to help, I'd say, "No, I'll do it."'

She coped with being an 'only child' by organizing her day-to-day life in careful detail. She told the *Mail on Sunday*, 'When I was a little girl, I'd write down my plans for the day, to the last minute. I'd go, "shower 8 a.m., dressed 8.15 a.m. . . ." I like to get up in the morning and have a plan, and know what I'm doing at any moment of the day.'

The next item on her schedule would have been breakfast before arriving at the Harwood Hill JMI and Nursery School at 8.45, in time for the first lesson of the morning, which was either maths or writing. The school was just two minutes' walk from the house in Sewells.

Alesha was a chatty and sociable little girl who got on well with the other children. 'She was always one of the popular girls,' observed one contemporary. She would join in at break time or after lunch when the favourite game was called 'semis', which involved a lot of running around the netball court. One person was 'it' and the safe place to stay in the game was standing in one of the semicircles drawn on the court. Alesha excelled at this because she was a very fast runner. Sport, in general, was encouraged at Harwood Hill and Alesha loved afternoon PE, as well as netball, from an early age.

Performing was also a passion and dance classes from the age of five revealed that she had a flair for invention and choreography. Even as a little girl she would make up her own dances – something she continued to do when her mother could no longer afford the lessons. When the school put on an ecological stage musical, called *Yanomamo*, about the destruction of the Amazon rainforest and its effect on the oldest Indian tribe living there, the Yanomami, Alesha was allowed to devise her own contribution. One classmate still recalls her dance: 'It was very different and very vibrant.'

The subject matter says much for the forward thinking of Harwood Hill. Her classmate observed, 'In the afternoons there would be time for the term's topic work. There was no national cur-riculum then, so the teachers got to choose it. One year, I recall, it was "Victorians" and, another time, "Apartheid". It was a very right-on, sweet school.'

After school there was the walk home with Beverley and the chance to play on the swings and slides with her friends in the small park at the end of her street. It was a scene played out all over the country – young mothers chatting and putting the world to rights while keeping a watchful eye on their happy kids.

Strangely, Alesha has never talked about of her time at primary school or even mentioned it by name. Perhaps it is a painful reminder of a time in her life when her father was no longer there and she missed him. Only her elder brother Mark has laid bare the hardship of the ensuing years in the Harris household. Much later, when Alesha was famous, he spoke dramatically – perhaps overdra-matically – of scavenging for pieces of bread in the kitchen and frequent nights when they went to bed hungry because there was no food in the cupboard. He also described sharing their room with two other children, who moved in with one of his mother's boyfriends. They lived a squashed-up existence in single beds with no room to swing a cat.

Alesha doesn't dwell on a distressing childhood, preferring always to stress her parents' good points. The most she has ever admitted is that it was 'lively' and that 'there was always something happening in the house.' She is not a 'poor me' sort of person and learned to take care of herself as a child and keep the people she loved and trusted close by. Instead of weeping and wailing, her neighbours mostly remember her famous laugh. She's always had it and describes it as a cross between a crow and the chuckle of Sid James, the star of so many *Carry On* films. One neighbour said, 'You could hear her in the garden laughing away the moment you turned into the street.' It was a laugh that always got her noticed.

The positive effect of becoming part of a single-parent family was the unbreakable bond Alesha formed with her vivacious, young-at-heart mother. She also became closer to her grandmothers, Beverley's mum Maureen and Melvin's Jamaican mother Clem. The latter would cook her young granddaughter the most delicious Caribbean meals, including salt fish and goat curry, which have remained her favourite dishes ever since.

Her father too was talented in the kitchen and he would take over cooking duties on the occasions when there was a family Sunday lunch: 'My dad's Sunday roast is amazing. He really experiments with cooking and seasons up the chicken the night before. And his roast potatoes are the best in the world.'

CHAPTER TWO

Don't Hit My Mum

Alesha was eight years old when she came home after school to find her mum sporting a nasty black eye. She instantly knew that her mother's current partner was to blame. She and her brother Mark would sit on the stairs in the evening, worried for their mum as they listened to the rows being played out downstairs. She could see Beverley trying to hide the bruises the next morning. But this was different: 'I kind of knew how it had happened so that couldn't have been the first time . . . and she said she fell and she banged her head on the cupboard . . . I knew straight away that it was her partner that had done that to her, so there must have been incidents before that, but that one always stands out because of the fact that it was so obvious and the fact that she gave me this blatant lie.'

There was nothing she could do. She was just a frightened little girl. Mark was only ten and the two children had to carry this burden around with them every day. More than twenty years would pass before they felt able to talk about their ordeal and the dreadful things that had happened to their mum. The image of the black eye stayed with Alesha because of her mum's desperate and futile attempt to keep the truth from her son and daughter, but it wasn't the worst violence Beverley suffered.

The abuse had been going on for a couple of years when one

evening she was beaten up in the street while her children looked on helplessly. Alesha would describe the event in heartbreaking detail for a BBC documentary called *Don't Hit My Mum*. She recalled her mum running out of their home pursued by her partner: 'She was crying and running out the house and my brother and I was sort of like pushed back and then he chased my mum down the road and I was thinking "run for your life, just keep running" and hoping that my mum would get away. But he caught her and started attacking her on the side of the street in front of us. That's my worst memory. I think that is the image that I have always carried.'

Her brother recalls the same incident, although he remembers it slightly differently, saying that they were watching the assault from a window. He told the *News of the World*: 'The guy started to attack her as she legged it out the house. I'll never forget seeing her running down the street, him leaping on her and breaking her ribs with the force of his body weight. We were screaming at him to get off our mum. That time she ended up going to hospital, but the guy didn't leave and the violence just continued.'

The next day Alesha had to drag herself the couple of streets to primary school and pretend to be the happy-go-lucky, smiling little girl that everyone thought they knew. She admits putting on a brave front when she was actually 'quite scared of everything'.

Alesha and Mark were too young to be able to stand up to this bully. She explained the feeling of helplessness: 'You feel weak, you feel useless, like you can't do anything.' Instead, after school, the brother and sister would scramble out of an upstairs window and sit on top of the gable at the front of the house and stare out at the street. Mark recalled, 'We would huddle together and secretly slag him off behind his back. It was our way of fighting him.'

By the time Alesha was ready to follow her older brother to Monk's Walk School, her mother had found the strength to split from her abuser. Mark revealed that eventually the police became involved and 'he was told never to come round to the house again.'

Alesha seized the opportunity to tell the man what she really thought of him: 'She didn't hold back and the rows got really heated although the guy never got physical.'

Neither Alesha nor Mark has ever named the man responsible for the assaults on their mother, although it must be an open secret in the very small world of Welwyn Garden City. Perhaps they were both sparing Beverley's feelings.

Amateur psychologists would have an opinion about the traumatic effect her mother's abuse had on Alesha. She herself talks of the frustration she felt at having to let it happen because she wasn't old enough or strong enough to do anything. As an adult, she would recognize that this frustration in other youngsters facing the same problem could lead to aggression and anger. She hopes she didn't follow that example: 'I would hate to think that I was ever aggressive towards other people but it definitely made me quite insecure.'

Looking back at her emotions then, she admitted, 'I would say that both my brother and I would carry a lot of aggression within us and I do think we did probably handle things differently but we were carrying the same feeling.'

Mark's aggression, if that is the right description, was channelled into fiercely protecting his sister at school. She recalled that he went 'berserk' when she was called a racist name. He didn't hear it directly from her but news of the unpleasantness spread rapidly around the school and her brother acted swiftly to sort out the culprit. Alesha recalls, 'I remember my brother actually having someone up by the neck outside the headmaster's office and dropping him on the floor.'

Experiencing some racism was almost inevitable for Alesha because she was one of a handful of black students in a large, mostly white, working-class school but for the most part it was what Alesha would later describe as 'mild' abuse: 'It was rude, but what could you do?'

A product of Alesha's outrage at what had happened to her mother, combined with the right-on approach of her early schooling, was a keenly developed sense of social injustice. She acknowledged, 'I believe every child has the right to grow up in an environment where they feel secure and fearless going into the world and I suppose I didn't feel that myself.' As a successful adult, Alesha would embrace more than her fair share of good causes, particularly those supporting women who are the victims of domestic violence.

Nobody at her primary school knew the problems Alesha faced at home. And the same was true later at Monk's Walk, where outwardly she appeared confident and extrovert. She admitted, 'I was pretending to be really confident, pretending to be really hard so nobody would pick on me.'

Alesha loved to sing. It's what her school friends remember most about her. She would sing going in to class and on her way home. She walked everywhere around the streets of her home town, trying to sound like her favourite artists, Michael and Janet Jackson, Diana Ross or Salt-N-Pepa, one of the pioneers of the American hip-hop scene in the late eighties. The very first record she bought with some birthday money was 'Push It', a huge hit for the all-girl trio in 1988. There wasn't much more to practise than 'Ooh baby, baby', but that didn't matter to a schoolgirl.

Secondary school was a fresh start for Alesha Harris, as she was known then. The family moved from Sewells, half a mile away to a bigger council property on a street called Ingles. The road itself was busier and was used as a cut-through by traffic but, conveniently, the Co-op was only fifty yards away. Her mother would continue to live in the street and shop locally long after Alesha had become successful and rich. The house had an extra bedroom so, generally, the family had more space to breathe. After her traumatic experience with her last boyfriend, Beverley found a new strength in her spirituality and began to show the serenity that her daughter continues to admire. She became a born-again Christian.

Monk's Walk School was a substantial change from the cosy local primary that Alesha had been attending for seven years. The sprawling aspect of the school reflects the nature of Welwyn Garden City itself. It's easy to understand why she was grateful for the protective presence of her elder brother. It was also reassuring that many other pupils from Harwood Hill had made the one-mile trip across to their senior school.

The school's motto is '*Vel Optima Cuique Praebere*', which doesn't exactly trip off the tongue. It means 'Excellence For All' – the sort of sentiment schools always promote but which, in recent times, Monk's Walk has gone some way to achieving with its best-ever exam results and a glowing Ofsted report in 2011.

The school uniform hasn't changed since Alesha's time: a navy blue sweatshirt worn over a white shirt with a black skirt or trousers. The advantage of a simple uniform is that everyone looks the same whatever their financial circumstances.

Beverley was struggling to bring up her children on benefits. Alesha now had a younger brother, John, who was born in July 1987. There was very little money around. As a result, Alesha recognized that she was the 'poor child in school'. She was the only person she knew whose family couldn't afford a telephone at home. Most of the time she accepted the situation; as she grew older it became more of a problem when boys asked for her number and she had to tell them she didn't have a phone. She laughs, 'They thought I was lying.'

She listened to what her mother told her: 'Them sort of things didn't bother me 'cos my mum would say, "You don't realize you are so rich. You have love, you have a home, you have food and there's clothes on your back." There are people in the world who are suffering who don't have that and I think it is really important to be happy without material things.'

It may seem a corny view in a materialistic age but it was an ideal that mother and daughter shared. Beverley never lost the respect of her daughter. On the contrary, Alesha admired her strength and courage in removing herself from her violent relationship and her subsequent efforts to do her best for her children. She maintains loyally, 'I didn't have a perfect childhood but it was still a great one – and I don't want anyone to think different. Mum always supported me and wanted me to be happy. I thank her for her absolute love.'

While she may not have had a pair of Levi 501s to wear like her friends did, she was the most vivacious of her group. She was even showing early signs of becoming a diva, as she demonstrated her dancing talents to the rest of the school.

At this stage of her life she didn't have an all-consuming ambition to be a star or to carve out a career as a performer. She wanted something dependable, even a little more respectable. Her father, whom she still was not especially close to, would have settled for her becoming a teacher.

She was bright enough academically but she continued to shine in the sports arena. She represented her age group in the 200 metres and 4 x 100 metre relay for Hertfordshire, and her hard-up mother always made sure that Alesha had the best trainers for running that she could afford. Alesha also excelled at gymnastics. She was so good that she was roped in to help coach the younger girls, including the children who used to be her next-door neighbours in Sewells, Sarah and Angela Reeve. Alesha had always been kind to the sisters – perhaps missing the fact that she didn't have a female sibling at home.

When she was younger she would often poke her head around the door of the Reeve family home and ask their mother, Sandra, if it was all right for her to take the youngest, Angela, to the park at the end of the street. Mrs Reeve, who was a teacher at Harwood Hill, would always agree. She recalls, 'I trusted Alesha. It was as simple as that.'

Alesha's three best friends at school were Paula Marshall, Tracy Brown and Victoria Skeggs and she remains close to them. Alesha didn't have a huge circle of friends but her winning smile led to her being accepted easily. Intriguingly, one teacher wondered shrewdly whether the big and ready smile was in fact a nervous one. Alesha's fellow teenagers didn't notice. One classmate, Natalie Lincoln, observes, 'Alesha always appeared to be a happy girl at school. She was very slim and used to wear her hair tied back. She was very pretty, not really any different to how she is now on television.' Everyone, it seemed, liked Alesha, so it's perhaps a little reassuring to learn that she was a bossyboots at school and could get into a dreadful temper sometimes.

One of the best criteria for judging how well a pupil did at school or how much they enjoyed their time there is whether they ever return. Alesha went back in 2009 with her friend the presenter and DJ Fearne Cotton, for an episode of her series entitled *Fearne and . . . Alesha Dixon*. They met the deputy head, Mr Kelly, who was one of the most popular teachers when Alesha attended. He said, 'Alesha was an absolute star.'

More interesting, however, was his revelation that he could remember Alesha 'having her strops' and 'diva moments'. He recalled Alesha getting upset when she was in the school hall rehearsing the dances she had choreographed: 'I remember the dance not going to your satisfaction and the tears and strops that followed.' Alesha seemed genuinely surprised she had behaved that way. Mr Kelly added, 'You were demanding two hundred per cent of yourself.'

She loved singing and dancing and was probably the best dancer in the school. She didn't foresee a career in show business, although she does confess to being inspired watching *Top of the Pops* one evening when she was ten and seeing Neneh Cherry perform her ground-breaking single 'Buffalo Stance': 'I remember turning to my mum and saying, "She looks like me!" I had never seen a mixed-race singer from the UK before her – it was important to have someone like her that I could identify with as a kid.'

Her reaction was nothing more than the secret dream of a young girl, the sort of wishful fantasy that swells the queues to audition for *The X Factor* every season. One afternoon after leaving school, however, Alesha was walking down a street in London's Earls Court after she'd been to the Exhibition Centre when she was handed a flyer for a street dancing class. It's the sort of thing that happens to Londoners a hundred times a day and few of the flyers are ever read properly before they are thrown in the nearest bin. But Alesha did read hers and thought it sounded something worth trying, so she popped it in her handbag. It was a decision that would change her life forever.

CHAPTER THREE

Discovered

Everybody needs a slice of luck to get started in the music business. Alesha Dixon was a teenager from Welwyn Garden City with no family background in entertainment and no prospect of a breakthrough. In any case, her career path had been mapped out for her – she was going to be a PE teacher and was set to go to Loughborough, the renowned sports university in Leicestershire. A degree from there would have been the best possible start. She was restless, however, and looking for a bit more excitement in her life.

The flyer she'd been handed was for a special deal on a class at Danceworks just off Oxford Street. She was hesitant about going because she wasn't confident away from her home environment. It took a while for her to phone up to get the details and then she had to borrow the train fare from her mother, who was still struggling to make ends meet. She recalled, 'She gave me her last few pounds to get a train to go to the class.'

Alesha was a nervous young woman in those days. She wasn't that keen on getting the train down to King's Cross. She explained, 'I was quite scared of everything – even to go on the train to London, just scared to pick up the phone and make an enquiry. I had a lot of fears and I wonder if it was because of not having a sense of security as a child.'

She made it to the dance studios in Balderton Street, however. They were among the best-known in London and the place where Victoria Beckham, Mel B and Melanie C had auditioned for the girl group that would become the Spice Girls. Alesha had no idea that she too would, in effect, be auditioning when she attended the class because she was being watched by a woman on the lookout for bright new black talent.

Louise Porter discovered Alesha Dixon that afternoon. She had identified a gap in the market for a British R & B girl group. Surprisingly for a woman so absorbed in R & B culture, Louise was originally a classically trained 'Charlotte Church' type of singer from Cardiff who had moved to London at eighteen to pursue a career in music as a singer-songwriter. She was signed by EMI in 1978, the year Alesha was born, so she'd had a huge amount of experience by the time she first met the girl from Welwyn Garden City.

As a songwriter, Louise had initial success teaming up with George Duke, the Grammy Award-winning American producer behind such classic tracks as 'Let's Hear It For The Boy' by Deniece Williams and 'On The Wings Of Love' by Jeffrey Osborne. Louise also worked with the smooth soul star Alexander O'Neal, one of the biggest vocalists of the eighties, whose 1987 hit 'Criticize' became one of the most familiar sounds of the post-disco decade.

Louise moved more into the R & B sector when she met an ambitious young producer called David Brant from Harlesden in North London. They decided to join forces when Louise was offered a deal with indie music publisher Reverb Music: 'I asked them if they would also sign Brant and they said yes. We received an advance to get a studio together. We started writing and at the same time I started putting together girl groups who would record the songs we wrote and produced.'

This aim was very important to Alesha's future career because Louise had discovered and developed a girl group before they had even met. The band in question was called N-Tyce – not to be confused with the American rapper of the same name. The four girls had a burst of success in 1997, beginning with 'Hey DJ! (Play That Song)'. Louise had signed them to her production company Big Out Ltd and secured a deal with Telstar Records. Their follow-up song, 'We Come To Party', was their biggest hit, reaching number twelve in September 1997, which was respectable but wouldn't give the Spice Girls anything to worry about.

Their sound was quite bland and the rapping came across as more college musical than street. They had four top forty singles but their debut album, *All Day Every Day*, which was released in August 1998, was a flop, only making number forty-four in the album chart. They had hoped for a breakthrough in the US and signed a deal with Sony, but only one single was released there before the girls split up. In retrospect they needed more of an edge to take them above the pleasant enough dance music that was so popular at the time. By then Louise and David Brant had already parted company with the girls in circumstances that were never properly explained. David recalled, 'We both got bumped off the project for political reasons, which pissed me off.'

Louise Porter had already seen the future as far as she was concerned. She had been intending to take six months off to recharge her batteries after the 'full-on work' breaking N-Tyce into a crowded and competitive music scene: 'But when I saw Alesha at that dance class, I couldn't resist her. I thought she had a lot of potential. I could see it just from her dancing. I built Mis-Teeq around Alesha. She was just a young woman attending a dance class. She wasn't a singer, songwriter or MC at the time.'

Louise was going on instinct backed by twenty years of experience. She approached Alesha on the spot, told her she liked the way she moved and asked if she could sing. She told her that she was putting a girl group together and wondered if she would be interested. It wasn't Louise's style to promote herself as if she were selling a second-hand car but Alesha had heard of N-Tyce and was sufficiently impressed to take Louise's card and promised to call her when she'd thought about it.

On the way home she was excited about what had happened when, in a bizarre twist, she was approached for the second time in one day. Another woman spoke to her on the train and wanted to sign her up for a girl group. When Alesha reached home, she couldn't wait to tell her mother what had happened. She ran through the door shouting, 'Mum, I think the universe is trying to tell me something!'

She decided to call Louise Porter back and so began the gradual blossoming of her talents. Louise explained, 'The first step was to train her properly in singing and writing songs and I asked her to learn to MC, which she embraced. I find it easier to teach other girls to sing and to write songs from a female perspective.'

Louise told Alesha that it would be a long, hard process to train to be ready. In some ways it would be just like doing a college course for three years to gain the right qualification. Before she could devote herself to music, however, Alesha had to convince her fiercest critic, her father, that it was a good idea to abandon her safer career path. He had dreamed of his talented daughter becoming an accountant or even a stockbroker, although he would certainly have settled for a PE teacher. He was particularly concerned that the colour of her skin might be a drawback in music.

Alesha recalled that he told her, 'I understand that you love singing, but you have to look at the market, and there aren't many successful British black artists.' She remembered replying, 'I can't make my decisions in life based on other people's successes and failures.'

Her dad's concerns made her even more determined to succeed: 'He helped me because I was like "I will be successful as a black female". My dad created the ambition in me.'

While Melvin had misgivings, he had unwittingly influenced her choice by taking her to the Notting Hill Carnival when she was younger. She loved the smells and the sounds of the famous annual event in West London and observed, 'All the dancehall records I saved up to buy, like Shabba Ranks and Buju Banton – I heard them at Notting Hill.' The former was a cult Jamaican DJ before reaching a wider audience with his 1992 hit 'Mr. Loverman', which featured his trademark cry, 'Shabba!' Buju Banton is one of the most controversial and popular Jamaican artists of recent times with a string of bestselling dancehall albums. In 2011 he was sentenced by a Florida court to ten years in jail for drug trafficking and firearms offences.

Alesha had moved on from childhood favourites like Diana Ross, Michael Jackson and Madonna. The artist who influenced her most as an older teenager was Lauryn Hill of The Fugees. Lauryn was only three years older than Alesha but had already achieved so much. She was born in South Orange, New Jersey, part of New York City commuter territory. Her father was a computer programmer and her mother a high school teacher, but they were both very musical and encouraged their children's talents. Lauryn met a Haitian boy, Prakazrel Michel, known as Pras, in high school and he introduced her to his cousin, Wyclef Jean. Together they formed a band called The Rap Translators, which would become the world-famous Fugees, short for refugees, by the time they released their first album, *Blunted on Reality*, in 1994. Their second, *The Score*, became one of the best-loved hip-hop albums of all time and brought international fame. Their version of the classic ballad 'Killing Me Softly', with Lauryn on lead vocal, went to number one in the UK and was the biggest-selling single of 1996, the year Alesha turned eighteen.

The opportunities around Welwyn Garden City to learn to MC were limited but fortunately Alesha could turn to her father's brother, Uncle Leroy, for some guidance. He helped get her started by showing her how to think up rhymes after she told him about her plans at a family party. She never forgot his encouragement: 'He inspired me but I found it hard to take myself seriously. I thought people would laugh at me.'

She took every opportunity to grab the microphone at parties and local clubs, although her initial efforts wouldn't have had the leading male rappers quaking at the female competition. Even though she was nervous, she found these early days exhilarating, especially when she put on her best short dress and took to the stage on a Friday night at Pulse, the town's most popular club at the time. One of the DJs recalls, 'She was very popular – just the girl next door to many of the kids there.'

Alesha admits that her raps then were cheesy to say the least. She told the *Daily Telegraph*: 'I had this one lyric I would do: "You're nicer than the chicken and the rice and the gravy. You're so damn lovely, I'll be your wife and I'll have your babies."'

Part of Louise Porter's strategy was to remain resolutely in the background and let her artists take the credit for their success. She clearly thought it was counterproductive to let the public think the group had been put together in a clinical fashion like the Spice Girls. It didn't suit an urban or garage image to be manufactured in any way.

Louise was prepared to back her judgement with her own money. She paid for the rehearsal time and, subsequently, the recording sessions that would be needed to attract the right deal. She hired choreographers to work with Alesha but did most of the vocal coaching herself.

The accepted history of Mis-Teeq is that Alesha met Sabrina Washington by chance at a class at another dance studio called Dance Attic off the Fulham Road. In fact, Sabrina was already in a rap duo called 4 By 4, who had won a talent contest at the Mean Fiddler in her home patch of Harlesden in North London, when she answered a magazine ad that Louise had placed asking for fresh young black talent interested in joining her production company. It was always assumed that Alesha was the rapper and Sabrina the singer but that isn't how it was at first.

Louise has only ever given one interview about her work – to the online site *HitQuarters*, where people serious about music exchange information and ideas and pay a subscription to belong. She told them, 'Sabrina started off as a rapper. I auditioned her and her partner. I told Sabrina that she was fantastic, but her partner wasn't what I was looking for.' It was a bit like one of those Simon Cowell moments on TV when he tells one half of a duo to ditch the other. Sabrina was prepared to do it. Louise added, 'Luckily she called me and came down to sing for me and Alesha, and we snapped her up.'

Alesha, it was clear, was the Gary Barlow of the arrangement and the one who, in Louise's eyes, would be the central figure of the band when it was finally formed. For the moment, Alesha and Sabrina were a duo and they would travel three times a week to Dance Attic to rehearse and improve so that they would be ready when Louise went knocking on record companies' doors.

Sabrina, who is three weeks younger than Alesha, was originally from Gravesend in Kent but was brought up in a musical family in the same neighbourhood as David Brant, whom Louise brought in to help develop the girls' songwriting abilities. Her father was in a reggae band with Buju Banton, who featured large in Alesha's record collection.

She too had taken her education seriously, and her parents had originally hoped that she would have a career in the law. She trained as a dental hygienist before deciding that music was where her future lay.

Rather like the Spice Girls, the two girls were bright and forceful personalities, full of life and energy, who formed an instant bond through their mutual ambition – a desire to make it and an intention to work as hard as necessary to accomplish that aim. They would be seeing a great deal of one another over the coming years so it was important that they enjoyed each other's company. The problem, as is so often the case with bands, particularly female ones, would be how they got on once they had achieved some success and were no longer driven by a shared ambition.

Three times a week Alesha, dressed in old jeans and trainers, would take the train from the centre of Welwyn Garden City to King's Cross Station, then catch the Tube to Fulham Broadway and walk a couple of minutes to the Dance Attic Studios in North End Road. It became a routine, as if she were commuting into Central London for a job. It required a certain dedication, as the journey took at least an hour and a half door to door.

Louise Porter was making sure the girls practised hard and started organizing personal appearances at clubs. At one show in Earls Court she thought the time was right for Alesha Dixon, her chosen professional name, to put her MC talents to the test. She wasn't keen. Sabrina recalled, 'She said, "Don't let me go up there and make myself look stupid, Bri!"'

At that time in British music a female MC was a novelty but Alesha's husky rap style received a good response. She recalled, 'The feedback was good and so I started taking it more seriously.' The crucial thing was that it gave the girls something different to offer record companies in the future.

Mostly, though, their time was spent rehearsing and training. On the way home from dance practice, Alesha liked nothing better than to pop into her favourite bar, The Cottage, which was just a couple of hundred metres from the train station in Church Road. Sometimes Sabrina would join her if they had plans to go on to a club later.

Alesha was a demon at pool. Most of the large pubs in Welwyn Garden City had tables, so you could usually get a game. Her dad was a good player and he had taught her the basics. Often her old friends from Monk's Walk would join her for a drink. One of her group recalls how she was impossible to shift once she had control of the table.

'It was funny. She would put her money down and win her game. Then these guys used to put their pound down on the side for the next game or the one after that and she would always beat them. They weren't too happy about it. They could never get control of the table from her.'

The major drawback to this comfortable routine was that Alesha didn't have any money and couldn't borrow from her mum because she didn't have any either. She tried dodging the train fare a few times but that was far too risky to become a long-term habit: 'I used to bunk trains sometimes. It wasn't very nice but I was just determined to get to London to do what I wanted to do.' A better idea was to look for part-time work that would bring in some cash and still be flexible enough to allow her to continue her training with Louise.

She found the perfect job working as a cashier at the Ladbrokes shop in Woodhall Parade. It was a two-mile walk from home but all the dancing was keeping Alesha very fit. The bonus of the job was that the shifts were flexible and easy to organize around her trips to London. Alesha was also well paid for a job that needed no qualifications – she was earning about £10 an hour. The drawback was that those were the days when smoking was allowed and at the end of a shift Alesha's clothes would stink. She hates cigarette smoke and found the small shop very 'smoky and stuffy'. For that reason, she would describe working in a bookie's as her worst job when she was asked ten years later.

This particular branch of Ladbrokes was very much a local meeting place and Alesha soon got to know the regular customers. Betting shops were not yet digital, so she had to punch in all the bets manually and the manager, Jamie Button, would settle the winners and losers at a separate table. Jamie had also been brought up locally and was a popular and friendly figure in the town.

Besides taking the bets, Alesha put up the advertising posters and wrote the day's special offers on a whiteboard. She also had to go out onto the floor to tidy the shop; she put all the pens back in their racks, swept the hundreds of scrunched-up losing bets off the tables and emptied the ashtrays. Alesha likes everything clean and neat – her friends call her Monica after the character in *Friends* who was fixated on cleaning – so it was all she could do to stop herself taking a mop to the floor of the betting shop. Sometimes after work she and Jamie would head off for a drink at The Cottage or he would go and support her when she was MCing locally.

Most often after work, though, she would run into the arms of her famous boyfriend waiting patiently outside.

CHAPTER FOUR

Damage Control

The struggle to the top is always an attractive story in pop – as millions of viewers of *The X Factor* know only too well. Every contestant seems to have a back story to bring a tear to the eye. Alesha had that too, but she was determined to keep the more traumatic aspects of her childhood well hidden from public scrutiny. Her mother's agony was in the past but never forgotten, and at this stage of her life she certainly didn't want it paraded for general entertainment.

The abuse wasn't the only family secret that Alesha preferred to keep close. Her youngest brother, Callum, who was born when she was seventeen, was diagnosed with cerebral palsy. He has spent his life in a wheelchair being cared for by his devoted mother, Catherine Gamble. Alesha is full of admiration for her father's partner, who is perhaps second only to her mother in the esteem in which she is held. She wrote in her personal thanks for *Lickin' On Both Sides*: 'Lots of love to Catherine and to the rest of the Gamble family – I love you all!'

Callum's condition is one of the major reasons why Alesha still lives close to where she was brought up. Cerebral palsy is an umbrella term for a number of neurological conditions that can affect a child's brain and is usually caused before birth. The damage to the brain affects the ability to control movement.

Alesha, out of respect for her family, has never spoken of her brother's condition, except in 2009, when she became an ambassador for the Variety Club, the show business charity that takes sick, disabled and disadvantaged children on day trips, and provides wheelchairs and other life-enhancing equipment to make things easier for families.

She observed, 'I've seen first-hand how difficult it is for parents to have disabled children and the effects of having a disabled sibling. I know how difficult it can be for parents, dealing not only with the physical difficulties of having a disadvantaged child, but also the emotional side of it.

'My little brother realized, when he got older, that he couldn't do the same things other children can do. He has been on a trip with the Variety Club – when they do these fun things, whether it's going to the theatre, the seaside or whatever it might be. It takes their minds off things. They need that escapism, they need to feel like they're living and they're no different to anybody else.'

Perhaps understandably, Alesha seems from an early age to have developed a compulsive desire to keep her life secret. The image she portrays has always been of an open, smiling, happy young woman and she has seldom wavered from that. Only when she became a successful public figure who could make a difference has she spoken about the highly personal matters that have so affected her family. The secrecy has spilled over into every aspect of her life.

She certainly didn't want the public to know that she was the girlfriend of a member of one of the most famous boy bands in the country. Incredibly, she managed to keep her relationship with Noel Simpson of Damage, her first serious love, entirely hidden for nearly fifteen years.

The image of Mis-Teeq was of talented girls struggling to make it. They religiously stuck with this story in interviews, making no mention of the financial support and musical expertise of Louise Porter or the input of her right-hand man David Brant. And that image would have had no credibility if everyone knew that at the end of Alesha's shift at Ladbrokes, Noel would be waiting patiently outside to pick her up. It would have been the dream of many a teenage girl to go out with someone in a boy band and Alesha was living it.

Damage were hugely popular in the late 1990s. In 1997 they were the first all-black band to feature on the cover of *Smash Hits* magazine, an edition that was the bestselling issue of the year. Three of them, Rahsaan Bromfield (known as Ras), Jade Jones and Noel, were students together at the Barbara Speake Stage School in Acton. Noel had struggled with dyslexia as a child so his parents had encouraged an education based more on physical expression than academic achievement. His father was also called Noel so his close friends and family always called him Junior.

Powerfully built and with a broad smile, Noel had ambitions to be the British version of Eddie Murphy, but when that looked unlikely, he developed his interest in music, listening to R. Kelly and Bobby Brown. 'Myself and Ras would always make up raps and come up with some choreography for school shows. There are videos of these floating around on the Internet and they need to be tracked down and destroyed.'

They recruited Jade when they were all sitting around one lunchtime and heard him hit the high note from 'If I Ever Fall In Love' by the American soul group Shai. They immediately realized he was a brilliant singer. The fourth member, Andrez Harriott, the son of Choice FM DJ Daddy Ernie, was at the Sylvia Young Theatre School when he and Jade appeared at the Old Vic together in the musical *Carmen Jones*. They found their fifth member, Coreé Richards, singing at a bus stop.

They were all fourteen and fifteen at the time and worked hard for three years before they found success. Their slice of luck occurred when Jay Kay from Jamiroquai heard them and volunteered to pay for the cost of their recording session and the subsequent demo tapes. They sent the song, a cover of Michael

Jackson's 'Anything', to Jazz Summers, one of the founders of Big Life Records. He signed up the boys in early 1995 but was in no hurry to rush out a record.

Instead, as Noel recalls, they toured small venues, the old way of securing a fan base before releasing a debut single: 'We started with a school tour, then a *Smash Hits* road show, an under-18s tour, the Birmingham Clothes Show, performing alongside other black bands like 5 Star and Ultimate Kaos.

'Maybe it's because we all came from performing arts backgrounds and had honed our skills over the years but I think we were more polished and professional than a lot of the other performers and we got an amazing reception wherever we went. We had all known each other for years and there was never any friction within the group. We were just so grateful to have the opportunity to perform in front of audiences. We were living the dream.'

By the time they released 'Anything' as their first single in July 1996, Damage were gaining a reputation for being one of the nicest bands in the business. The track reached only number sixty-eight in the charts, but these were not yet the days when record companies dropped an act after one poor sale: 'The label didn't force us to churn something out and then turn us away if it failed.'

That patience was rewarded when their next single, 'Love II Love', was much more successful, reaching number twelve in the charts and cementing their future. Noel recalls, 'It took us to a different level of success. It never felt like work. It was crazy. The girls were screaming wherever we went, asking for snotty tissues or eating our discarded apple cores.'

To celebrate their success, they threw a big family party at which their parents would be meeting for what they thought would be the first time – only for them to discover that they knew each other from the seventies and eighties when they were West Indian teenagers on the London music scene or had gone to school together.

Damage were touring the world but unusually never let success go to their heads. Instead, within the industry they were known to be polite and friendly, without resorting to being mean to others. Noel is too well mannered to say if Alesha asked him for a half-eaten apple core when they met but he now looks back fondly on his former girlfriend.

'From the moment I met Alesha, she was the way she is now: headstrong, beautiful, with an amazing heart. She would always stand up for what she believed was right. She was grounded and humble, and she hasn't changed.'

Noel gives much of the credit for Alesha's character to her mum Beverley, whom he always got along well with when they stopped for dinner at her home: 'Her mother always helped her keep her feet on the ground. She was a lovely woman.'

He would travel up to Welwyn Garden City whenever he could: 'I used to take taxis to see her, and charge them back to the label. Suddenly, they were like "hang on, you're taking these taxis out of London!" I was busted but it was good while it lasted! I used to wait outside of Ladbrokes for her to finish her shift and then we would go off together.' If they weren't going to see Beverley, then it would be back in the taxi and down to London for a night out at one of the fashionable underground clubs that Alesha enjoyed so much.

Damage were doing well. By the end of 1997 they had released three top ten singles, including a mellow cover version of Eric Clapton's 'Wonderful Tonight', which reached number three. All the songs were on their debut album, *Forever*.

The album was romantic and soulful, with more of the smooth harmonies of the American band Boyz II Men than the urban edge of The Fugees. As one critic wrote of the title track, 'This would be the perfect song for the first dance at a wedding.' In the UK the album peaked at number thirteen, but around the world it was a huge hit and was number one for thirteen weeks in the Philippines.

At the end of the title track, Jenny Francis, the 'Lady of Soul' on Choice FM, has a brief voiceover in which she gives some 'special mentions' – the first is to Alesha and Junior – before giving a name check to the other couples in the band at the time. It was a simple gesture but refreshingly different from the gushing acknowledgements that artists tend to write on album sleeve notes about their partners, loving words that are often regretted after a break-up.

The group were keen to forge a bond with their fans through competitions and personal appearances. They also wanted to 'give something back' by supporting new talent. They invited fans who had bought *Forever* to submit songs they had written and the best one would be the B-side of their next single.

Noel recalls, 'We listened to hundreds of songs before picking out the best one, which really stood out from the pile. We invited the person down to the recording studio in West London. A shy, chubby teenager turned up with his mum to record the track, clearly petrified and in awe of the situation, and we kept having to remind him that we were regular guys like him. It was Craig David. He was really sweet and we were pleased to see his career grow like it did and proud to have given him a break into the industry.'

The smooth progress of Damage met an unexpected obstacle when their record company, Big Life, went into administration. Recording their second album was put on hold and they concentrated on touring with *Forever*. Inevitably time apart put a strain on Noel's relationship with Alesha and the two split up for a while, as Noel jetted off all around the world.

Musically, Noel and Alesha were not that well connected. While he favoured the smoother sounds of R & B, she was becoming enthralled by garage and the edgier side of urban music. Fortunately, Sabrina shared her enthusiasm and they both loved Lauryn Hill's debut solo record, which had more influence on their future sound than any other.

The Miseducation of Lauryn Hill is one of those classics that should be in everyone's collection. Alesha was mesmerized by the fusion of soul, reggae and hip-hop, and both she and Sabrina would always name it as their favourite record in interviews. They weren't the only ones. The album, released in August 1998, eventually sold more than eighteen million copies worldwide and won five Grammy Awards, including Album of the Year. Lauryn's lack of new material since then has probably increased its almost legendary status.

Alesha observed simply, 'Lauryn is my biggest idol.' She told the National Literacy Trust why she so admired her: 'I love Lauryn Hill because she is not scared to talk about real life. She may say things that are slightly controversial but she gets people thinking and gets people talking. Not only is she an amazing singer, she's an amazing rapper. And I love the fact that with her what you see is what you get.'

While she and Sabrina, calling themselves Face II Face, were becoming better known around the clubs of Hertfordshire as a sort of rapping, Home Counties version of Salt-N-Pepa, they were both becoming impatient to reach a wider audience.

Louise Porter was always on the lookout for the right third member of the band. It took two years for her to find Su-Elise Nash. Louise recalled, 'We'd been looking for a long time and auditioned lots of girls until we found Su-Elise. I just bumped into her at the Dance Attic one day. She'd actually been auditioning for another girl group. But, luckily for me, I was able to snap her up.'

Fortunately, Su-Elise was already an experienced dancer, having been taught at the Royal Ballet School and studied at the Italia Conti Academy of Theatre Arts in Clapham, so she wouldn't need the amount of training that Alesha and Sabrina had undergone. She was born in Dulwich and, like the others, was of Caribbean descent. She had enjoyed dancing lessons so much as a child that it was always her ambition to start her own dance school, and she had started a business course at Middlesex University when her pop aspirations took over.

No sooner had they found a third member for their group than they found a fourth, a backing dancer from Birmingham called Zena McNally, who had answered another of Louise's advertisements. Zena had already worked with well-known black acts like Beverley Knight and Busta Rhymes and she, too, would not need the same level of training as Sabrina and Alesha. N-Tyce had been a four-girl group, so at the time that set-up seemed to work best for the new band too.

Louise has auditioned hundreds of girls over the years. It was nothing like trying out for *The Voice* or *The X Factor*. She preferred them to bring in photos and a biography, and she liked them to be on time because that would bode well for the hectic schedule that pop hopefuls have as they dash here and there trying to get noticed at showcases and promotional visits. She usually asks the wannabe to sing a cappella and do a short dance routine. Zena, who was very striking-looking and had a stunning voice, ticked all the boxes.

Louise came up with the name Mis-Teeq when they were sitting around one day trying to think of one. Alesha recalled, 'You know we had all come up with different names but that was the only one we could agree with and we all thought that we had something a little mystic about us as well.'

The most pressing thing was to write some original material that they could record for a demo. David Brant had composed a track with other Reverb writers, Maryanne Morgan, Ron St Louis and London-based American Alan Glass, which seemed promising. Alan was a very experienced songwriter who had composed for both the Lighthouse Family and Aswad since he had settled in the UK.

The song was called 'Why?' and it would provide the girls with the breakthrough they needed. Louise Porter recalled that every time they recorded a new song, the girls improved vocally. They started doing more live shows and their style began to evolve. When David offered Louise 'Why?', the girls were ready. But it's all about connections in the music business.

Mis-Teeq had a lucky break. When they were recording the demo, they were overheard in the next studio by David's friend, the DJ Darren Stokes, who had enjoyed his own moment of fame with the electronic dance hall duo Tin Tin Out. He liked it and offered to play the track for Pat Travers, head of A & R at independent dance label Inferno Records, which was based in Acton and took its name from a rather hot table sauce. Pat, in turn, played it to the label boss, Steve Long, who also liked it and picked up the phone to Louise. After more than two years of hard graft, it took this rapid sequence of events to take Alesha's career to the next stage.

Meanwhile, Noel was back recording a new album in London and he and Alesha decided to resume their relationship. The deal with Inferno meant that Alesha could at last give up her job at Ladbrokes and start living the life of a pop star, albeit one who had yet to release a record.

Damage had grown up and moved on from being a boy band that had a silly media rivalry with Blue and become a proper R & B group. They were picked up by EMI and were feeling 'on top of the world' when they finally released another single, 'Ghetto Romance', which was Noel's personal favourite of all their tracks and their fourth top ten hit in July 2000. Noel said, 'It was exciting because we had always seen ourselves as an R & B group and not a boy band.'

The group had moved up a division by supporting Mariah Carey on her European tour. Ras was going out with one of Mariah's best friends and over dinner one night had told the superstar that he was in a band. She suggested Damage do the tour without hearing any of their music or seeing pictures. Noel recalls, 'We jumped at the chance. It was only a short tour but we chilled with her and she was lovely. Don't believe the diva stuff about Mariah.'

It might seem strange that Alesha hadn't joined forces with Noel when he'd been doing so well. They did, in fact, collaborate on a garage track called 'Rumours'. He recalled that he fought to get

Alesha involved because he was concerned that the song wasn't right for the band and needed some of the extra sparkle she could give it: 'We were still going out when she did this with the band. It was our one attempt at a slightly garage-flavoured single but it didn't really work.

'Damage was under a lot of pressure at the time to jump on the garage bandwagon, which was really big at the time. We didn't feel comfortable about it. I was in Ayia Napa when the finished track came through, and I knew straight away that it wasn't quite right. If it had been a remix of an existing track, it would have been great – but not as a stand-alone single. We're an R & B band, not a garage band, and we shouldn't have jumped on the bandwagon. Our fans didn't react positively either so we stopped attempts at garage after that.' In retrospect, Noel is being harsh about 'Rumours', although he was right that the fans didn't like it. It peaked in the charts in October 2000 at number twenty-two, which was very disappointing.

Alesha was in her element, however. The track was produced by K-Gee, Karl Gordon, who recalled, 'I produced a couple of tracks for Damage and one of them was "Rumours". They told me there was this girl they wanted to feature on the track, but I'd never heard of her. They sent through her tape and I was like what is this scratchy, strange-sounding voice? But, as I listened to it more, I began to think she really had something. She had a unique sound to her voice. I liked it. Alesha was really young. From the moment I met her, I could see that she was very talented, very focused and very driven. She knew how to push herself.'

She loved making the video with the boys and there's no doubt it improved her profile. Noel observes, 'She looked amazing. It was important for her to get her face seen as much as possible as she was just starting out, and this was another platform.'

It wasn't the most creative video – just everyone lounging around chatting while the camera flitted from scene to scene to show the various members of Damage singing the song. Noel, for once, was not wearing a hat, but looked muscled and fit in a white shirt, gold jacket and yellow aviator sunglasses. For the most part, if you blinked, you missed Alesha, in a lemon T-shirt, until she started a rap towards the end of the song and lit up the screen. She had changed into a shimmering silver dress and oozed star quality during a twenty-second rapid-fire rap – the kind that she would later become famous for.

Noel and Alesha were still keeping their relationship private. The media weren't concerned about them because she had yet to make an impact. Instead, their focus was on Jade Jones and his new girl-friend, Emma Bunton of the Spice Girls. They didn't become a big 'celebrity' couple but perhaps Damage could have achieved greater fame if they had.

Noel observes, 'We could have exploited some opportunities more ruthlessly. It was always kept separate from the band. That was the way Jade and Emma wanted to run their relationship and we respected them for that, but, sometimes, I don't think we took advantage of every opportunity as much as we could have.'

Emma and Jade must have been doing something right because they are together twelve years later and the parents of two young children. The relationship between Noel and Alesha, however, had run its course. They had dated, with a short break, for more than two years.

A legacy of their time spent together was the development of Alesha's social conscience. The newly formed Mis-Teeq would appear with Damage at many charity concerts. Noel observes, 'We both had a sense of gratitude for what we had and we wanted to give back, so we took up any opportunities there were to perform charity gigs, as it was our way of doing this.' The most memorable was when they both appeared on the bill at the Hammersmith Apollo for a charity concert in aid of disadvantaged and disabled chil-dren – a cause close to Alesha's heart. All the acts performed Michael Jackson songs and the man himself turned up unexpectedly.

Noel recalls the excitement, 'He had decided to make his way down to the gig with no entourage or warning to the organizers. There was no special box for him so, instead, they set up a special place by the side of the stage where he watched everyone perform. I remember there were loads of kids in wheelchairs in the front row. It was tense, making sure I nailed the harmonies while he was standing there watching. I also remember him walking behind us on stage while we were performing, which was so unprofessional but we gave him a pass!'

Damage continued to tour and their second album, *Since You've Been Gone*, was finally released in April 2001, exactly four years after their debut. The *NME* thought the break had done them good: 'They've left behind the pop that laced their debut (though they will deny until the end that it even existed), and replaced it with something more classic.' It reached number sixteen in the charts, but deserved better.

In his section of the sleeve notes, Noel pays a simple and heartfelt tribute to Alesha: 'Thank you for your love and confidence in me. You give me a feeling I can't explain in words. I love you with all my heart.'

Noel continued to see Alesha at concerts, including one in honour of Lamont Dozier at the Hammersmith Apollo, when Mis-Teeq provided the highlight of the night by singing three Supremes songs. But while Mis-Teeq were on the up, Damage had reached a plateau. They were becoming tired of the constant touring and living in each other's pockets for fifty-two weeks of the year.

They were unlucky that their record company experienced financial trouble when it did – a problem that Alesha would know all about in the future. Surprisingly, they didn't all embark on solo projects. Three of them, including Noel, began helping young people. Andrez obtained a criminology degree and worked in youth justice, helping to prevent young people from reoffending after they left prison. He works closely with a team helping to support those wanting to exit gangs. Ras became a Prince's Trust Team Leader, overseeing a twelve-week self-development programme. He also introduced Noel to youth work.

Noel explained, 'He invited me to a session he was giving on music production for young people. I went along and loved it and wanted to figure out a way of doing it full time. So now I run a youth club.'

He runs the Dedworth Manor Community Centre, Windsor, as well as Inspire, a local scheme to help young people find full-time employment. He says, 'I found my niche working with young people. I know what it's like to do badly when you're at school. That's why it's important for me to be there to show these kids that the sky's the limit, that no matter what challenges they face, they can pursue their dreams.' Noel's positive attitude to life clearly rubbed off on Alesha Dixon.

After they split, there was no acrimony and the pair continue to be friends; Noel doesn't have a bad word to say about his former girl-friend. Damage were among the good guys and a far cry from the dark side that Alesha was about to be drawn towards. Who could say how things would have turned out if she'd stayed with Noel?

CHAPTER FIVE

The First Ladies of Garage

Mis-Teeq were building a good reputation with their frequent live shows but there was still no sign of a debut single, which was frustrating. David Brant's production of 'Why?' had led to their deal with Inferno but that progress was in danger of stalling. Steve Long decided to commission a garage mix and brought in two of the leading figures in the genre, DJ Face and Matt 'Jam' Lamont, to do it. They were the first garage DJs to break through into the mainstream with a weekly radio show on Kiss FM, and Lamont was described as the 'UK Garage Godfather' by *NME*.

Louise Porter told HitQuarters, 'Once we had the mix the whole thing just blew up. We knew then we had a really hot act. We knew we were going to have a big hit and that's when the major labels started to get interested and offered us some really good deals.'

In the end, Louise and the girls decided to go with Telstar Records in conjunction with Inferno. Telstar had also signed Louise's previous girl group, N-Tyce, so there was already a connection there. It was a good decision at the time but would later prove to be an unfortunate one. Telstar had spung to prominence in the early eighties with a string of bestselling compilation albums – including the infamous Jive Bunny – before expanding in the nineties into long-term artist development. The company had a reputation for attracting artists by offering large advances.

They also took on acts in joint ventures with other labels. They had Craig David, for instance, on their books through a deal with Wildstar Records. He gave Telstar their first number one when 'Fill Me In' reached the top in April 2000. His success as a breakthrough garage artist made the prospect of joining Telstar more attractive to Mis-Teeq.

The Telstar deal guaranteed Mis-Teeq the chance to make an album, the first of five in their new contract, with enough money to make the kind of record they wanted. 'Why?', meanwhile, launched them into the mainstream, despite being a garage remix. The original R & B production had performed disappointingly but that instantly changed with the release of the new garage version. It was now a fast dance track. *AllMusic* online praised Alesha's humorous and effortlessly cool, quick-fire MC skills. The *NME* called it a 'nimble re-rub'. It also said the remix had 'lifted the beseeching sentimentality of the original and stuffed credibility, unfamiliarity and depth into the dissected melody'.

Radio 1's Dreem Team started playing it, calling the track 'bad, bold and sassy'. The Team were a group of three DJs – Spoony, Mikee B and Timmi Magic – who had started out in pirate radio before hosting an award-winning show on Radio 1 in the early noughties. As a result of the exposure, 'Why?' went from being an underground hit to a chart one in April 2001, peaking at number eight. Mis-Teeq and MC Alesha Dixon had arrived.

The charts remain a big deal, especially to artists desperate for a hit. Alesha spent that particular Sunday afternoon listening to the countdown at her mum's house in Ingles with other members of her family gathered round. It was an emotional moment when they realized 'Why?' had made it. Alesha recalled, 'I started crying. My nan started crying. We were all bawling.'

They had made videos of both versions of the song – the R & B mix and the garage remix. In the first and rarely seen video, Alesha barely features. It's a little reminiscent of Victoria Beckham, who seemed slightly pointless on the Spice Girls' first hit, 'Wannabe'. Alesha looks fantastic in the little we do see of her, with her hair straight and wearing a slinky black cocktail number. The rather unexciting action was filmed underground in what appeared to be a disused railway station and her outfit hardly matched the dark surroundings. Sabrina sang the lead vocal and the whole song revolves around her.

Sabrina was again centre stage for the video of the remix. This time they had moved outside and Alesha was much more in evidence in a black trench coat, gold corset and white hot pants. Leading fashion writer Alison Jane Reid, of *The Lady Magazine*, observes, 'I guess this is an attempt to make her appear a little more hard-edged but the result is still impossibly cute.' Alesha announces, in her distinctive deep and throaty rap style, 'It's the remix' – her very first Mis-Teeq solo. She had two proper rap breaks in the song, which raised the track up a notch, urging everyone to 'pump up the tempo': 'Here we go, here we go. Move to the beat and go with the flow.'

The difference between the two versions couldn't have been clearer – the first was laidback; the second was urgent and made you want to get up off the sofa and dance. The soulful side of R & B restrained you, whereas the rhythms of garage released you. Alesha's outfit reinforced the sense that this was a more current version. She wore a fashionable, long black leather coat that she could have borrowed from Noel.

From Alesha's point of view, the remix was much more desirable, as she was now at the front of the group next to Sabrina and not on the sidelines. The chief sufferer appeared to be Zena and, with hindsight, she looked less comfortable in the remix video. No sooner had the four girls made their breakthrough than they became three. Zena McNally left the band after just one record.

Everyone did their best to paper over the cracks except Zena, who revealed that there were more disharmonies than harmonies within the group. She told *The Situation* online that her opinion was the final one taken into account when it came to making decisions: 'Sabrina and Alesha were there prior to me being there. There was an imbalance in the group. It was like 'cos they'd been there the longest, the production company just leaned more to them. I had a lot of good ideas and I write a lot too. I know I'm talented.'

Zena felt that she was being told what to do. She was even more outspoken to the *Daily Record* a couple of years later, particularly regarding the tension between herself and Sabrina: 'Mis-Teeq was a clash of personalities and there was a lot of friction between us as a band. The record company wanted me and Sabrina to share the lead vocals.

'People said she felt threatened but we were four beautiful girls who were all equally talented and wanted to get on. I was more angry than depressed because I'm a very strong person. It's a shame it happened, but it's water under the bridge now and if I saw Sabrina I would talk to her.'

The immediate consequence of Zena's departure was that Mis-Teeq made their debut on *Top of the Pops* as a trio. Jamie Theakston introduced them and the three girls performed as if they had been singing together as a trio for years. They couldn't believe how much smaller the *TOTP* studio was in real life than it looked on television – it was something Alesha would get used to over the years.

She was quite clear when she spoke to the *Guardian* about Zena's departure: 'We didn't kick her out! We had a single out and a video out with four people in them. We looked stupid. But there were other issues in her life, and it made us stronger.' The sleeve of the CD single is a collector's item because it's the only record with all four girls on the cover.

Louise Porter was diplomatic about Zena's departure. She explained, 'When you're putting together a group and people don't want to work with each other, you can't force them. It was all very friendly and nice, but Zena pursued another avenue.'

It didn't sound particularly friendly – or nice. Zena didn't disappear without trace, however. She had ambitions for a solo career and eventually signed with Mercury Records in 2002, spending most of her time in the US recording with some of the leading producers of the time, including Bobby Brown, the husband of Whitney Houston. She was also much in demand for roles in pop videos.

When her album *All of Me* failed to catch fire, she moved into presenting, hosting *In The Mixx* on Sky and BBC Radio 1Xtra's breakfast show with Trevor Nelson. She married American soccer international Cory Gibbs in Miami in 2008 after meeting him while he was under contract to Charlton Athletic in East London and she was living in Canary Wharf. The couple moved back to the US and now have their main home in West Palm Beach, Florida. Using her married name, Zena Gibbs, she is a director of GibbsWorld Realty, a property company, and is promoting a new career as a photographer. Her life now is a world away from garage music. She still refers to Alesha as a 'friend' and shot a promotional portfolio for Su-Elise, which the latter called 'beautiful'.

Splits and divisions are commonplace early on in careers, particularly with girl groups. The Spice Girls, for instance, originally included a girl called Michelle Stephenson and not Emma Bunton but she didn't gel with the other four. Their manager at the time, Chris Herbert, explained that she seemed 'separated' from the others. In the US, Destiny's Child had very similar upheavals. They were originally four but, after a series of musical chairs, ended up as three.

Mis-Teeq had to suffer many comparisons with that famous American R & B group, mainly because they each contained three stunning young black girls. They took it with good grace. Alesha said, 'It's a positive thing for us.' Musically they were very different, with Mis-Teeq achieving their breakthrough as the first female UK garage act. They had purposely made themselves as different as they could be to popular American acts like Destiny's Child.

These days everything tends to be brought together under the umbrella of urban music, but when Mis-Teeq began recording in 2001, award ceremonies would have separate categories for R & B, garage and hip-hop. Usher, Alicia Keys and Destiny's Child were R & B; P. Diddy and Ja Rule were hip-hop, while So Solid Crew and Mis-Teeq were garage – the raw end of urban music. If you went out to a club in London in those days, as Alesha liked to do, many of them would have an R & B room and a separate garage room.

Mis-Teeq, meanwhile, literally had to regroup. Their immediate concern was recording their first album, which needed to reflect a new direction as the UK's premier girl garage band. They took another catchy track by David Brant and friends called 'All I Want', which they had recorded the previous year, and gave it a garage twist with a remix by Sunship, a production collective that had been the brainchild of Ceri Evans and was at the forefront of the UK garage sound. Sunship had been responsible for the garage remix of Craig David's 'Fill Me In', so it was quite a coup for Mis-Teeq to be one of their next projects.

The resulting version of 'All I Want' was earmarked as their follow-up single and their debut record as a threesome. They also shot their first video without Zena. It begins with Su-Elise trying on an outfit in front of a magic mirror, which promptly sucks all three girls into different outfits. Alesha wore distressed jeans and a top in eye-catching pale yellow with big hoop earrings, demonstrating how great she looked in strong colours. She delivers a rapid-fire rap to get things moving: 'M with the I with the S–T double E Q . . .' Her style was now firmly established: it was very fast, almost raucous, and delivered with a blend of Caribbean and Welwyn Garden City. She explained, 'With me, you get passion and fun and that's what it's all about.'

'All I Want' was one of the big summer hits on Ayia Napa and sped to number two in the charts when it was released in June 2001. It was beaten to the number one spot by Shaggy featuring Rayvon with 'Angel'. The girls' song didn't please everyone, with *NME* declaring, 'It's not a patch on "Why?".'

Alesha seemed to have grown in stature as an MC in a few short months and was full of energy when they performed the song on *Top of the Pops* in October 2001. The audience had the chance to appreciate Alesha's famous legs for the first time as she danced in a white shift dress and matching boots. As well as featuring more prominently, Alesha had the additional benefit of a songwriting credit on the remixes, which would greatly improve her bank balance.

The first album was taking shape, thanks to the use of dynamic and fashionable producers. The group flew to Trondheim in Norway to work with the producers known as StarGate, who were part of a thriving Scandinavian music scene and had the golden touch in the British charts. The team consisted of Tor Erik Hermansen and Mikkel Storleer Eriksen, who had decided to call themselves the more consumer-friendly StarGate for their UK work. Together with their songwriter collaborator Hallgeir Rustan, StarGate first tasted international success with 'S Club Party', a 1999 hit for S Club 7. That may not have seemed cutting edge – nor did their work with Atomic Kitten and Blue – but they knew how to fashion chart hits. They also allowed their artists room for self-expression. This suited Alesha, who was feeling more confident about her own contribution after 'Why?'. All three girls received credit for their work with StarGate.

Alesha explained how the collaboration worked. The six of them would sit around informally with a Dictaphone and pads of paper. StarGate would devise the backing track and from that the song would take shape. 'Someone would chip in with a chorus or a verse or one line, then someone else would add another line and build it up like that.'

'One Night Stand' would be Mis-Teeq's next single and third top ten hit in a row. The media were beginning to sit up and take notice of the girls they were calling 'The High Priestesses of Garage', which sounded good for a group who had yet to release an album. Alesha observed, 'Before us there hadn't been a girl group fronting garage music so that makes us stand out from the rest. We got in there at the right time.'

Using StarGate demonstrated Mis-Teeq's forward thinking. Unusually for Scandinavian producers, they had grown up listening to R & B and hip-hop. Within a few years, the Norwegian team would be superstars, fashioning hits for the biggest acts in the world. They produced 'Unfaithful' and 'Rude Boy' for Rihanna, 'Firework' for Katy Perry and 'Irreplaceable' for Beyoncé.

Back in England, Mis-Teeq worked with Rishi Rich, a pioneer of Indian R & B, and Mushtaq, another leading Asian producer who had first sprung to prominence as a member of Fun-Da-Mental. Mushtaq, who was born in London to Bangladeshi and Iranian parents, had already worked on Damage's album, producing three tracks, including 'I Don't Know' featuring Emma Bunton. With Mis-Teeq, he co-wrote a track called 'B With Me'. He then produced it, programmed the drums and played all the instruments.

The most interesting collaboration on the first album, however, featured Mis-Teeq and So Solid Crew, the most talked about new act of the year. The track 'They'll Never Know' featured raps by Alesha and two of the charismatic members of So Solid, Asher D and MC Harvey. The 'Harv man' would have a huge impact on her life.

PART TWO

Mrs Harvey

CHAPTER SIX

Son of a Bullit

Michael Harvey is not every mother's dream for their daughter. Like Noel, he was in a boy band but as MC Harvey he was one of the leaders of So Solid Crew, the most notorious male group in the country. They were nothing like One Direction or, even, Damage. He wore the clothes of the street, had razored eyebrows, a tattoo proclaiming 'In God I Trust' and a nasty scar on his neck from the time he'd been stabbed with a broken glass and nearly died during a bar brawl in Aiya Napa in 2000.

He was born Michael Junior Harvey in Plymouth on 1 May 1979, the year after Alesha. By a weird coincidence he was known as Junior to his friends and family – just like Alesha's former boyfriend, Noel Simpson Junior. Like her, his father Michael was Jamaican and his mother white. Michael Harvey Senior was in the Royal Navy stationed at nearby Devonport when his son was born. He achieved some fleeting television fame as Bullit in *Gladiators*, which became one of the most popular television shows of the nineties, presented by Ulrika Jonsson and John Fashanu.

Each of the gladiators had different stage names, like Rhino, Shadow and Wolf, and their own theme music, which would blare out whenever they took on the contestants in a series of very silly challenges. Bullit, whose signature tune was 'Unbelievable' by EMF, was particularly adept at Atlaspheres. Contenders and gladiators were trapped in two-metre circular pods, which the former would attempt to manoeuvre onto sensor pads to score points, while the gladiators tried to prevent them.

Bullit, who had been a successful athlete for the Navy, a champion amateur boxer and a bodybuilder, was in the original live shows at Wembley in 1993 before being dropped for the subsequent television series. He went into acting and had some minor roles but, more importantly for his son, he began his own production and management company called Artiste Promotion & Management. Father and son look uncannily alike.

Michael Junior also inherited some of his father's athletic prowess and was a very promising young footballer, who was on the books of Chelsea Football Club Academy at the age of eleven. Despite his father's brush with celebrity, there wasn't much spare money at home across the Thames in Battersea where the family had settled. Michael, who grew up with a South London accent, had to manage without the 'best trainers or cool clothes other kids had'. His upbringing, though, was stable and happy until his family life was shattered when he was fourteen and his parents split up: his father had got another woman pregnant.

Michael told the *Daily Mail*, 'Suddenly my mum went to live in Plymouth with her family and left me with my dad. I didn't understand. As soon as she went the house felt unstable. Dad sometimes didn't come home until midnight. When you're fourteen years old and stuck in a house on your own, it's weird.

'Then three months later my dad brought home a baby and said: "This is your brother." I knew it took nine months to make a baby so I didn't get it – especially when the woman involved had been coming to my house pregnant when my mum was there. He'd been having an affair.'

His father subsequently remarried and his mother returned to Battersea. Michael moved in with her on the Winstanley council estate, where residents were serenaded to sleep by the sound of police sirens.

The violence and the downside of street life were the source of inspiration for the often disturbing lyrics of So Solid Crew but, as a teenager, Michael's life was built around a career in football. He had spells at Barnet and Aldershot, which might not have been as glamorous as he had hoped for but it was still very early days. He scored his first-ever goal playing in a cup match for Basingstoke against Rochdale and a photograph of that special moment had pride of place in his bedroom at home.

At this stage of his life music wasn't an ambition. He explained, 'I was rapping and stuff when I was young but I was mainly concentrating on my football; music was never a big thing in my life. I always had the potential but I never really got deep into it.'

That changed when a badly broken ankle finished his long-term football aspirations but kick-started his musical ones. He started hanging out more with his friends from the neighbourhood, including a former classmate called Marvin Dawkins, who used the street name Romeo on account of his smooth chat-up lines.

Michael would join Romeo at club nights and became more absorbed in music than football, so when his contract wasn't renewed he was ready for a new challenge. The friends would join up with other like-minded young men to form a musical 'gang' that would hang around pirate radio stations like Garage FM and, in particular, Delight FM.

Originally the collective went by the name of SOS but that proved to be a problem because a DJ on another station had already taken that title. One of the leaders of the group, Dwayne Vincent, who performed as Megaman, came up with So Solid Crew and everyone liked it, so it stuck.

Michael started calling himself MC Harvey and that is the name he has always used in public. Alesha preferred Michael rather than Junior, which was perhaps a little too close to home after Noel.

Modestly, the newly styled Harvey admitted to the *Western Mail* that he was not the best MC to begin with: 'We all met outside Spar in Battersea and then went to the radio – I was absolutely rubbish. My hands started sweating and my knees were going. I did not want Megaman or Romeo to pass me the mic, it was like a hot flame. But you soon find yourself finding your flow and I started getting good.'

Gradually the collective grew larger – twelve MCs, eight DJs, five vocalists, seven producers and four kids. They would drift in and out of the crew but when they launched their first album there were thirty members involved. A core group of ten would become the best-known. They also set up So Solid Kids, a younger version of themselves aimed at harnessing the talents of children from the neighbourhood.

Although they were at pains to point out the originality of the concept, So Solid Crew were admirers of the Wu-Tang Clan. Harvey, in particular, would listen to their work, which he described as 'deep'. He told fans in a webchat that he would definitely want to work with the famous and influential New York City collective.

Harvey said, 'We get compared to the Wu-Tang Clan because of the number of people involved and what we're talking about. But they started like us. They've got their own brand and albums and they've done individual stuff. So it's an honour to be compared to them.'

At Delight FM, they steadily built an enormous underground fan base of mainly school-age fans, thanks to their So Solid Sundays, when the DJs would take over the station from lunchtime until 10 p.m. and play a collection of 2-step garage tracks. The MCs, including Harvey, would contribute marathon rap sessions – sometimes up to two hours at a time. Unsurprisingly, they quickly achieved cult status. Harvey was a major part of their first mixtape, entitled *MC Harvey and DJ Swiss of So Solid Crew Present UK Garage Mafia.*

Coincidentally, So Solid's best-known vocalist was the stunningly pretty Lisa Maffia, a young mum from Brixton. She sang vocals on their first single release, 'Oh No (Sentimental Things)', and quickly became a key player within the group.

Harvey met Alesha Dixon in a club in Watford one spring night in 2001. It's a bit of a grey area as to how long she'd been a single girl again before hooking up with Harvey. Both were on the edge of fame. Alesha told the *Observer*, 'Harvey was a little bit drunk and we were in the VIP section of this club, and you know what that's like, and I was not the only girl he'd chatted to that night, so I wasn't interested. I'm not stupid. But we kept bumping into each other in different clubs. And then one time he bought me a glass of champagne and we had a dance, and that's when I gave him my number.'

She didn't actually say that they fancied each other from the start but they were both extremely attractive and made an eye-catching couple. They also found they had plenty to talk about – not least Alesha's developing MC style. She recalled, 'When Harvey first heard my MCing, being an MC himself, he always said I had potential, but there was a lot of things I could improve on. One day he wrote me a lyric. Sometimes I'd write something and I'd ask him what he thought and he'd say, "That bit sounds a bit dodgy. Switch up your flow," or whatever.' Harvey did wonders for Alesha's confidence by taking her with him when he MC'd for So Solid Crew at big club nights and making sure she had time at the mic.

By the time they were acknowledged as a couple in public, Harvey was as well known as his girlfriend, thanks to the astonishing success of So Solid Crew's second single, '21 Seconds', which went straight to number one in August 2001 with sales of more than 118,000 in the first week.

The track was a landmark record in the development of urban music in the UK. The title highlighted the twenty-one seconds that each of the MCs had to rap about themselves. Harvey went before Romeo. There's not much you can rap in twenty-one seconds, so after a few rhymes involving break and snake and flow and toe, it was on to the next. But the concept was original and bright and captured the imagination of its target audience.

The problem for the whole So Solid Crew project was that the darker side of street culture began to beg for attention. In May 2001, one of the MCs, Neutrino, was shot in the leg during a fight outside a nightclub. It was a strong hint that guns would become persistently linked to So Solid Crew and ultimately lead to their demise.

Ironically, Neutrino, with another MC, Oxide, had already released a single entitled 'Bound 4 Da Reload' that was banned from many radio stations for its inflammatory lyric, a spoken sample that declared 'Aah I've been shot'.

The problem for So Solid Crew was that they became more notorious for their links to guns and shootings, knives and stabbings than for their music. Richard Pendlebury in the *Daily Mail* wrote, 'They had become standard bearers for taking the violence of the "ghetto" into a wider world. Instead of appreciation for their music, they began to generate fear.'

There was worse after Neutrino. Another leading member, Ashley Walters, who rapped under the street name of Asher D, was on bail when '21 Seconds' was released. He had been arrested the month before, after a confrontation with a traffic warden in the West End. Armed police were called and stopped his car in the Haymarket; they found a loaded gun hidden in a sock in his girlfriend's handbag. The gun, a Brocock ME38, was a replica of a Magnum revolver but had been loaded with five rounds of modified ammunition that turned it into a lethal weapon. Asher D was just nineteen, a father of two with a third on the way, when he pleaded guilty to firearms charges at Southwark Crown Court the following March and was sentenced to eighteen months in a young offenders' institution. His girlfriend, Natalie Williams, the mother of his two children, was given twelve months community service after admitting possessing the gun.

So Solid's urban world seemed a million miles away from the manicured lawns of Welwyn Garden City. Mis-Teeq represented glamour and elegance and certainly didn't sing about 'taking you to the morgue'. Fortunately, the bad publicity that So Solid Crew attracted failed to tarnish the image of the girls.

For a while Alesha and MC Harvey were called the black Posh and Becks, which may seem pretty ludicrous now but is an indication of how big they were back in 2001. Nobody seemed to mind the link between Mis-Teeq and the perceived bad boys of the urban music scene, and their collaboration 'They'll Never Know' was well received. Harvey described it as a 'bangin' track'.

Alesha and Harvey were in competition with each other when the nominations for the 2001 MOBOs were announced. The Music of Black Origin Awards were extremely big news in the music industry and this was public recognition that both had arrived in a very short space of time. They were contesting the Best UK Act and Best Newcomer categories; So Solid Crew were also up for the Best UK Garage Act. For some reason Mis-Teeq were overlooked for that award, despite being the 'High Priestesses of Garage'.

The MOBOs are probably ranked second only in prestige to the BRIT Awards. They were founded in 1996 by Kanya King, an inspirational woman who turned a dream into a commercial phenomenon with passion and acumen. She was from North West London, the youngest of nine children with a Ghanaian father and an Irish mother. She was thirteen when her father died, making things financially difficult for her family. She worked in a bakery for a while before embarking on a career in television as a lowly researcher, but she persevered and eventually became a senior researcher with Carlton Television and a founding member of the production team on *The Chrystal Rose Show*, an early nineties talk show.

In the mid-nineties, she started developing an idea for an awards show that would showcase the talent of black artists. Her vision was that black music needed a platform. The performers, she felt, were not getting the recognition they deserved in a music business still dominated by *Top of the Pops*. She started the MOBO Organisation from the bedroom of her home, which she remortgaged without telling her mother. She couldn't afford an office, so she would try to raise sponsorship through phone calls she made while lying on her bed in her pyjamas.

A few months later she had guaranteed enough funding to hold the first ceremony at the New Connaught Rooms in London. The Fugees were the big winners on the night, although Lionel Richie received a Lifetime Achievement Award. In retrospect, the biggest name in black music to win an award then was the late hip-hop artist Tupac, who won Best Video.

The original awards were exclusively for black musicians and that was still the case in 2001 when Mis-Teeq and So Solid Crew were nominated as Best UK Act. They were up against Sade, Craig David and Damage, which could have been potentially embarrassing for Alesha if her former boyfriend had walked off with one of the premier awards. Perhaps luckily Craig David won. So Solid Crew did win the two other awards they were nominated for, however, while Damage also missed out as Best R & B Act, which was won by Usher.

Mis-Teeq's performance at the MOBOs in September 2001 was perfectly timed to give them a burst of publicity before the release of their debut album, *Lickin' On Both Sides*, at the end of October. They arrived on stage astride matching Ducati motorcycles. It was a neat advertisement for the album, which coincidentally featured a cover on which the girls, wearing vixen-like red and black, draped provocatively across a pair of the hot bikes. The album title sounded raunchy enough, even if it just meant simply 'listening' on both sides or, more likely, the switching between R & B and garage mixes.

Just six months after the release of the Damage album *Since You've Been Gone*, in which Noel declared that he loved Alesha with all his heart, he didn't rate a mention on her own debut. Instead she gushes about her new boyfriend, the 'Harv man'. She thanks him for being positive and bringing joy and inspiration into her life before concluding 'I love you.'

Their exposure at the MOBOs guaranteed Mis-Teeq review space where, ordinarily, they might have only gathered a line or two. The response was mixed. The *London Evening Standard* was irritated by the combination of R & B and garage. Chris Leadbeater wrote, 'It switches continuously and schizophrenically between its two chosen styles.' He did, however, think that their So Solid Crew collaboration 'They'll Never Know' was 'as good as anything Destiny's Child have done. The *NME* also liked this track, calling it 'a tough and characteristic slice of pure pirate material'. Alex Needham thought the girls should stick resolutely to garage: 'As a garage girl group, Mis-Teeq are at the top of a field of about four. As an R & B girl group, they are probably around halfway down a field of several million.' The fusion of R & B and garage was their strength and their weakness, it seemed.

UK Mix online thought they spanned both genres with 'confidence and style', however, and praised Alesha for her 'unmistakable talent' for MCing. Describing the album as an 'incredible achievement' was perhaps a little strong but the record-buying public were behind it and the album went straight into the charts at number three in the first week of November 2001. The release of three top ten singles before the album came out might have had a negative effect on sales but that proved not to be the case. Eventually, *Lickin' On Both Sides* was certified as double platinum, which really was an achievement. It also turned Alesha, at twenty-three, into a very wealthy young woman – certainly the richest person in her Welwyn Garden City world.

The success of the album and the publicity from the MOBOs combined to make Mis-Teeq flavour of the month in media terms. The press had woken up to the fact that three beautiful young black women made a good interview. Alesha, in particular, was noticed. She was voted tenth in a one-off *Smash Hits* poll entitled the '100 Sexiest', won by Rachel Stevens of S Club 7. Again, it was a rapid rise to recognition.

Their concert date book was also full. The big disappointment of the year was the cancellation of MOBOFest, where Mis-Teeq were scheduled to appear on the same bill as their hero, Lauryn Hill. Alesha had been so excited, 'I can't believe we will be on the same show as her. If we end up performing on the same stage as her, I know I'll faint immediately.' It fell through without explanation.

Mis-Teeq ended a wonderful year with a well-received sell-out concert at Scala in London's King's Cross, where they were reviewed in The *Guardian*, a sure sign of their increased artistic credibility. Betty Clarke observed, 'Working one section of the crowd as she punches the air, titillating another with a hands-on-hips stance, Alesha is a woman who takes no prisoners. She comes armed with a London twang and a look of determination, and her rapid-fire MC style is fierce.'

Max Bell in the *London Evening Standard* noted the 'none-too-subtle reference to oral sex' during the track 'One Night Stand'. He added, 'The slinkies in green, red and blue maintained the thrust of their poppier side without completely dismaying the adult-orien-tated nature of the crowd.'

The *Guardian* also made the point that whereas So Solid Crew caused controversy, Sabrina, Alesha and Su-Elise were the garage girls it was safe to love. Almost imperceptibly Alesha had taken over as the centre of attention in the group. Traditionally it's the lead singer who catches the eye, but Mis-Teeq were an unusual group because of Alesha's rapping. The *NME* reviewed the concert, noting that 'Alesha is one of the country's most talented young MCs.' It didn't mention Sabrina.

The celebrity of her boyfriend didn't do Alesha's profile any harm either. She was certainly ending the year in better career shape than MC Harvey. The triumph of the MOBOs must have seemed a million miles away when So Solid Crew's first nationwide tour was cancelled amid a blaze of negative publicity. It was one thing after another.

One of the singers, Skat D, real name Darren Weir, who had featured on '21 Seconds', pleaded guilty at Cardiff Crown Court in October to assault causing grievous bodily harm on a fifteen-year-old girl. He had punched her in the face after she had slapped him, apparently spurning an invitation to join the group in their hotel following a gig in the Welsh capital. Her jaw was broken in two places and surgeons needed to insert two metal plates to repair it. He was identified when one of the girl's friends who'd witnessed the incident recognized him in a So Solid Crew video. The court heard how the performer had a previous conviction for actual bodily harm for assault on a bus conductor in March 1999.

The judge decided not to send Skat D to jail, however. Judge Christopher Llewellyn-Jones said, 'You are a young man on the brink of a career which may be extremely successful – we do not know. I am satisfied on the evidence that a prison sentence would undoubtedly have a significant, adverse effect.' Instead he ordered him to pay £3,500 compensation to his victim, a fine of £1,500 and £500 in prosecution costs.

Afterwards MC Megaman was outspoken, 'He was lucky to get away with a fine because he could have easily fucked his career like that. So Solid and our management company have sent their apologies to the girl's family so hopefully we can look over that and move on with life.'

So Solid Crew could have done without this following on so soon after Asher D's conviction. But there was worse to come at the end of October. It was reported that two men were shot inside the London Astoria where So Solid Crew were performing as part of a birthday celebration for MC Romeo. Two shots were apparently fired towards the stage.

Perhaps it was just the sheer numbers involved with So Solid Crew but they seemed to have an unerring ability to find trouble. The release of their debut album, *They Don't Know*, was completely overshadowed by controversy even though it made number six in the charts. Perhaps there is such a thing as too much publicity being a bad thing because their album fared less well than *Lickin' On Both Sides* despite the column inches they commanded.

Their nationwide tour was scrapped before it began when pro-moters started to pull out, fearing that violence might break out at concerts. The day after So Solid Crew pulled out of the tour, the headmaster at White Hart Lane School in Tottenham banned a visit from Harvey and three other members of the crew over security concerns. They had been due to give a 'community workshop', a common practice among bands, who perform a few songs and try to inspire the children to make the best of their lives.

Alesha gamely tried to stand up for her boyfriend's band, she told the *Daily Mirror*: 'I think the whole thing has been blown out of pro-portion. They're not the painted picture the media likes to create. Trouble happens everywhere in the country in all types of music . . . People are entitled to their opinion. It takes two to make a night, doesn't it?'

She also told the *Daily Telegraph* how upset Harvey was when the tour was stopped but that they would come back and do a bigger tour in the future – something that was destined never to happen. Revealingly, she confided that these days she avoided raves and would only go to see Harvey perform at a university. And she doubted whether she would let her own children go out and see So Solid perform live.

Alesha was beginning to give the impression that she and Harvey were quite domestic away from the spotlight. They certainly watched the first-ever series of *Pop Idol* together when television became acquainted with Simon Cowell. She was outraged when Zoe Birkett lost out to Darius Danesh. She was a big fan of the eventual winner Will Young, observing, 'He can sing, he's got a beautiful voice.' She was not so complimentary about one important aspect of the show: 'The thing that really gets me about *Pop Idol* is the bloody judging.'

CHAPTER SEVEN

Follow Love

For the one and only time in her life, Alesha was happy enough to be completely unguarded about her personal feelings. She was in love with Michael Harvey and she didn't mind letting the world know it. She gave the *Observer* a glimpse into their home life: 'After we came back from our last promo trip, I was desperate to see him and I couldn't get hold of him. I was having dinner with the girls. I was so depressed I hadn't even brushed my hair, and who walks in the door? Harvey! I couldn't believe it. I put my head in my dinner.'

She also revealed Harvey's romantic nature: 'Last night I was on the computer for about two hours and he was upstairs cleaning my room. When I came out of the living room there was a sign in the doorway that said "Follow Love" and as I got to the top of the stairs, it said "Getting close". When I went into my room, there was a sign in front of my bed that said "Harvey loves Alesha" with a picture of me and I just started cracking up.'

It was a sweet story told by a 23-year-old girl who had every reason to be happy. She was already far richer than she would ever have been as a PE teacher. She could easily afford to buy her man a Burberry washbag for Christmas or a £1,500 leather Prada jacket. She still maintained that her favourite shop was Miss Selfridge but did admit that she once spent £2,000 on a knee-length white dress from Versace.

She was one of the most successful young female artists in the UK. Mis-Teeq had been nominated for two MOBOs, they were about to embark on their first arena tour supporting Shaggy and they had just received the news that they were up for a BRIT Award. No wonder she felt confident enough to tell the newspaper her feelings for Harvey. 'I love him,' she said.

She was also becoming used to featuring in newspaper stories that would sometimes make her choke on her cornflakes. The most memorable was that she had snogged Usher. She laughed, 'I'd never even had a conversation with the man.' At this point in her life she could see the funny side of the media merry-go-round. That would not always be the case.

For the moment Mis-Teeq were absorbing the news that they had been nominated for a BRIT Award in the Best Newcomer category. So Solid Crew were also in the running in a bewilderingly broad and random list that included Blue, Elbow, Gorillaz, Turin Brakes, Starsailor, Zero 7, Tom McRae and Atomic Kitten. Alesha stated the obvious, 'We'd love to win the BRITs and I think anybody who says they don't is a liar.'

They dusted off another single from the album to coincide with the publicity from the BRITs. 'B With Me' was released just two days before the big night at Earls Court. They chose the Bump and Flex remix by Grant Nelson, one of the most famous names in UK garage. This version again gave Alesha the chance to shine when introducing the track with her catchphrase, 'It's the Mis-Teeq ladies'. The Jamaican twang to her rapping suited the Caribbean feel that was enhanced by the use of a steel drum. The accompanying video featured the girls dancing provocatively on a beach and Alesha, in particular, had a much sexier image. The track reached number five – the fourth top ten hit from *Lickin' On Both Sides*.

Mis-Teeq didn't win the BRIT Award, which was chosen by

Radio 1 listeners, who went for the safe option with Blue. The boy band were chart friendly and not the least cutting-edge. So Solid Crew won Best British Video for '21 Seconds', chosen by the readers of *Smash Hits*, perhaps an indication that the establishment had given up on the band long before their fans.

The BRIT Award is actually far less important than the chance to attract new fans with a blistering live performance. Adele's sublime rendition of 'Someone Like You' in 2011 arguably was the spark that made her the most successful recording artist in recent times. Mis-Teeq chose to perform their motorcycle version of 'One Night Stand' but with a twist: they did a mash-up of both the R & B and garage versions of the song.

They were introduced as the 'multi-talented' Mis-Teeq by Frank Skinner who, somewhat bizarrely, was hosting the awards ceremony that year, and had to make their way, in black evening gowns split dangerously high, down a long flight of steps. Afterwards they confessed they were terrified of falling and spent the whole time gazing down at the floor to make sure there were no disasters.

For the first half of the song Sabrina was in the middle, delivering her mellow vocal, but halfway through Alesha took centre stage as MC when they moved up a gear for the garage version. You couldn't take your eyes off her because she looked like an angel and rapped like a man.

These were the golden days for Mis-Teeq. Their first major tour around the UK culminated in a performance at the Shepherd's Bush Empire in April 2002. Harvey was there to watch his girlfriend. Simon Price in the *Independent* said Mis-Teeq were 'the best, least patronizing kind of pop act: they're of the kids, not just for the kids.' He had noticed the group's rapport with their audience. Alesha, in particular, was able to make a connection, a gift that would serve her well in the future.

Alesha featured a lot in interviews. She always seemed to have something to say. The *Daily Telegraph* observed, 'When Alesha Dixon makes an announcement, it stays announced.' She was quick and entertaining without the bland veneer that affects so many American stars. One day she would reveal that her favourite part of a man's body was his buttocks, the next she would launch into a frenetic freestyle rap on *The Big Breakfast*, impressing presenter Johnny Vaughan with her ability to find something to rhyme with vinegar.

During a Radio 1 interview with Jamie Theakston, who had recently been exposed in a Sunday newspaper for visiting a Mayfair call girl, he inadvertently described Mis-Teeq as 'old pros'. Alesha was the first with a comeback, laughing, 'Well, he should know.' It was just a minor quip but an early indication that she had a natural flair for broadcasting.

The winning smiles and friendly nature of Mis-Teeq disguised the fact that the three young women were entirely focused on maximizing their chance of success. They would happily spend four hours in hair and make-up before a television appearance to make sure their image was exactly right. But they didn't pass the time talking about their nails. There were accountants to see and solicitors to brief. Deirdre Donovan of the *Observer*, who interviewed them before they appeared on *Blue Peter*, said, 'Mis-Teeq's look takes serious maintenance. It's because of this that even solicitors' meetings are conducted surrounded by tables covered in trainers and pots of glitter.'

The previous year the girls had sacked their management team, Asylum, who promptly turned round and sued them. Louise Porter, perhaps sensibly, never involved herself in management, preferring to concentrate on development and production. Asylum had been set up by Steve Gilmour, who had guided the career of the popular boy band 911 in the nineties. He had also signed up Darius Danesh from *Pop Idol*. Mis-Teeq, however, decided they didn't need him. Su-Elise, who had been intent on studying business before joining the group, explained, 'It's our career and it's in our hands. We realized we don't actually have to have management because we're doing fine ourselves.' The sheer pressure of work made it impractical though and they appointed new management, Twenty-First Artists. The legal action with Asylum was settled quietly behind closed doors, as is so often the case in the music business, and the details were not made public.

Meanwhile, Alesha, who had grown up with one pair of jeans in her wardrobe, had discovered a love for shopping. She revelled in her new life and observed, 'Give us twenty minutes and we'll go shopping.' Fortunately Harvey was equally at home in the department stores and they liked to choose clothes for each other. She said, 'He's got great taste and always gets my size right, which is unusual for men.' She treated him to a trip to Milan for his twenty-third birthday and bought him a designer suit with all the trimmings. She observed, 'He looked gorgeous.'

She didn't shout about it but Alesha, it seemed, was happy to spend her money on a glamorous lifestyle. She had expensive tastes and Harvey would teasingly call her a diva. He summed it up: 'She's high maintenance – you can't take her to Nando's.'

Now that they were practically living together they liked to do the usual couple things. They would sprawl out on the sofa to watch favourite television programmes like *Sex in the City*, *Ugly Betty* and *Lost* – at least those were Alesha's favourites.

They also had their own MC battles – 'clashing' at home while watching MTV, which was good practice as well as fun. They had been inspired by watching *8 Mile*, the 2002 hit movie starring Eminem, who was Alesha's favourite rapper. They still enjoyed going out dancing, in particular to Pangaea, a basement club in Piccadilly, which was very popular with celebrities.

The club may or may not have been the venue for some spontaneous sex. Alesha told *FHM* magazine, 'I've done it in the ladies' toilet at a really posh bar in London.' She also admitted that, like Sabrina, she had enjoyed sex in the back of a car. She then confided, 'Once I tried it with handcuffs but they were too small so that didn't really work for me.' She didn't specify whether Harvey was her part-ner for such action or if it had all happened when she was younger.

It was time to get engaged. Mis-Teeq were on tour in Sweden when Harvey decided to fly over to surprise her. He took the impressive diamond ring out of his pocket, went down on one knee to propose and Alesha started crying with happiness. He said simply, 'I knew I loved this girl. She said yes, thank God.' A delighted Harvey described the ring: 'It's the sparkliest thing I've ever bought – all diamonds. I was broke for two months afterwards but it was worth it.'

Alesha had always wanted to get married – something neither of her parents had done, either to each other or to other partners. She also wanted a home of her own and the couple started house-hunting close to Welwyn Garden City. Harvey apparently enjoyed the peace and quiet of Hertfordshire after growing up in the urban madness of South West London.

She was not, however, about to put marriage before her career. She may have had a blingtastic ring but she had no plans to name the day. She couldn't even find the time for an engagement party. She explained to the *Daily Record*, 'Michael and I haven't set a date yet because I'm far too busy to plan anything that big. The fact he is in So Solid Crew means he understands and is very supportive. 'I don't think I could have a boyfriend who wasn't doing anything because it would be an unbalanced relationship.'

By a strange coincidence, all three members of Mis-Teeq were engaged at the same time. Sabrina's fiancé was a fireman called Ian Mitchell, while Su-Elise had become engaged on her twentieth birth-day to a millionaire property developer called Charles Gordon, who had progressed from humble origins in South London to become one of the most successful black businessmen in the capital. He liked to keep well away from the limelight generated by his pop star girl-friend. For a while there was talk of a triple wedding, which would have been a nice gimmick but was hardly practical. It held the media's interest for a while, but only Alesha would eventually walk down the aisle.

Her first priority, however, was the biggest concert that Mis-Teeq would ever perform in – The Queen's Golden Jubilee concert on 3 June 2002. The concert, entitled Party at the Palace, starred Paul McCartney, Eric Clapton and Elton John among the biggest names in popular music. Most memorably, Queen guitarist Brian May opened the event by performing his arrangement of 'God Save The Queen' from the roof of Buckingham Palace. It was cheesy and wonderful in equal measure. McCartney closed the show with the reassuringly familiar 'Hey Jude', which enabled the thousands packed into the Mall to join in and for everyone to go home with a warm glow.

Unsurprisingly, So Solid Crew weren't invited. Mis-Teeq, who were stealthily moving away from garage, proved the point by sharing a stage with Ricky Martin, whose camp disco style was about as far removed from the urban scene as it was possible to get. They sang 'B With Me' with a distinctive rap from Alesha before scuttling off so that Ricky could deliver 'Livin' La Vida Loca', his signature hit from 1999. Later, by themselves, they performed 'Stop! In the Name of Love', The Supremes' classic. They all wore shimmering sixties-style dresses and had tucked their hair up into bob wigs.

The girls met the Queen as well as Prince Charles, who told them how much he liked their Missoni-designed dresses. Alesha was even more excited to meet the singer Annie Lennox, who asked for an autograph for her daughter, she told I Like Music online: 'It is really surreal to be giving an autograph to a big star like Annie. I had dinner with her. She told me she was nervous about the show and the simple fact that someone of her status was nervous made me feel better.'

Afterwards, Alesha observed, 'It is the best gig I have ever played at. We were like little girls'. She recalled the moment before the show when she was relaxing with her publicist, Laura: 'We started crying! It was one of those surreal moments; Paul McCartney was doing a sound check, we were in the palace getting ready to perform, and we knew how many people around the world were going to be watching and saw the crowds. It was one of those moments, it was really powerful. I'll never forget that.'

Shortly afterwards they received a reality check from the newspapers when it was reported that a charity event had to be postponed because they had demanded a fee of £10,000. This was unfortunate publicity because Alesha would eventually become one of the most active celebrities in the world of good causes.

All three girls took part in the Soccer Six charity tournament at Chelsea's Stamford Bridge ground. Their team had no trouble thrashing the opposition and didn't concede a single goal in the competition. Afterwards Alesha was scathing about the opposition players, who included members of Atomic Kitten and Hear'Say: 'We were playing girls that were very much, like, "Ooh, don't break my nails" kind of thing. We went there and we just kicked butt.'

Alesha had found a kindred spirit in Su-Elise, one of the few girls she knew who was her sporting equal. Su-Elise was a whizz at lacrosse and swimming, and had represented Surrey at cross-country when she was younger. She was also a devoted Arsenal fan and liked to play football in the park. Alesha had the advantage of being engaged to a former footballer, although Harvey was never too keen on having a girl join in when he was playing football with his mates. Domestic harmony was assured, however, when Harvey's team won the men's competition.

Mis-Teeq's final single from *Lickin' On Both Sides* was timed to cash in on the estimated television audience of 200 million around the world who had watched the Jubilee concert two weeks earlier. 'Roll On / This Is How We Do It' reached number five in the charts, the fifth top ten hit from the album. It seemed to be almost a greatest hits album, yet it was only their debut release.

The track was all over the radio when the band played for the first time at Glastonbury, which any other year would have been the biggest music event of the summer. Nowadays it's commonplace for pop and urban acts to perform alongside the rock greats but in 2002 it was still a bit of a novelty.

Mis-Teeq performed in the Dance Tent while Stereophonics were on the main Pyramid Stage. *BBC News* online reported, 'They were one of the most charismatic and energetic groups at the festival, and they certainly outperformed some of the rock bands. They were jumping around and pumping out their hits on stage in the Dance Tent – and the big crowd was giving the group one of the most rapturous receptions of the weekend.'

The summer festival circuit was becoming an increasingly important showcase for the modern pop act. After Glastonbury, Mis-Teeq played Party in the Park, the annual concert in Hyde Park in aid of The Prince's Trust, Mardi Gras at Hackney Marshes and the Creamfields festival near Liverpool. The latter was a traditional summer mudbath, and the girls didn't want to walk to the stage in their designer high heels. The organizers promptly laid on a Mini and the three of them squeezed in. Unfortunately, it became stuck; the girls refused to budge and had to be pushed ignominiously to the stage by security staff.

Alesha's gradual rise to prominence within Mis-Teeq culminated in September 2002 with her first important job away from the group. She was signed up to be the host of the MOBO Awards at the London Arena. Mis-Teeq were again shortlisted, this time for UK Act of the Year and Best Garage Act. They were up against So Solid Crew in both categories. It would be a return to the spotlight for Harvey, who had been rather in his girlfriend's shadow throughout the summer.

He was quite outspoken about their plans to have children. He told the *Independent*, 'Me and Alesha will do three albums each, then I'll do a film and then we'll have kids.' He added that they couldn't agree on a name for their first child: 'I like the name Trinity but Alesha doesn't. So that's that.' His views did not necessarily match those of his fiancée, who had said shortly before that she was too busy to plan her wedding.

Alesha had been a bag of nerves on the day of the awards ceremony, especially working with her co-host, LL Cool J, whom she had never met. She learned her script by heart, but the veteran American rapper and film star said he didn't need to do that and would just read his lines from the autocue. That only made Alesha more nervous: 'He was very overconfident. But he's a legend and been around for ages and I felt privileged to be presenting with him.' In the end, she needn't have worried because they worked well together. She recalled later, 'Afterwards, I saw him being interviewed about the show and he said some really nice things about me.'

Harvey, meanwhile, had been trying to move on from So Solid Crew by launching his solo career. Both he and Alesha were aware they needed to appeal to a wider, mainstream audience to achieve any long-term success.

The year could hardly have gone better for Mis-Teeq: although they didn't win the MOBO for Best UK Act, which went to Ms Dynamite, they were named Best Garage Act. It ended on a sad note, however, when the popular John McMahon, who had looked after them on tour, was killed on Christmas Day. He was behind the wheel of a Chrysler people carrier that left the road and crashed into a telephone pole near his home in Stafford. He died at the scene, aged forty-three.

McMahon had also worked with Ms Dynamite and Craig David and at the time he was just starting to look after Girls Aloud. The papers carried a grisly picture of the battered vehicle with 'Girls Aloud' painted on the side. Sabrina said, 'We are deeply shocked. John was a lovely man who will be sorely missed by us and everyone he worked with.' Mis-Teeq would dedicate their second album to him.

CHAPTER EIGHT

Scandalous

Mis-Teeq recorded their most famous track, 'Scandalous', at a time when everyone was trying to stay as far away from scandal as possible. Part of the master plan to reach a wider audience was to secure a foothold in the lucrative American market. That was never an easy prospect but was particularly daunting for a black female group competing against some of the most popular acts of the time, including Destiny's Child and TLC.

The pattern for Alesha's future career path as a mainstream entertainer was set in these early days when Mis-Teeq were riding a wave of popularity. The ability to recognize a need for change when things are going well would stay with her even when she was established as a popular judge on *Strictly Come Dancing*.

Mis-Teeq had managed to avoid being bracketed with So Solid Crew even though Alesha was engaged to its most charismatic member. But it was clear that UK garage had a shelf-life because of its limited appeal. It wasn't just Harvey's collective that couldn't match the peak of their first album: Ms Dynamite, arguably the biggest female star of the genre, won the prestigious Mercury Music Prize in 2002 for her album *A Little Deeper* but never again reached those heights. Nobody knew it at the time but when she won the BRIT Award in 2003 for Best British Female, her best days of commercial success were already behind her.

Ms Dynamite had become good friends with Alesha through her connection with So Solid Crew. Alesha observed, 'We'll see in her next album what she's really capable of.' As it turned out, Ms Dynamite wouldn't release that album until 2005 and it failed to make the top twenty.

Already Alesha was trying to position the band away from the very narrow perception of Mis-Teeq. She told the *Daily Record*, 'People have called us a garage act but we aren't, we incorporate lots of different music from reggae to ragga, hip-hop, slow ballads and R & B.' That covered just about every sort of contemporary music.

The second album would be the key for Mis-Teeq and their ambition to broaden their appeal. Their first had been a success beyond their expectations but appearances on *Top of the Pops* and the endless promotional days were no longer a novelty. It had been a conveyor belt and there was a danger of the public becoming tired of so much Mis-Teeq. Their record company had suggested a Christmas release for the follow-up but the girls wanted more time. Alesha explained, 'You have to develop your sound, not just churn stuff out.'

After 'Roll On', nine months would pass before 'Scandalous' was released in March 2003. The track was another collaboration with StarGate and took just two hours to compose during one of their chilled-out writing sessions. Alesha explained that the song was light-hearted: 'It's about how you can really fancy a guy but they are a bit bad. Some women like a bit of scandal with their man.'

Everything about the track was glossier and more sophisticated than their debut. The *Daily Record* called it their finest music to date. Julie MacCaskill enthused, '"Scandalous" is a stonking fusion of dance, pop, R & B and garage which is as infectious as the flu. Positively oozing sex appeal, the heavy hook gives the girls' garage sound much-needed weight without ever becoming overbearing.'

The video was also a classier affair. The action begins with a lone man running through an unwelcoming urban area while a vicious-looking dog snarls menacingly. He runs into a secret nightclub, where Alesha begins the song sprawled on the bar. The girls smoulder through the whole track, which is quite repetitive in a hypnotic sort of way. Alesha still raps but in a softer style and there's no sense of cranking it up with a 'And, here we go.' There's just a suspicion that the production is not as fresh and individual as some of their earlier hits.

The video was their second collaboration with Jake Nava, who was fast becoming one of the most sought-after directors in music. He had also worked with them on 'B With Me'. The same year as 'Scandalous', he directed the Beyoncé solo breakthrough, 'Crazy In Love'. His work with Mis-Teeq would lead to a nomination for Best Video at the 2003 MOBOs.

The exposure was almost instant and 'Scandalous' featured in many advertisements, including, most notably, in a £5 million campaign for Coca-Cola. Usually it was Pepsi that was linked to music so it was big news when Coke entered the marketplace with their TXT for Music promotion, a major breakthrough for Mis-Teeq. In the commercial, they are shown being led away from their dressing room by a roadie, who takes them to Coca-Cola Music HQ, where the group Busted are recording. It's not a particularly exciting ad but the timing was excellent and the opening bars of the song became instantly recognizable.

'Scandalous' reached number two in the charts in March 2003. This time it was only a couple of weeks between the release of the first single and the album *Eye Candy*, which also made the top ten at number six. Reviews were mixed but generally positive for Alesha. The *Scotsman* said, 'Were it not for the blaring vocal contributions of the fabulous Alesha, whose strident, foghorn reggae toasting supplies Mis-Teeq with about 95 per cent of their edge, *Eye Candy* would just be another lame example of the Brits copying what the Americans do better.'

Interest from national newspapers was an indication that Mis-Teeq had made the jump into the mainstream and were more

consumer friendly. They were no longer relying on specialist magazines or online sites to notice them. Even the *Sunday Mirror* gave the
album nine out of ten.

The *Guardian* thought *Eye Candy* was a sharp career move, but
one with 'humanity and depth.' The paper's reviewer, Dave
Simpson, also noted that Mis-Teeq had shifted 'further from their
garage roots towards the more internationally lucrative R & B'. That
was exactly the intention. They had recorded parts of the album in
the US in order to obtain a polished feel.

Thinking ahead to their American push, they brought in the
renowned Newark-born rapper Reggie Noble for a remix of
'Scandalous' entitled 'Sumthin' Scandalous'. Under the stage name
of Redman, he was best known for his work on 'Dirrty', the number
one for Christina Aguilera. They also went to New Jersey to record
with Joe Thomas, the acclaimed producer and R & B singer usually
credited simply as Joe. He featured on the track 'Home Tonight'.

It was all part of the plan to give the band international credibility. Alesha still had big ambitions for Mis-Teeq: 'We want to release
three albums and carry on, not implode and split up before the third
one is released like so many British female groups.'

Eye Candy didn't produce as many hit singles as their first album
but the follow-up to 'Scandalous', 'Can't Get It Back', still managed
to make number eight – their seventh top ten hit in a row.

Harvey hadn't been faring so well musically. Things had looked
promising in 2002, when he had signed a reported six-figure deal
with the independent label Go Beat. He too had been trying to present a more acceptable face to the masses by appearing on a *Smash
Hits* tour alongside Darius and H & Claire from Steps. He also joined
Melanie C and Russell Watson to record a version of the classic
Queen song 'Bohemian Rhapsody'. His first solo single, however,
'Get Up and Move' barely made any impression when it was released
in the autumn.

Then his label went bust, which delayed the release of the album he had already made. He would have to re-record it if he ever wanted to fill the shelves of the record stores. The fragile nature of the music business was confirmed just a few weeks later when Relentless Records, the label that had launched So Solid Crew, went into liquidation. His musical career went from bad to worse with the news that for Christmas he was recording a rap song with Princess Diana's notorious ex-lover James Hewitt. It was called 'Ding Dong'.

Unsurprisingly, Harvey started to widen his search for stardom away from music. He took part in *Celebrity Fear Factor*, in which he decided against putting his head in a tank full of maggots. He started presenting *T4*, Channel 4's weekend slot aimed at the teenage and youth markets, and appeared in a straight-to-video action movie called *Out for a Kill*, starring Steven Seagal, in which he was credited as Michael Junior Harvey.

More promisingly, he took part in another reality show called *The Games* on Channel 4. He was one of a group of celebrities, including comedian Bobby Davro and chef Jean-Christophe Novelli, who competed in a series of Olympic-style events like diving, weightlifting and gymnastics. Harvey collected the gold medal, which was no surprise to Alesha, who said, 'I knew he'd win. I was so proud of him.' It was a pity Alesha didn't have time to take part as well. Instead she was busy rehearsing for Mis-Teeq's first headlining UK tour.

In October 2003 Harvey resumed his football career when he signed with AFC Wimbledon in the Combined Counties League. It was a far cry from his schoolboy days with Chelsea, but within six months he was playing at an even lower level, for Lewes in the Ryman League.

Perhaps surprisingly, Alesha and Harvey together weren't as much in demand as might have been expected for the black Posh and Becks. They were a well-known couple but their relationship didn't seem to benefit their careers. Singly they were glamorous and charismatic, but they didn't appear to be creating a joint brand the way the Beckhams had done so successfully.

They had finally found the house they wanted on the outskirts of

Welwyn, just ten minutes from Beverley. They bought the four-bedroom modern house, mortgage free, for £317,000 in October 2003. At today's prices it would probably fetch upwards of £450,000, but Alesha has never been tempted to sell it. Their new home wasn't particularly glamorous but was a good place to start their life together. The small development of new houses had the air of a gated community even though there was no official security. You wouldn't guess that anybody famous lived there.

Harvey's personal popularity was high. He was described by the *Western Mail* as a 'heartthrob for a generation.' He also seemed proud of Alesha's achievements: 'That is my woman, the love of my life.' It was a sentiment she had echoed in the acknowledgements of *Eye Candy*: 'Individually we are strong. Together we're amazing. Always and forever baby.'

Apart from such public slushiness, Alesha went back into her shell regarding her private life in 2003. She preferred to keep her personal life and public image separate, making sure nobody knew when she and Harvey jetted off for a holiday in Barbados with Romeo and his girlfriend. They were in a family resort with lots of children around but nobody bothered them. Harvey even helped to organize some football games for the kids.

By the end of the year she was even more reticent to talk about her private life than she had been previously. She put a reporter from the *Cambridge Evening News* firmly in her place for asking if Harvey would be watching her gig that night. The question wasn't particularly intrusive, especially as the following day was her twenty-fifth birthday, but Alesha snapped, 'Maybe, why are you so nosey?'

Alesha's mood was not improved by the final release from *Eye Candy*, another StarGate production called 'Style', which failed to make the top ten. She declared it to be her least favourite Mis-Teeq track of all time. She explained, 'We were kinda pressured into doing it.'

The prospects for 2004 were promising, however, especially after she received a call from Pharrell Williams inviting her to be in the new video for his band N.E.R.D. The charismatic Williams had gained a reputation as one of the most exciting talents in the music business through his production work with his old mate from Virginia, Chad 'Hip Hop' Hugo. As The Neptunes, they had written 'I'm A Slave 4 U' for Britney Spears and 'Girlfriend' for 'N Sync. He was a close friend of Justin Timberlake, who Alesha had always said was the artist she would like to work with.

Pharrell was a fan of Michael Jackson and once had a bizarre radio conversation with the man in which he called him 'Sir' throughout. He shared Jackson's belief that music is a gift from God. The Neptunes were keen to move out from behind the mixing desk and make their own records. They formed N.E.R.D (No one Ever Really Dies) in 2001. Pharrell wanted Alesha for 'She Wants To Move', which would be the first single from their second album, *Fly or Die*.

Pharrell had seen Alesha on the front cover of *Arena* magazine and decided she had the look he wanted for the video, despite American casting directors looking for a better-known supermodel in the US. Alesha didn't hesitate: 'I got the call on the Wednesday and on Thursday I was on a flight to LA.' She knew that Pharrell had a reputation as a player but she told *RWD* magazine that he didn't try it on with her: 'I'm in a happy relationship and that would have been an awkward situation. But one thing I must say is, that man is professional. Before I went out there, everybody told me he'd be a womanizer but he was totally the opposite of what everybody had said.'

Her decision to do it was made easier with Harvey's support. She confirmed he was the first person to encourage her to go, despite press reports that he was mad at her for agreeing to fly across the Atlantic to film with Williams. Alesha observed, 'He's not an insecure person.'

That was fortunate because Alesha spent the three-minute video dancing on a podium in a silver-fringed micro dress that left little to the imagination. The song itself was a little monotonous, with Pharrell and co watching Alesha shake her booty while they sang 'She's sexy' over and over, although they did include the immortal line 'Her ass is a spaceship I want to ride.'

Alesha loved the experience, calling it 'brilliant' and 'amazing' and 'a complete honour'. It was also a very shrewd move because it remains one of the landmark moments in her career. Perhaps because of her contribution, 'She Wants To Move' reached number five in the charts, N.E.R.D.'s biggest UK hit.

When the video was released, up and down the country people were asking, 'Isn't that Alesha from Mis-Teeq?' The important thing from a career point of view was that Sabrina and Su-Elise weren't in it.

CHAPTER NINE

MC^2

Telstar Records folded on 5 April 2004. The label announced it was going into administration with debts of £8.5 million. At the time much of the blame was laid at Victoria Beckham's door and the poor performance of her double A-sided single 'Let Your Head Go/This Groove', which had failed to reach number one despite a huge promotional campaign. She had signed a contract with a £1.5 million advance, which demanded something better than number three in the charts. It was the last record she would ever release. Su-Elise joined the criticism: 'I think there was far too much hype surrounding her project with Telstar and obviously it didn't pay off at all. It's really sad as everyone we worked with at Telstar has lost their jobs because of the situation.'

Victoria was an easy target. While her recording potential was wildly overestimated, she wasn't the only disappointment. Craig David, arguably, had peaked and his second album, *Slicker Than Your Average*, had failed to top the charts. Telstar pointed to the changing face of the record industry and the trend for people to download music from the Internet as the key reason for their demise.

Alesha could be forgiven for thinking the whole business was an unsteady deck of cards. Her ex-boyfriend Noel's label went broke, as did Harvey's and So Solid Crew's – and now hers. You never knew what was going to happen next. One minute Alesha was on top of the world, appearing in Pharrell's video and relaxing with Harvey in sun-drenched Dubai, and then this.

The collapse of their record label was bad timing for Mis-Teeq, not least because royalties they were expecting from the sales of their second album would instead be used to pay off creditors. Lawyers and administrators were now the key players while their management team, Twenty-First Artists, tried to claw back their recording assets. Their five-album deal was worthless.

Telstar's juddering demise wasn't expected to be the end for the group, who were putting all their energies into breaking into America. The early indication was that their first single there, 'Scandalous', was going to be a major hit, despite the marketplace being so crowded. The initial breakthrough was achieved by chance when the popular and influential American DJ Carson Daly heard the track while he was on holiday in the South of France and started playing it when he returned home, convincing Reprise Records that they should sign Mis-Teeq.

The Atlantic is full of British acts who thought they could just turn up in the US and match their British success only to sink without trace. Robbie Williams, Blur and Oasis are some of the biggest names who failed to make an impression. It really is a case of putting the time in, so Alesha, Su-Elise and Sabrina went to the States for two months to try to get noticed and promote the single.

Sabrina recalled in the *Guardian*, 'We were told the song was being played on the radio and we were like, yeah, right. It was only when I got to New York and heard it being played in a shop that I realized it really was. It's pretty amazing.

'We're not going to go out to America and try and imitate what Americans do, because they do it best. We don't sound American – our sound is very British. They love the English accent, so we want to keep sounding as British as we can.'

'Scandalous' reached number thirty-five in the *Billboard* Hot 100 when it was released in May 2004 and also made number four in the dance chart. This was quite good but not desperately exciting. If it had been a Destiny's Child recording, it probably would have been the biggest-selling record of the year. Intriguingly, on the specially designed cover for the US, Alesha featured in the centre of the trio and not to the side as she usually did.

The album that was launched two months later fared less well, only managing a lowly 125 in the *Billboard* chart. Called unimaginatively *Mis-Teeq*, it was a compilation of the best bits from their first two albums, including most of their hit singles, although for some reason 'Why?' was left out. The additional publicity obtained when 'Scandalous' was chosen as the theme tune for *Catwoman*, starring Halle Berry, made little difference to sales. It might have helped more if the film had been better received. It won the Golden Raspberry Award as the worst film of the year, so being associated with the movie was nothing to be pleased about.

The American critics were lukewarm in their response to the album. The *Cincinnati Post* observed, 'From an American point of view, Mis-Teeq's wild British success is a mystery.' *Time* magazine referred to them as a 'spelling-impaired British hip-hop trio'.

The *Desert News* of Salt Lake City was not exactly unkind, suggesting the album was 'worth a listen' but the review also identified a key problem: 'When they're singing together their style is reminiscent of Destiny's Child ...' Mis-Teeq could never escape being compared to the superstar group and, in America itself, that was a huge barrier to success. A second US single, 'One Night Stand', failed to match the impact of 'Scandalous'.

The only upside of their trip was the shopping. Alesha loved New York in particular, calling it her favourite place in the whole world. They spent far too much money in Gucci stores, and chose the latest Louis Vuitton bags. They may have missed home but seemed genuinely to embrace the size and opportunity of America. Su-Elise observed simply, 'Everything is bigger.'

With hindsight, perhaps they played it too safe. They had grabbed attention in the UK by being part of the garage scene and by promoting Alesha's ability to MC. They didn't do that in the US and, as a result, were not offering anything different. The American online site *VH1* pointed out patronizingly, 'The girls even do a little rapping' and proceeded to call them the British version of Destiny's Child.

The group returned to the UK not exactly to lick their wounds but deflated. They had missed most of the big summer festivals but, in any case, they didn't have any new material to showcase. They didn't even have a MOBO nomination to look forward to. Ironically, those awards were overrun by American acts in 2004, with Kanye West and Usher the big winners on the night. Garage music, meanwhile, had been dropped from the awards altogether – a clear sign that this particular branch of urban music was now history.

This was the first year they introduced white acts into the nominations, which some commentators thought softened their appeal. Joss Stone, for instance, was nominated for Best Album for *Soul Sessions*, prompting one commentator to call the awards a 'patronizing piece of ghettoization'.

It seemed unlikely that Mis-Teeq would be nominated again any time soon and certainly not in an album category. They didn't have one. After the bankruptcy of Telstar, work on their third album had ground to a halt, which was disappointing as this time they had been working with Guy Chambers, who had co-written many of the most memorable Robbie Williams songs, including the crowd-friendly anthems 'Angels' and 'Rock DJ'. Alesha had been excited by the collaboration: 'Guy has brought out a different side to us'.

Not everyone was impressed with the work in progress on the album. Harvey would later tell the *Daily Mirror* he didn't think the music was right and he would convey his doubts to his fiancée: 'She said: "Babe, what do you think of this song?" Because I'm an honest freak, I don't mince my words. I said: "Babe, I don't like it." Alesha needed a lot of support. She's a sensitive girl who takes her work very seriously.'

Alesha's comment about recording the tricky third album was generally upbeat: 'We're going to take our time and make sure we get it right.' It looked like Mis-Teeq had all the time in the world without a new record deal.

Alesha went back to her house in Welwyn to think about the future. The first big decision she made was to set a date for her wedding to Harvey. They announced that the big day would be on 19 June 2005, which allowed plenty of time to plan ahead and determine Alesha's next career move. She now had the time to sort out the wedding arrangements; she was no longer too busy. She wanted the occasion to be 'simple and lovely'.

Five years is very much a generation when it comes to pop music and many famous boy and girl bands have split up after that length of time. They can often spend as long pursuing success as staying together after they have found it. Take That split up five years after the release of their first single. The Spice Girls lasted five years after signing their first record deal. 'N Sync and Blue were two other famous groups who didn't make it into a sixth year of recording. Mis-Teeq joined the list in January 2005, when they announced they were disbanding. It wasn't a big surprise. It's always easier to get on when ambition is shared.

Girl bands were acknowledged to be particularly difficult to keep harmonious and some, like Sugababes and Atomic Kitten, were forever changing line-ups. Louis Walsh, who used to manage Girls Aloud, observed, 'Girls are high maintenance, it's easier to manage boy bands – less hairspray, less make-up, less baggage.'

The official statement read: 'They've done it so they can explore other opportunities. But the band loved their time together and they'll remain friends.' Exploring other opportunities was a polite way of saying that they had been together long enough and wanted to pursue solo careers. One theory was that they didn't want to relocate to America, but things really hadn't gone well enough there to warrant such a move in any case.

In the years since their split, various stories have cast a little doubt on the party line that all was sweetness and light. Harvey, who always seemed to be less discreet than Alesha, told the *Daily Mail*, 'Being with two girls every day of your life can be hard. Women are a nightmare as it is. They weren't getting on. It was silly things, things like who was going to wear that outfit.'

Alesha was reported in the *Daily Record* as saying that she no longer spoke to the other two because they were bitter about her superior talent: 'There's not a lot of love lost, because there was only one in Mis-Teeq who was going to shine.'

Sabrina was quoted in the *Sun* as saying, 'A lot of people say Alesha should have stuck to MCing because her voice isn't that strong and I agree.' She later told *Live From Studio Five* that she had been misquoted and the media couldn't be trusted to tell the truth.

Mis-Teeq was unusual in that the lead singer was undeniably Sabrina, whose soft, honeyed vocals always led the melody. But it was Alesha who had gradually taken over the group due in part to her devastating good looks but also largely because her machine-gun MCing had given the band their identity. By the time they split, she had become the central figure, which might well have frustrated Sabrina.

It's usually important to be quick off the mark as a solo artist and it was soon announced that Alesha had signed a three-album deal with Polydor worth a reported £500,000. She had been taken on by Colin Barlow, the forward-thinking boss of the label's British division. The extent of any negotiations before Mis-Teeq split was never revealed. Sabrina wouldn't release a record until 2010, while Su-Elise has yet to make her solo debut. Instead, she trained as a dance teacher and opened her own stage school, which now has six centres in the Home Counties.

Before it was all over, Mis-Teeq sang a version of the old Andrews Sisters' favourite 'Shoo Shoo Baby', which appeared on the

Presenting Alesha Dixon . . . champion dancer, award-winning singer and television star.

Alesha with her mother Beverley, who has been her inspiration and the most important person in her life.

She has always been close to her half-sister Leyanne, her only female sibling. They are all smiles walking home with Mis-Teeq's Capital FM Award for Favourite R&B Artists in April 2004.

Nobody in the media realized she was the girlfriend of Noel Simpson from leading boy band Damage. Noel is on the far right of this band shot, taken before a Radio 1 concert on Plymouth Hoe in August 2000.

Damage's current line-up after re-forming in 2009. Noel, who is wearing the hat, remains good friends with Alesha.

With her Mis-Teeq bandmates, Sabrina Washington (centre) and Su-Elise Nash (right), Alesha performs The Supremes' classic 'Stop! In The Name Of Love' at The Queen's Golden Jubilee concert at Buckingham Palace in June 2002. Alesha said it was the best gig they ever played.

Alesha is centre stage when they perform 'Sumthin' Scandalous' featuring Redman for the MOBOs at the Royal Albert Hall in September 2003. It was a remix of their biggest hit, 'Scandalous'.

The girls decided not to dress up when they performed at the Christmas lights switching-on ceremony at the Lakeside Shopping Centre in December 2003.

From chavtastic . . . at the Trafford Centre, Manchester, in December 2003.

To fantastic . . . before the BRITs at Earl's Court in February 2004.

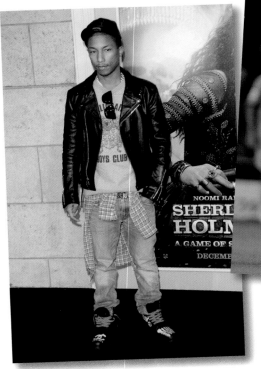

Three of the men in Alesha's life. Top: MC Harvey, pictured on the left with his So Solid Crew bandmates, was the real deal. Middle: Footballer John Carew was her boyfriend for two months. Bottom: Singer and producer Pharrell Williams . . . maybe.

A match of two halves – Alesha with MC Harvey, who would become her husband.

Alesha with Javine Hylton, Harvey's co-star in *Daddy Cool*. They are pictured at the musical's opening night party in September 2006, two months before he confessed he was having an affair.

Javine is pregnant when she and Harvey attend the premiere of *Hancock* in Leicester Square in June 2008.

Alesha is delighted to see Arlene Phillips at the National TV Awards in October 2008. There were no smiles a year later, when she controversially replaced her as a judge on *Strictly Come Dancing*.

Performing with Bruce Forsyth, who has always supported her, at the Help for Heroes concert at Twickenham in September 2010.

Dancing up a storm with fellow judge Bruno Tonioli at the launch of the 2010 season of *Strictly*. Even Craig Revel Horwood would have given them a perfect ten.

soundtrack of *Valiant*, a Disney cartoon about an heroic wood pigeon in World War Two. The song was pleasant enough but as far removed from UK garage as it was possible to get. It featured as a bonus track on their *Greatest Hits* album, which was released on the Universal label in April 2005.

The album was a commercial opportunity to cash in while Mis-Teeq were still fresh in the memory. The *Daily Mirror* described it as a 'nostalgic trip through recent British urban pop at its most vibrant'. Most fans already owned the songs, though, and the album only reached number twenty-eight in the UK album charts.

In the age of celebrity weddings you might have expected the Alesha Dixon–MC Harvey union to have been one of the big *OK!* or *Hello!* events of the year. They may not have commanded the £1 million paid to Posh and Becks but in a world overpopulated by soap stars they were refreshingly glamorous. Alesha was determined, however, that her big day was not going to be a diversion for fans of glossy magazines.

The newspapers barely carried the story and certainly no pictures were published. It was almost a secret wedding despite the fact that the ceremony was in a lovely Hertfordshire village where anybody could have strolled past the church. Alesha's desire for her day to be completely private could have been motivated by a number of factors.

Firstly, the sort of pictures a glossy magazine would want might have proved tricky when relations between her mother and father weren't particularly close. Alesha, too, had seen very little of him during the past few years, especially since he had split from his partner, Catherine, and left Welwyn Garden City to begin a new life as an electrician in Thailand. On Alesha's wedding certificate, the space for the bride's father has been left blank. He isn't acknowledged at all. Alesha described herself as a musician, while Harvey lists his occupation as 'entertainment business'.

Secondly, Harvey, who had so far managed to avoid the So Solid Crew malaise of getting into trouble with the law, had finally done just that in Welwyn Garden City. He had been involved in a confrontation in January after a policeman had seen him driving his black 4 × 4, a VW Toureg, while using his mobile phone. Harvey had apparently stopped his car, jumped out and demanded to know why he was being followed. A scuffle followed and Harvey was arrested.

His appearance at St Albans Crown Court was scheduled for the beginning of June, just a few weeks before his wedding. He flew back especially from Ibiza, where he had been joined by a dozen of his closest friends for his stag weekend.

The court heard that Harvey had called the police officer a 'fucking pussy', grabbed him by the throat and tried to pull his tie off. Police had to use CS gas twice on Harvey in order to subdue him. He was found guilty of assault, using threatening behaviour and driving while disqualified and having no insurance.

He was sentenced to 150 hours' community service at a separate appearance twelve days before his marriage. Harvey was also banned from driving for nine months, fined £400 and ordered to pay £50 compensation. District judge Alistair Perkins said, 'You are clearly a very talented person with a bright future ahead of you.' The *Daily Mirror* noted that he had arrived at court with his flies undone.

Afterwards he put on a brave, even cheerful, face for the media: 'Getting married and going to court at the same time is very stressful, even for a relaxed person like me. But I like giving back to my community. I'm going to make old people happy.'

Alesha could breathe a sigh of relief that her husband-to-be wasn't languishing in jail as she set off down the aisle in her beautiful white wedding dress. She had always been determined to have a white wedding – although the dress did have some red silk in the design. She chose the Nigerian-born couturier Yemi Osunkoya, the man behind Kosibah, to design the gown. He had set up the design house in 1991 and named it after his mother. He was named Bridal

Designer of the Year at the Mahogany Bridal Awards in 2002 and 2004.

He spent nine months creating the gown, which was made of white duchesse satin, with a hand-embellished bodice in tiny Swarovski crystals. The dress followed a classical A-line silhouette and flared to a stunning fishtail shape in white with inserts of burgundy satin. Alesha had been keen to have a two for one dress. For the church ceremony she had a detachable underskirt which sat on top of the main dress. In the evening when it got too hot, Alesha was able to whip off this piece and, hey presto, it was as if she was wearing a new dress.

Alison Jane Reid wasn't impressed: 'The dress you wear on your wedding day should be the epitome of style and elegance. Isn't that every girl's dream? The designer has made some wonderfully restrained and elegant gowns, but this isn't one of them. It is trying too hard to be elegant and fun at the same time. I like the bodice, with its delicate embellishment, but the fishtail with its rather too extrovert red inserts is more *Annie Get Your Gun* than serene bride.'

Yemi maintained that his inspiration was celebrating the female form: 'Growing up in Nigeria, West Africa, I was used to seeing women of all shapes and therefore feel very comfortable designing for "real" and curvaceous women.' His design for Alesha's dress certainly celebrated her curves and femininity. He was there on the morning of the wedding to help Alesha get dressed and ensure she felt 'beautiful, luminous and confident' on her big day.

Harvey wore a matching white suit, which might have been more fitting for a wedding on the beach than the beautiful St John's Church in Lemsford, on the edge of the famous Brocket Hall Estate. The village, which has a large watermill over the River Lea, is renowned as one of the prettiest in the area and the church itself is picture postcard perfect for a summer wedding. Alesha walked down the aisle, accompanied by her two bridesmaids dressed in red – her sister Leyanne and best friend Victoria Skeggs. Harvey's best man was the Premiership footballer Sean Davis, whom he had grown up with in Battersea. A talented midfielder, Sean had made a promising start to his career at Fulham before transferring to Spurs, but major injuries harmed his chances to fulfil his potential.

Harvey thought his bride looked 'amazing'. He admitted, 'When I saw her walking down the aisle I was gone. I cried my eyes out and Sean was crying too.' The ceremony was conducted by the local vicar, the Reverend Edward Cardale. It was of particular significance to her mother Beverley, who had never married but was a devout Christian. She had found comfort in her faith in recent years and was in a happy, long-term relationship.

All the reports of the wedding claimed that Alesha and Harvey were married at Brocket Hall and not this delightful English church setting. The reception, however, *was* held at the splendid stately home and the bridal party posed for pictures by the lake. You can walk through the grounds of the estate from the church to the hall but Alesha was never going to do that in her wedding dress.

The new Mr and Mrs Harvey slipped quietly away for a dream honeymoon in Hawaii and Las Vegas. She told *Top of the Pops* magazine, 'I'd never been to Hawaii and it always sounds so romantic and it really is and it's beautiful. Las Vegas I'd never been to either and that was just a completely mad place. I mean it's crazy and four days were enough there!'

While her wedding to the man she loved had been wonderful, it didn't immediately change her life. They were already living together and her home routine wouldn't change, or so she thought, until she started a family. She remained fiercely ambitious as a performer and wanted the new Mr and Mrs Harvey to be financially more secure first.

Her most pressing problem, therefore, was to decide what sort of performer she wanted to be. In the end she would spend a year working on her first solo album. She had seen from her Mis-Teeq days that comparisons don't necessarily help. She was already concerned at the media calling her the 'British Beyoncé' long before Bruce Forsyth did. She was nice enough about it to Top of the Pops online, claiming to be flattered, but wanted to distance herself from the American superstar: 'Musically I think we are very different. Beyoncé is very much R & B – that's her style and she owns it – but I'm trying to do something slightly left field and break out of some of those stereotypes that have been put onto me.'

The first priority was to make sure she sang more. She didn't want to be a rap star and vocally needed to step away from Sabrina's shadow. Then she needed to decide her musical direction. Everybody would be expecting R & B, especially as that was the route Mis-Teeq were following. Alesha chose to ignore R & B completely. Instead she explored funk, the music from her youth, when her mother had moved on from Diana Ross and introduced her to the records of James Brown, the godfather of soul and singer of 'Get Up I Feel Like Being A Sex Machine'. She added a touch of the reggae sounds that her father used to play for her. Alesha described her new direction as 'pop funk reggae', which covered most bases.

In the UK, the biggest influence on her new sound was the producer Johnny Douglas, who was best known for his work with Kylie Minogue on her albums *Light Years* and *Body Language*. Together with songwriter Nina Woodford, they wrote a track called 'Fired Up', which she loved so much she decided to make it the title of the album. Gone were the drum machine and techno wizardry of R & B and in their place were real musicians playing in the studio. Alesha loved the live feel of the recording when she joined Nina and Johnny to stand at the mic and shout 'Fired Up' as the band played behind them.

She flew to Stockholm to meet the Swedish songwriter and producer Anders Bagge, who worked closely with Colin Barlow and had written for Jennifer Lopez, Whitney Houston and TLC. He encouraged Alesha to have the confidence to be herself. She acknowledged to I Like Music Online that he made a big impression on her: 'The nicest way to make music is to just be free and let yourself go and have no fear. And that's what Anders allows you to do, because his personality is so crazy, and he's exciting to be around and it makes you feel excited.'

During one of their last sessions in the studio Anders gave her a backing track to listen to in her hotel room. She was by herself, in a foreign country with nothing to do but write a lyric. She recalled, 'I was all excited and I was ringing up my mum and going, "What do you think of this hook? I think it's really catchy?"' Beverley, it seemed, was still the first person she rang.

CHAPTER TEN

Knockdown

MC Harvey's career plan seemed to be to turn himself into a one-man variety show – you had no idea where he was going to turn up next. Since his initial success with So Solid Crew, he had been a television presenter, a movie actor, a reality show contestant and resumed his career as a semi-professional footballer. He had combined the last two for a Sky TV series called *The Match*, in which a group of celebrities competed for a place in the starting line-up in a special match against a team of former players, modestly called The Legends.

Harvey was on the losing team in 2005 and again in 2006, when he played on the left wing and dyed his hair red, ensuring he was one of the most noticed celebrities. The final was played at St James's Park, the home ground of Newcastle United, in front of a crowd of 58,000, which was a step up from the usual attendance at AFC Wimbledon or Lewes Football Club.

While his solo music career may not have been progressing, he never seemed to be short of work. Some of it was not quite what he had hoped for – he had to serve in a charity shop near Alesha's mother's house as part of his community service. He couldn't even drive himself home, and had to wait for his wife to arrive to pick him up.

In November 2005 he was announced as one of the stars in a new West End musical called *Daddy Cool*, based on the music of Boney M., who had a string of disco hits in the seventies, including 'Rasputin', 'Brown Girl in the Ring' and 'Rivers of Babylon'. 'Daddy Cool' had been their breakthrough hit in 1976. The idea was to copy the success of *Mamma Mia!* and *We Will Rock You*, although it was always doubtful whether Boney M. had the same enduring fan base as Abba and Queen respectively.

One of Harvey's co-stars was the gap-toothed singer Javine who, like Alesha, had a white mother and a black father. She had made a big impact on the 2002 show *Popstars: The Rivals*, a pre-*X Factor* competition to discover a girl group and a boy band. In the final, Javine seemed to stand out from the other five girls: she was taller, black and possessed a more powerful voice. She was a strong favourite to make the winning line-up but the viewers thought differently and voted for Cheryl Tweedy, Kimberley Walsh, Nicola Roberts, Nadine Coyle and Sarah Harding ahead of her. These five would go on to have huge success as Girls Aloud.

When the result was announced, there was genuine surprise in the studio. The show's presenter, Davina McCall, told her, 'You are too good for the band. You are a star in your own right.' At the time Javine did seem to have something extra and that was perhaps her downfall: nobody felt sorry for her. She was almost overpraised – to the extent that viewers thought she would make the final five easily. Perhaps the public weren't so sure about the prospects of the lovely Geordie, Cheryl, who would become one of the biggest stars in the country.

Initially the prospects for Javine did indeed look rosy. She was chased by record companies and her debut single, 'Real Things', was released on the Innocent label in July 2003. The song made it to number four, which was a respectable start but, as it turned out, would prove to be by far her biggest hit. She was in the charts at the same time as Mis-Teeq featured with 'Can't Get It Back'. Her debut album, *Surrender*, was finally released in June 2004 and featured some of the names closely associated with Alesha, including StarGate and Johnny Douglas. Sales were very disappointing, however, and having managed only number seventy-three in the charts, she was dropped by her record label.

Her new manager, Jonathan Shalit, persuaded her to take part in a competition to choose the next Eurovision Song Contest entry for the UK. He specialized in using television opportunities to secure maximum publicity for his clients. He convinced her it would open doors, although in recent years Eurovision seemed to be more a kiss of death than anything else.

She won *Eurovision: Making Your Mind Up*, beating, among others, Katie Price (Jordan), who had been hoping to launch a singing career. Somewhat ironically, the famously busty Katie was over-shadowed by controversy surrounding Javine's boobs. While performing, Javine's right breast popped out of her skimpy dress. Afterwards she said, 'I think it only came out for a split second.' Shalit claimed it was a genuine wardrobe malfunction, although media sceptics pointed out that her breasts had been on view earlier in the week during a holiday in the Canaries.

There was no malfunction repeat during the final in Kiev, when she scored eighteen points and was placed twenty-second. The track, 'Touch My Fire', which had been produced by Johnny Douglas, was released as a single and became a minor hit, reaching number eight-een in the charts. Her career, it seemed, was in danger of stalling when she entered *The Games* in early 2006, just as Harvey had done three years earlier. And, as he had, she won the gold medal.

Daddy Cool was not the first time she had taken to the stage. She had appeared as Nala in a West End production of *The Lion King* before she pursued a singing career in *Popstars: The Rivals*. Neither she nor Harvey was the star of *Daddy Cool* when it opened at the Shaftesbury Theatre in September 2006, nor was either of them the biggest name – that belonged to Michelle Collins, who had been

Cindy Beale in *EastEnders*. Harvey played a character called Shakespeare, who spent most of the musical rapping or taking off his shirt to reveal a rippling physique. His participation ended abruptly when he was shot. Javine was a pole dancer and would-be singer called Asia Blue, who fancied him.

Harvey was much in demand for interviews as part of the promotional campaign for the show. In one, for the *London Evening Standard*, he had to answer some rapid-fire questions, choosing from two alternatives. He chose vodka rather than gin and preferred cash to credit cards. He was then asked, 'Jamelia or Javine?' He replied, 'Oh man, why are you doing this to me? They are both my friends. OK, I'll say Javine because she's like a sister to me.'

While Harvey had been rehearsing for his West End debut, Alesha had been busy preparing for the launch of her solo career. In July she appeared on the last edition of *Top of the Pops* performing her debut single 'Lipstick'. She wore a very short black sparkly dress that looked like something supplied by the costume department of *Strictly Come Dancing*. She was backed by a guitar-led band and the overall effect was nothing like Mis-Teeq. The song was a bit of an old-fashioned belter full of 'Hey, hey, heys' and 'Whoa, whoa, yeahs', making it difficult to judge the strength of Alesha's vocals away from her MC role in Mis-Teeq.

Unhelpfully, it had taken more than eighteen months since the demise of the band for the record to hit the shelves amid reports that the first choice had been changed. Originally it was scheduled to be a track called 'Superficial', a song reflecting her views about the music business, but at the last minute 'Lipstick', the song she had written in a Stockholm hotel room, was chosen instead, which was not a good sign. She had decided to style herself Alesha and not Alesha Dixon for this new stage of her career. Perhaps fortunately she had decided not to change her professional name to Alesha Harvey.

Alesha did a flurry of interviews and television appearances but perhaps she had lost the attention of the public during her time away from the spotlight. She even answered the obligatory baby questions with good grace. Female celebrities have to face these questions constantly, especially when they get married, have a new boyfriend or turn thirty. Kylie Minogue and Jennifer Aniston must have their response on repeat. Alesha told *RWD* magazine, 'I would like a baby, but not right now because I have to focus on getting myself established as a solo artist. Obviously once that has happened I can deal with children.'

After babies, the second most popular question she was asked was how married life with Harvey was going. She praised her husband of a year to *BBC News* online: 'If I get wound up about something he is very good at keeping me relaxed and it's helpful to have that at home. He's been through his own strife and it's good to have someone who can relate to how I'm feeling. I don't know what I'd do without him.'

'Lipstick' was an interesting choice for her solo launch because it's a powerful, strong song and, as she was intending, not a mellow R & B track. Alesha explained, 'I wanted to hit the public with a "bam!" in your face ... I'm back.' *BBC News* online described it as a 'hi-octane sisters-unite anthem'. *I Like Music* online thought it 'cool and sassy' and praised the song's message that women needed to stop bitching about each other and unite. Alesha explained: 'It's about self-respect and being confident in yourself and in who YOU are.'

Clearly, this was an important song for Alesha and not just for the obvious commercial reasons. She told *I Like Music* that she cared about the way women address each other: 'I think it's really ugly ... you know how women can be quite jealous of each other ... But why do we see each other as competition? All for the attention of men, it's just silly. I just think it's a nicer trait to have to support each other. I like myself more when I'm happy for people. I don't wish bad on people, you know. I just think girls should be taking it easier on each other and stop blaming each other for everything.'

'Lipstick' deserved better than its chart peak of fourteen. Sales were harmed by confusion over its release date and an absence of steady airplay. Alesha gamely told Radio 1 that she was 'glad to be anywhere in the top twenty as a new artist'. It remained to be seen whether her record label took the same view.

Alesha dusted off that disappointment in September when she went to the MOBO Awards at the Royal Albert Hall where, among others, she was photographed with Javine. Alesha received a nomination as Best UK Female, which was a surprise because her debut single had been in the shops for only two days. She lost out to Corinne Bailey Rae, a newcomer who was flavour of the year in 2006.

The very next night she went to support Harvey at the premiere of *Daddy Cool*. The *Independent* was not enthusiastic about the production: 'One can't feel affection for anyone here' and noticed a 'lack of reality in this story of Notting Hill gangs that don't swear or use drugs'. *The Sunday Times*, however, was more impressed: 'The production lives or dies, as such catalogue musicals do, by the amount of goodwill, dancing in the aisles and nostalgic tears it generates. Judging by the packed audience I witnessed, this will be a hit.'

Charles Spencer in the *Daily Telegraph* loved it: 'Javine sings up a storm as the pole-dancing femme fatale. Michelle Collins treats us to another of her languidly sneering cockney über-bitches as Ma Baker, while Harvey raps with spectacular speed, fluency and wit, almost persuading me that this most unlovable genre of pop music might actually have some merit in it.'

Alesha and Harvey made a glamorous couple as they were photographed together at the after-show party at Floridita in Wardour Street. Harvey also had his picture taken with his co-stars Michelle Collins and Javine.

While Harvey had to get used to performing nightly on stage, Alesha had the difficult task of finding a second single from her upcoming album that would do better than the first. 'Knockdown' was a reggae-influenced track she had written with the Kent-based production unit Xenomania. She explained, 'It's a pick me up record. It's about when things are just getting too much and you just need some space to sort yourself out.'

Disastrously, Radio 1 didn't playlist the song, which resulted in hardly any airtime. Official Alesha Dixon, her online fan site, complained that this had 'a bad knock-on effect' when it came to chart position. Polydor were losing faith and pressed a mere 4,000 copies, which were sent only to Virgin and HMV stores, making it virtually impossible for the track to be a hit. But the reality was that Alesha's solo career was stalling before it had barely started. By the time 'Knockdown' was officially released on 30 October 2006, Polydor had already decided to cut their ties with her.

Alesha made a video in which she again revealed her dancing skills, moving easily and sexily with her backing dancers while wearing a spangly gold top and a bowler hat. The video wasn't particularly imaginative but it did confirm that 'Knockdown' was a catchy, modern tune with a chorus that stuck in your head to be hummed all day. TeenSpot.com was enthusiastic and said the song was a 'sure fire hit'. Disappointingly, but not unsurprisingly considering its lack of exposure, the track managed an almost embarrassing number forty-five in the charts. Ironically, bearing in mind that it sank without trace at the time, the video has been viewed more than 2.3 million times on YouTube.

Alesha had already given interviews to publicize the single and her debut album, which would be called *Fired Up*. The *Observer Music Monthly* had even published a positive review of the album: '*Fired Up* comes on like a charged-up assault on the beige British pop landscape, bristling with feelgood charisma.'

Incredibly, the album that had been her principal preoccupation for more than a year was never released in the UK. Alesha was rumoured to have secured all the rights and *Fired Up* was eventually released in Japan.

The commercially astute Alesha had already recorded remixes so that the album would be acceptable to specialist urban stations. The remix for 'Knockdown' was produced by K-Gee, Karl Gordon, who had worked with Alesha on the Damage song 'Rumours' five years earlier. Karl was a great admirer of Alesha's drive and talent and the two had remained friends. By coincidence he had been dating Javine for about ten months.

One morning Karl popped round to see Javine at her house and discovered Harvey in her bed – at least that's what the *Sun* claimed, although the guilty lovers both denied that was the way their secret affair had been exposed. Karl apparently called Alesha to tell her what had happened and she confronted her husband later when he returned home.

Both Harvey and Javine have since had plenty to say about what happened. Javine told the *Daily Mirror* a year later that they were not caught in bed: 'We weren't swinging from chandeliers. My boyfriend didn't walk in and see us naked on top of each other. One morning, Karl decided to come to the house. He walked in, saw Harvey, who had been staying in the spare room, and that was it. There was no fighting, no confrontation. Then Karl called Alesha and told her.'

Harvey was equally outraged at the suggestion that he and Javine had been caught in bed together. He told his story to the *Daily Mail* in December 2007, claiming, 'It's utter bullshit. That's the thing that's got to me, all these lies.' He maintained that Karl had simply seen his car outside Javine's house and told Alesha. He admitted his relationship with Javine: 'It was physical once – not three times or five times.'

According to Harvey, he was completely honest with Alesha and confessed to the affair: 'I could have lied, but I didn't want to be in the marriage any more. I knew I loved someone else and my heart was gone from my home. So I told her the truth. It's the hardest thing I've ever done in my life.

'I've performed in front of hundreds of thousands of people, presented national television, I've done films with Hollywood actors, but this was ten times worse, telling her I'd slept with another woman.'

Harvey would later recall that after he told her, he sat there like a zombie while she shouted at him for two days. He left the marital home and stayed with friends until he moved in with Javine two months later.

Inevitably, there would be opposing points of view where cause and blame were concerned. Alesha stayed in bed with the curtains closed and listened to her CD of *The Miseducation of Lauryn Hill* on repeat.

As news of her marriage break-up spread, it soon became apparent that public sympathy was entirely with Alesha. By contrast Harvey and, in particular, Javine were condemned for what had happened. Karl produced the most memorable quote on the sorry business: 'He's just traded in a Bentley for a second-hand Skoda.'

The singer Jamelia called Javine 'a slag' during an episode of *Never Mind the Buzzcocks*. She also made the point to the *Sun*: 'Alesha is a beautiful, fantastic person and her husband has been sleeping with Javine behind her back. Javine is a slag. I have no time for her.'

Javine did her best to stand up for herself, declaring that she was not a home wrecker because the home was already wrecked. The general public's feelings, readily expressed online in this digital age, were of shock and sympathy that anyone could cheat on someone as lovely as Alesha. The superficial reactions were remarkably similar to the outrage when Ashley Cole allegedly cheated on his wife Cheryl.

Harvey tried to justify his behaviour by suggesting that he and Alesha had different views on when to start a family and that this undermined their relationship. He wanted children before he was thirty: 'She said she wasn't ready. She didn't think we were financially stable enough.'

PART THREE

The Alesha Show

CHAPTER ELEVEN

Survivor

Alesha couldn't throw herself into her work – she didn't have any. Her whole world had been turned completely upside down within a few days. Her career and her marriage were in tatters. She told Fearne Cotton, 'I felt like dying . . . everything I had worked hard for and wanted in my personal life and in my career was just gone. I actually, for a short period of time, felt like my life had been pulled from under my feet.'

At least she had her family and loyal friends close by. Her grandmothers, Maureen and Clem, were keen to make a fuss of her. Her father, too, was on the phone from Thailand and the two put any lingering differences aside. She even made plans to fly out to see him. Alesha observed, 'As you get older, you realize your parents are human beings – not superheroes – and they're allowed to make mistakes. As a child, though, you're selfish, just thinking about your needs. Dad was always a part of my life.'

Her mother, in particular, was a rock when she needed her most. Alesha didn't want to talk publicly about what she would always call 'the worst time in my life', but five years later she was able to pay tribute to Beverley for helping her through it: 'Mum would never tell me what to do, but she was a huge support at that time. She kept telling me I would be strong enough to do whatever I needed to do – and she was right.'

They would take walks together near her house. One field had horses in it and the two women would stock up with carrots and apples and go down to feed the animals and talk things through, she described it to I like Music Online: 'It's quiet, it's peaceful and it keeps you back to basics with what's important in life. It's quite a therapeutic thing to do and, even better, it's my local area.'

Six weeks after the split, Harvey was living with Javine, when Alesha was seen out for the first time enjoying herself at Boujis in London. The newspapers reported that she was 'over her cheating hubby', which was not the case at all.

She admitted that Christmas 2006 was 'quite a dark time' as she contemplated the loss of her marriage and her career. She told the *Guardian*, 'You can't help thinking, "What have I done?" Because I tried to be a professional, I tried to treat people respectfully, I was a good wife, so what have I done? I believe you reap what you sow, so in my gut, I can't help feeling like something was trying to be flushed out of my life. I worked hard, I put my heart and soul into it, I've got a good mental attitude and my life was, like, pulled out from underneath me. I didn't know where to step. I was just lost. Within two weeks it felt like the world had collapsed on my head.'

Understandably, Alesha's moods and ability to handle things varied from day to day. In another interview, with the *Sun*, she said, 'I refuse to be depressed. It's just a waste of time. By the time New Year came round I was already feeling better. I'm very good at talking myself out of feeling down. I'm good at healing quickly. Plus, I didn't feel I was the victim, even though it was portrayed like that. My morals never changed, I'm a good person and I was a good wife. I shouldn't hold my head in shame. Why should I be miserable?'

Alesha's list of New Year's resolutions would have made interesting reading at the start of 2007. They might have included: get out more, redecorate the house and don't forget the divorce. Sorting out her home without Harvey was a good place to start. She decided to get rid of all signs and memories that would remind her of their life together. Harvey recalled, 'One day I came back and she had renovated the house. All my stuff was in bin liners. She even took my So Solid platinum disc down.'

She decided not to throw out her wedding dress. Instead she listed it for sale on eBay with a reserve of £2,000, the proceeds to go to charity. She even threw in the veil. The listing included a statement from the seller: 'As some of you may know due to recent press articles I am no longer happily married so I've decided to sell this beautiful one-off dress which I designed myself. It would be a shame for it to go to waste! Good luck and I hope you enjoy. Lots of love, Alesha.'

Harvey was upset when he found out: 'I was gutted when she sold the dress. It was heartbreaking because it was a huge part of our special day and it caught me by surprise.'

In the end Alesha didn't sell the dress after all but didn't bother to tell Harvey. She accepted the highest bid of £7,500, but much to her annoyance it turned out to be a hoax. She told the *Observer*, 'I've still got the bloody thing, unfortunately.'

Publicly at least, Alesha was putting a brave face on things. She was seen out and about at various London nightclubs. She was reportedly with a mystery man at Chinawhite, and on another night was looking the 'worse for wear' at Opium. She apparently told the *Daily Mirror* that Pharrell Williams was fit and she was hoping for a date. These stories may or may not have been true but at least they were keeping Alesha's name in the media.

Alesha did have a new housemate – her beloved dog Roxy, whom she found at a local RSPCA rescue centre just as her marriage shattered. They were a comfort to each other. She described the collie cross as a 'shy' and 'gloomy' dog who needed to regain her confidence. Her experience giving the dog a loving home led her to become a strong supporter of dogs' charities. Roxy was fiercely protective of her owner. Alesha told Chris Moyles, 'She's a trouble-some dog and only I would put up with her. She's got this growling temperament at night that scares my guests.'

In February 2007 Alesha left Roxy at home when she dressed up for the BRIT Awards at Earls Court, which were broadcast live for the first time since 1989, but with a 30-second tape delay to avoid any bad language from overexcited pop stars reaching the viewers. Alesha was part of *The BRITs Red Carpet* presenting team along with DJ Lauren Laverne, comedian Russell Howard and Matt Willis of Busted, who had just won *I'm A Celebrity . . . Get Me Out Of Here!*. She wore a white silk dress with a deeply plunging neckline, matching shoes, a dazzling crystal necklace, flowing hair extensions and a wide smile. She looked ravishing – as if she didn't have a care in the world.

Alesha had succeeded in getting out more and had banished all signs of Harvey from her home, but she had yet to kick-start her life. Out of the blue, she received a phone call from the notoriously pub-licity-shy Brian Higgins, the man behind Xenomania, who had written and produced 'Knockdown'. Fittingly, he would provide the pick-me-up Alesha so desperately needed. She would acknowledge her debt to him on the album *The Alesha Show*: 'You'll never know how much it meant to me the day you called me out of the blue and asked me to write with you again.'

Originally from the Lake District, Brian had spent much of the nineties as a keyboard player with the excruciatingly named Motiv8. He wanted to concentrate on writing and producing, however, so he set up his own concern, Xenomania, and promptly wrote his first hit, 'All I Wanna Do', for Dannii Minogue, which reached number four in 1997. Brian is a little vague about his odd choice of company name, only explaining that it's the opposite of xenophobia (a hatred of foreigners or foreign things): 'It means a love of everything – of all cultures.' Nobody liked the name and he was continually being urged to change it until he became a success and then everyone loved it.

His second hit was the million-selling 'Believe', which was number one in the UK and the US for Cher. In a classic pop story, he missed out on producing the track because he was too embarrassed to invite the famous diva to his grotty flat above a shop. He wasn't the man who decided to put the dreaded vocoder on the record – that dubious accolade goes to Brian Rawling, who ended up as the track's producer. It was part of a learning process for Brian Higgins who, during a painful fifteen years, realized he needed to be in control to produce the sound he wanted. He left London and moved to a rectory near Westerham in rural Kent, and set about recruiting a like-minded team of artists, writers, musicians – and accountants – all under one roof. His ambition was to create Motown UK.

The breakthrough year for Xenomania was 2002, when the company produced and wrote two number one hits, 'Round Round' for the Sugababes and 'Sound of the Underground' for the group he was most closely associated with, Girls Aloud. It's a pity Mis-Teeq split up before his golden years, as it would have been fascinating to see if he could have found a number one for them as well.

The other key figure at Xenomania was chief songwriter Miranda Cooper, a stunning blonde ex-dancer who, like Alesha, knew all about the advantages and disadvantages of being an attractive woman in a male-dominated business. Her father was a director of the royal jewellers Asprey, and she was far more likely to appear in the pages of *Tatler* than in the tabloid newspapers. Despite their very different backgrounds, she and Alesha got on famously. Alesha called her 'my little star', as well as a 'genius' and 'an inspiration'.

Miranda too had been 'discovered' at a dance studio – in her case by Dannii Minogue. Until she met Brian, her biggest claim to fame was performing as one of the backing dancers on Gina G's Eurovision winner 'Ooh Aah . . . Just A Little Bit' in 1996, a credential Brian never tired of reminding her about.

Brian is a strong believer in the development of long-lasting creative relationships and had been working with Miranda since meeting her through Dannii in 1997. He explained the Xenomania dynamic to *Music Week*: 'We are a very restless group of people. We rarely celebrate success, we just enormously enjoy working together. Invariably, when a record comes out and becomes a hit, we are too engrossed in the record we are currently making to really register anything but relief that the hit has been achieved.'

Xenomania is not a pop factory. That suggests churning out hit after hit on a conveyor belt with little regard for the end product. Their philosophy is simple: each song is special and different. It was a way of thinking that suited Alesha, who felt completely at home on the many trips she would take around the M25 to work at the studio complex in the coming year. Miranda observed, 'It's not remotely rock 'n' roll.'

Alesha has always enjoyed writing as part of a team and Brian was a producer who encouraged the ideas to flow. She prefers to work on the lyric first and try to capture a spontaneous moment. She already knew that process would work with Xenomania because of her experience with 'Knockdown', in which the first and second verses, as well as the chorus, ended up exactly as she'd first 'freestyled' them into a Dictaphone: 'The more you overthink it and revisit it, you lose that original magic that you found.'

By the time they'd finished, she had completed eight tracks that would find their way on to her next album, including her best-known song, 'The Boy Does Nothing'. The plan was to finish a whole album and then find a record deal.

Before she could organize that, however, she was offered the chance to appear on *Strictly Come Dancing*. The BBC's Saturday night flagship was incredibly popular and one of those shows that seemed like an institution from the very beginning, even though it had only begun in 2004 – the same year as *The X Factor*.

The great British public took an instant liking to the rather old-fashioned dance show. Kevin O'Sullivan, the television critic of the *Sunday Mirror*, observes, 'People love dancing and ballroom dancing in particular. It's always been sort of special to the British – a Fred Astaire–Ginger Rogers thing. It's in our DNA.' The original *Come Dancing* was one of the BBC's longest-running shows, spanning nearly fifty years from 1949 to 1998.

One of the great mysteries is how the contestants are chosen. The very first series in May 2004 had just eight contestants, including the rugby player Martin Offiah, the classical singer Lesley Garrett and the newsreader Natasha Kaplinsky, who was the winner. Series two, the same year, secured the autumn slot that became the norm and puts the show in direct competition with Simon Cowell's juggernaut. The winner was actress Jill Halfpenny, who beat, among others, Esther Rantzen and the comedian Julian Clary.

One of the most popular winners was Darren Gough, the England cricketer, who had one of the most striking journeys to success, transforming himself over the weeks of series three from an amiable no-nonsense Yorkshireman into a charmingly modest twinkle-toes. Kevin O'Sullivan explains, 'The most important words in reality television are "the journey". The producers don't really care that much if you can dance. They even sort of prefer it if you come to the table with no dancing experience whatsoever. And then you can go through the reality ride.'

Another cricketer, the smooth Mark Ramprakash, triumphed in series four over an odd bunch that included Emma Bunton, Mica Paris and DJ Spoony, who had given Mis-Teeq's career such a boost as one of Radio 1's Dreem Team.

The number of contestants had gradually swollen so that in 2007 the producers were looking for fourteen celebrities to dust off their foxtrots, quicksteps and jives. But why would they want Alesha Dixon, who just five years before had been part of one of the premier garage acts in the UK? She wasn't currently in the charts and didn't even have a record deal.

The producers always have a wish list of superstars whom they would love to get. Top of that list for years, according to a programme insider, have been Dame Shirley Bassey and Rod Stewart, but they never get them and they almost certainly never will. In 2007 they managed to sign the next best thing to Rod, his wife Penny Lancaster, and the Dame Shirley larger-than-life vamp role was filled by the actress Stephanie Beacham. The programme has always wanted to tempt Vince Cable to appear because it's widely known he is a keen and accomplished dancer but they've had no luck persuading him. Peter Mandelson once rashly said he would love to be on the show and so has to excuse himself politely every year.

After the customary failure to sign their Santa list, it's really pot luck and much depends on who is available, how well the celebrity's agent lobbies and who has received a favourable mention at production meetings. You aren't going to get rich appearing on *Strictly Come Dancing*, simply because the programme knows that the publicity is the carrot. The average contestant receives an estimated £25–30,000. The winner of the show doesn't actually win anything at all. The attraction of it is that, like the majority of celebrity-based reality shows, it has the potential to give careers a boost – either to those that are fading or those that have yet to blossom fully. Perhaps Alesha fitted both categories.

If anyone connected with the programme had ever watched Mis-Teeq, seen Alesha on *Top of the Pops*, watched her dance on the podium for Pharrell Williams or in her own video of 'Lipstick', they would have identified someone who could make an impact on the show. Kevin O'Sullivan observed, 'She was batting on a decent wicket. She is very, very attractive. And she came with dancing skills, which also helped – they don't want everybody to be completely inept. She also brought the potential to attract younger viewers.' And Alesha had a sob story, in her case the humiliating end to her marriage. It was reality television gold – the brave woman fighting back from adversity.

It seemed that Alesha was a perfect choice. The only problem was she wasn't sure if she wanted to do it. Her priority was still her music and she loved working with Xenomania. Would appearing on a middle-class BBC show presented by Bruce Forsyth, who was turning eighty, destroy her artistic credibility? 'I didn't want people to stop taking me seriously as an artist.'

She needed some wise professional advice, but she was no longer with Twenty First Artists and desperately needed a new agent. She had kept in touch with a shrewd Scotsman called Malcolm Blair, who had looked after Mis-Teeq on the road in 2001. They bumped into each other again in London. Malcolm remembered, 'She had just been dropped by her record label, her publishing deal had expired and she was getting a divorce. She said, "I've been offered the chance to go on *Strictly Come Dancing*, what do you think?" I said, "I think you should do it."'

Malcolm would become a vital fixture in Alesha's life. He came from a family with a strong musical tradition. His father, Jimmy Blair, was a famous musician in their native Glasgow. He ran a renowned music school in the Charing Cross area of the city. He'd also been a star on Scottish television in the sixties, when his band headlined a show called *Jig Time*. It was, for his son Malcolm, an early example of the power of TV and how it could bring almost instant popularity and success.

After leaving school, Malcolm worked in construction in the Middle East before coming home to try and fashion a career in music for himself. He began by forming a company that hired out luxury minibuses to bands and then became a driver for big names like U2 and Prince when they came to Scotland.

He moved on to be a tour manager for Wet Wet Wet, Iggy Pop and the American R & B singer Kelis. He later worked as production manager for James Blunt. In 2001 Telstar asked him to look after Mis-Teeq on a promotional tour of Europe and he met Alesha for the first time.

He told the *Glasgow Evening Times*, 'We just clicked right away. She was young then, about twenty-two, and so full of energy. If we were somewhere like Paris, we'd go and see the Eiffel Tower together. We'd eat together or go to the movies.' And echoing the sentiments of her former mentor Louise Porter, he added, 'I realized right from the start Alesha was the star.'

When Mis-Teeq split, Malcolm became the manager of the ABC concert hall in Glasgow, which is now the city's O2 arena. He was looking for a change when he met Alesha again in London. Professionally, he was just the sort of solid citizen she needed in her life – astute and experienced.

He understood the importance of television for the modern artist. Alesha would be able to negotiate a much better record deal if she were being noticed every week on the BBC's top-rated programme. Based on his advice, she agreed to do the show. It also helped that her two grandmothers and her mother were huge fans and were keen for her to do it. Alesha recalled having lunch with her nan Maureen: 'She held my wrist and said, "Do it for me."' Alesha is not soft when business and her career are involved, but she decided to call Malcolm to tell him she was going to go ahead.

Malcolm officially became Alesha's manager and has master-minded her rise through the television ranks: 'We're a team. I look after the business side of things and Alesha looks after the creative side. It works well. It's like a second marriage.'

CHAPTER TWELVE

The British Beyoncé

While she was throwing herself into getting fit and starting rehearsals for *Strictly Come Dancing*, Alesha received the news that Harvey and Javine were expecting their first child together. Harvey shared his thoughts with *Hello!* magazine: 'I believe that Javine and me were meant to meet and have children. Our destiny was mapped out. I know Alesha's been told. I'm sure she'll move on and have kids with someone who will make her very happy, but I don't know how she's taken it. No doubt people will say this is yet another blow to Alesha, but it's a year now. You have to move on.'

People did say it was another blow. One columnist memorably described it as applying 'vinegar to the wound.' Little more than nine months had actually passed since her life had been turned upside down, so she would have been superhuman not to feel a pang of disappointment at what might have been.

Alesha is very careful about how she behaves and rarely betrays her feelings. Javine did reveal that she'd seen Alesha once since Harvey left her: 'It was awkward but we are two women who aren't going to be seen fighting in public. I'm sure she wanted to give me a few slaps around the head. But we conducted ourselves really well.'

One of the ironic aspects of the whole mess is that whenever

Javine and Harvey were interviewed, it seemed that Alesha was the only topic people were interested in. In a bizarre way, Javine's pregnancy was good publicity for Alesha, although at the time she was focused on making sure she wasn't knocked out of *Strictly* in the first round.

Now that she had been confirmed as a contestant, the priority for Alesha was finding out which professional dancer would be her partner. She had to hope there would be a chemistry between them because, without that, the competition would represent an impossible task.

The dancers are the hired hands of the show. Most are paid similar wages to the contestants, although the higher-profile ones like Anton Du Beke and Brendan Cole receive considerably more. The show is as much a shop window for them – a stepping stone in their career – as it is for the contestants. The producers have the upper hand in any pay negotiations because they can always replace a dancer for the next series.

Alesha was paired with Matthew Cutler, a handsome former world amateur Latin champion from Essex. He had danced in the two preceding series but hadn't set the stage on fire. In 2005 he was partnered by actress Siobhan Hayes from *My Family* and they were the first couple voted off. He fared better the next year, when he survived until week nine with television presenter Carol Smillie. He was delighted to be given a partner with so much potential for his third series: 'I knew quite early on that we were going to go far. Working with someone like Alesha makes my job so much easier.'

In August, fully a month before the show was due to begin, Alesha had to visit a bleak industrial estate in Croydon for her first meeting to discuss what she was going to wear on the show. She took in pictures of designs by some of her favourites, including Gucci, Roberto Cavalli and Dolce & Gabbana. She needed to have fourteen separate costumes in case she made it to the final.

The outfits for all the female contestants were created by a team of eleven dressmakers under the guidance of the BBC's costume designer, Su Judd. It is painstaking work in a world where traditionally sequins are more essential than buttons. You could be forgiven for thinking the dresses were the most important part of the show. While Alesha thought her legs were her best feature, Su revealed to Liz Jones of the *Daily Mail* that she 'absolutely hated her feet'. It's nothing to do with their size. She never gets her feet out in sandals or flip-flops, because she'd had an operation in the early Mis-Teeq days to straighten a bone and it left a huge scar. The dresses Su's team made for Alesha were so striking that her feet were the last thing the TV audience noticed.

No dress was ever worn more than once and the majority of them were snapped up by viewers for a minimum of £1,400 the moment a celebrity had finished with them. Some of the ones Alesha wore were so short, it seemed the buyers were barely getting their money's worth. For the jive she wore a tiny green mini, which prompted Bruce Forsyth to comment, 'A lovely dress – pity they didn't have time to finish it.'

The contestants were announced two weeks before the series began at a special press launch. Alesha was asked if her time in the girl group Mis-Teeq would be an advantage, which wasn't a good start for getting the audience behind her. Alesha was quick to point out that the band's routines were street dances and not ballroom. While that was technically true, she was a highly trained and experienced performer who had practised hard for several years. She knew how to rehearse and how to present herself in front of an audience.

Mis-Teeq hadn't had a top ten hit for more than four years so, professionally, Alesha had dropped from sight. In comparison, the stars of soaps like *Coronation Street* and *EastEnders* were on TV week after week. She barely rated a mention in media previews, most of which concentrated on Rod Stewart's wife Penny. Bookmakers rated Alesha 12/1 eighth favourite behind even *GMTV* presenter

Kate Garraway and footballer John Barnes. The front-runner before the competition began was Gethin Jones from *Blue Peter*.

Alesha was given a relatively easy first week when the series got under way on 29 September 2007. Only the gentlemen had to dance in the first programme. The ladies took part in a group dance in which all the contestants, dressed in variously styled bright red dresses, moved uncertainly around the floor to the sounds of the *Strictly* house band performing the Ella Fitzgerald classic 'It Don't Mean A Thing (If It Ain't Got That Swing)'. It was all rather confusing as you tried to pick out some familiar faces.

Kelly Brook was definitely there. The model, who has forged a very profitable career from her photogenic figure, already looked a rival to watch. The judge Bruno Tonioli, at his theatrical best, exclaimed, 'How to pick a jewel from all these wonderful girls, but I would say the two hot brunettes – Alesha and Kelly.'

The competition began properly for Alesha the following week when she and Matthew performed the rumba. Before they danced, they were shown in a short piece they had filmed during their rehearsals. Alesha was keen to dispel the thought that she might be semi-professional. In between running, jumping and laughing, she explained, 'Being in Mis-Teeq changed my life. We had seven top tens and we had two platinum albums and also a top ten hit in America. We were very street, very urban. I have danced in videos and on stage but it's more sort of gyrating. Doing *Strictly Come Dancing* for me is living a childhood dream. I don't like to use the word poor but Mum couldn't afford to put me in stage school and stuff, so it is my crash course in professional dancing.'

She didn't mean it as a dig against those contestants who had been to stage school but at least two of them, Letitia Dean and Matt Di Angelo from *EastEnders*, had attended the Sylvia Young Theatre School, and Kelly Brook went to the Italia Conti Academy of Theatre Arts. Perhaps it was no surprise that these three would provide Alesha's strongest opposition in the coming weeks.

Matthew Cutler had the difficult task of reining in Alesha's natural energy: 'It's never-ending. It's like bouncing off the walls. I can't control her. Rumba is slow and romantic and I need to calm her down so she can dance the routine properly, otherwise she will go wild.' Alesha promised that she would be focused on Saturday and wouldn't waste the moment.

From this two-minute introduction, it was already clear that she was going to make a connection with the public. The camera loved her – her unique laugh, her big ready smile and her naturalness. She was an ordinary girl, albeit a very beautiful one.

She kept her promise to Matthew and focused on the night, her whole face a study in concentration as they danced to 'Hurt', Christina Aguilera's melancholy song. Alesha's mini-dress was a shocking pink and showed off her legs – a sight the audience would get used to in the coming weeks. Craig Revel Horwood, the notoriously hard-to-please judge, seemed to like Alesha from the outset, and described the dance as 'absolutely gorgeous, very sexy without being lascivious'. Bruno Tonioli told her, 'You have the seducing powers of Salome.' Len Goodman, the elder statesman, thought she was a contender despite it being her first dance. They placed her third behind Kelly Brook and Penny Lancaster.

Afterwards, Alesha was elated: 'I love Len. I came off the floor and I just exploded. This dancing malarkey is just great. It's brought out the competitive spirit in me.'

The producers had evidently spotted that Alesha's grandmothers supporting her in the audience would make great television in the coming weeks. Nan Maureen declared, 'Alesha always puts her heart and soul into everything she does. Once she started to dance tonight, my wildest dream came true.' Maureen was a good judge of her granddaughter's ability, because she was very active as an actor and director at the Barn Theatre in Welwyn Garden City.

Matthew soon realized that Alesha had a work commitment like no other. She would literally practise until they were both ready to collapse, happy to train and rehearse for six hours a day if she thought they needed to. She even wanted to train on Sundays, which Matthew wasn't so keen on.

The second week was the jive, which was more within Alesha's comfort zone, as it involved shaking her booty in a way that was a reminder of her video for Pharrell Williams nearly four years before. They danced to 'Shake Your Tailfeather', which Ray Charles had sung so memorably in the 1980 cult classic *The Blues Brothers*. Len Goodman thought it 'fun, fast and fantastic'. Arlene Phillips, the choreographer and the only woman on the panel, enthused, 'You're rocking, you're rolling, you're jiving, you're shaking your tailfeathers. Jive is associated with youth and I hope you get the youth of Britain up on their feet and jiving.' Clearly that wasn't going to happen, although it was a sensational performance. Arlene was reflecting the view of the BBC in general – that Alesha was in touch with young people even though she would be thirty on her next birthday.

The judges gave her four nines, which was the highest mark of the week, just beating Kelly Brook, who danced a tango. The two women were the last to perform, transforming a lacklustre show. Perhaps if Alesha had danced after Kelly rather than before her, she might have achieved a maximum score. They did seem a class above the others. Kelly was receiving far more media attention, however, so that the first few weeks seemed like *The Kelly Show*.

Alesha was ecstatic with her score: 'I knew when I got the nines my family would be bouncing off the walls. My nan says she is going to charge the BBC for the damage to her ceiling.'

While it seemed unlikely that Alesha would suddenly drop into the bottom two, she understood that you couldn't rely on last week's marks the next time round. Her nan Maureen advised, 'I told her, "That week is over. You wipe the slate clean. It's a new dance and you have to start from the beginning again."'

She wasn't looking forward to the American smooth, her first attempt at ballroom: 'It's like a new world to me. I was scared because I knew people might presume I would be better at the Latin and I really wanted to go out there and prove I can do ballroom as well.'

The training was difficult and Matthew had to tell her, 'We need a little less of the "yo dude".' It didn't help that she had hurt her knee during the jive, which requires a lot of jerky knee movements, and needed physio. *Strictly* fans didn't know at the time but for a day it was touch and go whether she would be able to continue, but fortunately she made a good recovery.

In the end her performance didn't match the jive, perhaps because she wasn't shaking any tailfeathers. Instead they danced to Fred Astaire's 'Top Hat, White Tie and Tails'. The judges were divided, with Len and Bruno bickering over the quality of her performance and Len calling Bruno a doughnut. They gave her thirty-three points, which was by no means a disaster, although Kelly and Matt scored more.

Afterwards, Alesha observed, 'Ballroom is a bit of a challenge for me because I'm not allowed to wiggle my hips. But once you nail it, when you get to the point in training when you're really feeling the dance, you fall in love with it.'

It would be even more of a challenge the following week, when she was scheduled to dance the foxtrot, arguably the most elegant of all ballroom dances. Alesha struggled to make a connection with it. It was a hard week of rehearsals but one bonus came with a trip to the *GMTV* couch for an early morning interview. Gradually, Alesha was becoming noticed more, as the media woke up to the fact that she could be a winner.

She revealed that she was having a nightmare with the foxtrot and rehearsals were going badly: 'I moaned all day. I just couldn't get it.' She also revealed that she had been in her comfort zone with Mis-Teeq but was finding *Strictly Come Dancing* far more stressful: 'I feel out of my depth, so before the show my hands start sweating and I genuinely get really nervous.'

Alesha wasn't being overdramatic about her nerves. She had always suffered with a touch of stage fright before a performance. She had even thrown up immediately before Mis-Teeq appeared on *Top of the Pops* for the first time, so this was no celebrity exaggeration. Her secret before going on to dance was a glass of white wine, which she told producers was apple juice.

She needn't have worried about the foxtrot because Bruno found it 'enchanting' and she scored nines across the board. Taking stock of the first few weeks of the competition, Arlene thought Alesha and Matthew were the most natural couple in the contest: 'I think they will creep to the top.'

Alesha, who was now the bookies' favourite to win the competition, came across as refreshingly normal in her interviews. She told the *Daily Mirror*, 'I don't mind getting my legs out but I'm still quite conscious of my cellulite. What makes me laugh is these magazines that put a circle around someone's cellulite as if it's alien to a woman!

'I'm sorry but there are more women with cellulite than without it. Of course I have cellulite and I'm not afraid to say it. I don't have a complex because I know all my friends have it too.'

She had to get her legs out again in week six for another Latin dance, the salsa, for which she wore a minuscule fuchsia pink dress. Bruno took his jacket off and shouted, 'Hot! Hot! Hot!'

Besides Kelly, Alesha's principal competition looked to be Matt Di Angelo, who played Deano Wickes in *EastEnders*. His salsa scored higher than Alesha's and, while he didn't have her natural flair, he was improving.

Almost inevitably the newspapers suggested there was a romance brewing between the two. The *People* claimed they were 'smitten with each other'. The story said they had been seen at a London nightclub and cited a source who revealed that they were 'really happy together'.

This is just the kind of publicity this sort of reality programme feeds off in a bid to boost ratings. Every year, for instance, *The X Factor* has any number of contestants playing musical beds. The great majority of such stories are fantasy, although one shouldn't necessarily jump to condemn the tabloid press – these revelations are often dreamed up on the inside by PRs and spokespeople keen to promote the show and their clients.

Ironically, Matt was indeed having a serious romance on the show, but it wasn't with Alesha. Instead he was involved with his dancing partner, raven-haired Flavia Cacace, who at the time was living with Vincent Simone, another of the dancers on the show. Matt and Flavia, who insisted they didn't get together until after she and Vincent had split up, remained in a relationship for three years.

Dancing is a very physical activity, as Alesha explained to *FHM* magazine: 'The ballroom dancing is very sexy. You can lean in and whisper to each other while you're on the floor. The Latin dancing is very physical and flirty. Just go to a salsa club.' She said dancing was 'like foreplay, but no actual sex. You're not getting any punani at the end!'

There was definitely nothing going on between her and dance partner Matthew Cutler but she graciously said he was the most fanciable male on the show and that she looked forward to training with him every day. Matthew was unattached since his divorce from his wife Nicole in 2003. She was also a professional dancer and partnered John Barnes in the series.

Alesha had been linked with surprisingly few men since her marriage breakdown. In July she was rumoured to have gone on two dates with Pharrell Williams while he was in London for the Concert for Diana. He performed two songs, including 'She Wants To Move', but, sadly, Alesha wasn't on stage at Wembley Stadium dancing alongside him. A more intriguing suggestion was that she was dating a nightclub doorman called James Chandler, who worked at Punk in Soho. He was described by the *Daily Mirror* as a 'good-looking hunk' who had won a competition for unsigned male models.

The *Sunday Mirror* went further and said the couple had been dating for seven months, which seemed an extraordinary length of time to remain undetected even for someone as secretive as Alesha. Considering how quiet they had kept things, it was amazing when James was quoted in the paper making some cringe-inducing comments about Alesha.

He said she gave him private dances at home. He revealed that they had met at a club: 'The first time I saw Alesha she was on the dance floor and I was hooked. I was watching her move her sexy body. Then I saw she had a great smile. I couldn't take my eyes off her. Alesha has a great personality and a great figure – what more can I say? She looks great in her sparkly dance outfits, but she looks even better out of them.'

Alesha has never spoken about James Chandler and following this flurry of stories he was never connected with her again. More importantly, Alesha had a waltz to dance to the uplifting ballad 'A Time For Us', the old Johnny Mathis hit. 'It gave me goose bumps,' said Craig. The performance earned her ten points from both Arlene and Bruno – the first two of eighteen maximum scores she would earn during the competition, which remains the record.

Arlene gave her view of the remaining contestants to the *Sunday Mirror*. Of Alesha she said, 'Watching her dance is like heaven with a pink bow on it. Strong body, great dancer and a joy to watch. She deserves to win and forge a new career for herself.' Arlene couldn't have guessed then that the new career would be forged at her expense.

The following week was even better when their cha-cha-cha earned her and Matthew thirty-nine out for forty points, with only Craig, for some reason, not giving the maximum. Their performance was arguably one of the all-time best on *Strictly Come Dancing*. They just pipped Matt and Flavia, who scored thirty-eight.

Alesha had taken to heart her nan Maureen's words of wisdom: 'I rang my nan for some advice on my cha-cha and she said, "Just give it some sex." I couldn't believe I was hearing this from my nan!'

The choice of music, Beyoncé's 'Crazy On Love', was inspired because it gave Alesha the opportunity to blend her new skills elegantly with her booty-shaking old ones. Arlene observed, 'This is a two-horse competition at the moment and you are one of the horses', which didn't come out sounding the best of compliments.

Bruce Forsyth memorably described her as the British Beyoncé, which probably wasn't exactly music to the ears of the woman who'd had to grit her teeth when Mis-Teeq were so often compared to Destiny's Child. She took the compliment with grace, however, telling Scotland's *No. 1* magazine: 'I love Beyoncé and am a massive fan but I don't think I am like her. I don't think anybody in the world could be like her. She is a unique artist and there is only one Beyoncé. It was very sweet of him to say it but I was rather embarrassed. For me it's quite a lot of pressure and I would never try to be her. I can only be myself.'

Kelly Brook had been left behind by Alesha as the competition progressed. Her cause hadn't been helped by criticism from Arlene, who in the interview with the *Sunday Mirror* observed that she wasn't sexual: 'Her smile, her hair, her teeth, her body, her legs – everything about her physically is stunning. But she doesn't exude sexiness.' Alesha, too, had given her opinion of Kelly, declaring that she was 'harmless'. She and her partner, Brendan Cole, were in the bottom two on the eighth show and had to be saved by the judges.

The following week, Kelly's father, Kenneth Parsons, died and, grief-stricken, she had to withdraw, unable to concentrate on the rigorous training the contestants faced every week. Understandably, she wanted to be with her family.

Her departure increased the attention Alesha was receiving and she was happy to give interviews with one proviso: her marriage break-up and the lurid accounts of Harvey's infidelity were off-limits. She must have been disappointed then to read the headline on an interview with Javine in the *Daily Mail*: 'You might win *Strictly* Alesha . . . but I won your man'.

CHAPTER THIRTEEN

Backlash

Alesha was more famous than she had ever been before. Every week she was being watched by millions of people on a show that was getting fantastic ratings. She sailed into the quarter-finals after more tens for the tango and a passable samba, although she personally didn't believe she had danced her best for the latter. There was the suspicion that she was beginning to feel the pressure. She and Matthew were practising twelve hours a day. She revealed on the show that she had now spent a total of 320 hours in his company and occasionally their partnership could be strained. She also admitted that she didn't know all the steps for one of the dances.

She wasn't joking, because she really did mess up the paso doble in the quarter-finals. Her first dance of the evening had been a Viennese waltz to 'Memory' from the Andrew Lloyd Webber musical *Cats* and that had been a triumph. Len, who has a way with words, exclaimed, 'If you don't get four tens for that I am going to go home and pickle my walnuts.' Unfortunately, only Bruno joined him in awarding a perfect score. He was at his most gushing, 'The fairytale is just beginning, I'm telling you that. How can anybody resist such beauty and such radiance? In your face you were telling the story. I lived the song with you.'

Elaine Paige, who had originally performed the song in the West

End, was in the audience and was taken by surprise when she heard it but said that Alesha 'danced beautifully to a beautiful melody'. Alesha hadn't been told Elaine was watching, which was just as well, because it would have made her even more nervous than usual.

Alesha wore a pink ball gown that was her favourite from the whole series: 'It had lots of layers and made me feel like Cinderella. It was beautiful.' Although she happily acknowledges that her legs are her best feature, this particular dress was floor length and they were completely hidden.

The paso doble, her second dance, was, in comparison, a disaster. Her green and gold flamenco dress was the best thing about it, although the judges liked the performance enough to award thirty-six points. Alesha, probably unwisely with the voting public watching, told co-host Tess Daly backstage, 'We really messed up – badly.' She thought the dance was her most embarrassing moment on the whole show because she had simply forgotten the steps: 'I made up the last thirty seconds but because Matthew is so brilliant, he just followed me and we got through it.'

The telephone voters were unimpressed and Alesha found herself in the bottom two. She was relieved when the judges chose her instead of her friend Letitia Dean to go through to the semi-final against Matt Di Angelo and Gethin Jones.

She also received the seal of approval from Vince Cable, who danced a quickstep with her at the practice studio in North London for a television segment. Vince couldn't have been more fulsome in his praise, 'Of the three who are left, Alesha is streets ahead in talent and performance as well as being drop-dead gorgeous. She is quite mesmerizing to watch, an astonishing performer, and I am rooting for her to win.'

Ironically, considering the future controversy over her expertise as a judge on the panel, Vince noted, 'Although she didn't necessarily know the names of the different steps, she was quick to pick up what I suggested.' They appeared together on *This Week*, the political show hosted by Andrew Neil. Alesha was poised and said, 'Politicians to us are a bit like Mars. You know that it's there but you don't quite know enough about it.'

For the semi-final Alesha had to dance the Argentine tango and the quickstep, which she had been practising when she met Vince. For the latter she skipped lightly and elegantly around the floor to the sounds of 'Valerie', the song made famous by Amy Winehouse. It was a winning combination of classic ballroom dancing and modern music, although the *Strictly* house band seemed to make any number sound like a performance at an OAP tea dance.

Alesha looked like a Hollywood star in a long, flowing white dress with her black hair scraped back from her face in the style of the great movie dancer of the fifties Cyd Charisse. Craig, who had been at his most cheerful when judging Alesha, again thought the dance was fantastic: '... full of syncopated steps. And what's more, you made it look really easy.' The studio cameras caught a glimpse of Maureen, her nan, in tears.

Her Argentine tango was even more dramatic. Bruno called it 'the irresistible power of subtle seduction'. She smouldered in a tight scarlet dress to 'I'd Be Surprisingly Good For You', another Andrew Lloyd Webber song, this time from *Evita*. Arlene described Alesha as 'one of the best storytellers we have ever had on *Strictly*'. Two more tens, making it four for the night, put her on top of the leaderboard. Matt won the dance-off against Gethin to join her in the final.

Afterwards, Alesha told the spin-off *Strictly – It Takes Two* what appearing on the show had meant to her: 'I actually thought 2007 was going to be crap. But because of *Strictly* my confidence is back – dancing actually saved me. I've got the real me back.'

Nothing, it seemed, could interrupt her serene progress to becoming *Strictly Come Dancing* champion – until her elder brother Mark sold a piece to the *News of the World* about their childhood. A company called Cash4YourStory claimed that he had approached them with his story and they had put him in contact with the newspaper to set up an exclusive deal. The company's website states, 'After much negotiation a deal was struck and the story appeared in the *News of the World* newspaper.'

The headline alone was shocking enough: 'TERRORISED ... BULLIED ... STARVED'. Underneath it continued, '*She fed off scraps in hell home*' and '*Star watched mum beaten black & blue*'. It was dramatic and made painful reading. Fearne Cotton summed up the substance of the feature in her 2009 television interview with Alesha: 'It painted an horrendous picture of Alesha's childhood with claims of a string of stepfathers, racist bullying and extreme poverty.'

Mark revealed that their mother had been beaten in an abusive relationship, something that Alesha herself would confirm and talk about extensively in the 2010 documentary *Don't Hit My Mum*. But he also made other allegations. He claimed that Beverley did nothing for a living: 'She never provided anything for us as kids. We often went to bed hungry. We'd come home and there'd never be any dinner ... We'd have to eat whatever we could find, usually buttered toast. There was never food in the cupboard because we didn't have any money.' He was also strongly critical of his younger sister, claiming that she changed when she found fame: 'When Alesha met and married MC Harvey the rapper she went into celeb overdrive and got very selfish.'

The article was extremely powerful. Alesha was absolutely furious and heartbroken for their mother. She told Fearne, 'That was the first taste of how fame can have a real backlash. I never thought that somebody from my own family could do that. It doesn't matter what goes on in families, it's between families. Everybody has family issues. Everybody. It's just unfortunate that yours has to be read by a nation.' She also revealed that her mum was 'really, really, hurt'.

She didn't respond to the allegations immediately. To do so then would have been even more of an unwelcome distraction. Only after the end of *Strictly Come Dancing* did she reveal that she no longer spoke to Mark and had cut him out of her life. She mounted a rigorous defence of her mother's reputation, starting in the *Sun* newspaper: 'The reason I don't talk to Mark is because of the way he is so disrespectful to our mum. I cherish her. If anyone is rude about her or says a bad word about her they won't be a part of my life. Unfortunately, that's how I feel about my brother.

'The last thing I would ever want is for people to think my mum is a bad mother – she's the most amazing mother anybody could ever wish for. I am fuming, because anyone who could accuse anybody of starving their children is just beyond ludicrous. Let's talk about Ethiopia – that's what real starvation is about.'

Mark's revelations certainly put a dampener on things. Her mother has never spoken about his allegations; instead she focused on supporting Alesha through the final stages of *Strictly*. It was all such a long time ago and she had never sought fame for herself.

Eventually, Alesha would forgive her brother. She told Fearne Cotton, 'If my brother was here now I would welcome him with open arms. Even though I'm hurt because of what he has done, because human beings make mistakes, none of us is perfect and the only way to move forward in life is to forgive. You never forget, but forgive.'

She had also forgiven her ex-husband, Harvey, and said, 'I am at peace.' She had been inspired by her mother's ability to forgive the man who had been violent towards her all those year before.

She and Harvey were on speaking terms and he was one of the first to call her when her brother's story appeared. He had been on a short plane journey from Newcastle to London when he read the paper. He told the *Daily Mail*, 'It was horrible... Her mum had a tough time, she went through a lot. But whatever she went through, she's a great person.'

When he rang, Harvey asked Alesha if she was okay and she told him that nothing surprised her with people any more. 'I said, "Look past him because karma will take care of him."'

During the competition, her family had taken it in turn to give their support in the audience, with her sister Leyanne joining the nans and Beverley to cheer her on. Harvey's mother, Jenny, also popped down to watch on one occasion. Alesha said sweetly that she was dancing for her grandmothers. Maureen observed, 'Once she gets on the floor and starts dancing, my heart just fills with joy.'

Alesha would need their support in the last week, which had begun so unpromisingly with Mark's story. And then her back went into spasm when she was practising a lift – a result of the punishment she had been putting it through with her rigorous training schedule. She needed further physiotherapy, a course of painkillers and some heavy strapping to ensure she would be fit for the big night. She was forced to watch Matthew practise the dances on his own and try to pick up as much as she could by watching him from the comfort of a chair.

Javine, now seven months pregnant, popped up to say that she really wanted Alesha to win and then to go over, yet again, the circumstances of Harvey being caught at her house, an incident that had happened a year ago.

Alesha was an odds-on 1/3 favourite to lift the trophy, which in betting terms was a certainty. The BBC crew member who had a betting slip worth £8,000 placed before the show began must have been feeling confident of a nice winter holiday.

Alesha needed to perform five dances in the Saturday night final: the waltz, cha-cha-cha and jive before the interval, in which the Spice Girls sang '2 Become 1' as part of their 2007 comeback; then the Viennese waltz and a show dance. She was as nervous as usual and admitted to having a weep with the sheer emotion of it all: 'I didn't even know why I was crying half the time.'

One of the reasons she was crying came out two years later, when she appeared on Justin Lee Collins's ITV chat show and revealed that she and Matthew had been out for dinner on the Thursday before the final and ended up at a party. She confessed that she was 'really drunk' and the effects resulted in her throwing up on the *Strictly* dance floor. She recalled, 'I couldn't tell the producers I was drunk. I told them it was nerves but really it was alcohol. It happened two or three times. I felt so ashamed, because the carpet was so nice and everybody knows I like a nice clean house.'

She had pulled herself together in time for her final performances. Her mother and grandmothers were all set to lend their support, but her father Melvin wasn't present. The official line from the BBC was that he now lived abroad and was unable to attend.

The final was mainly a reprise of some of the best dances from earlier in the series. Matthew and Alesha began with their waltz. Her sparkly, backless dress was named the nation's favourite *Strictly* dress in a poll in 2011. Their performance was again nearly flawless – missing out on a full score of forty only because a grumpy Len gave it nine. Bruno said the performance 'sends shivers down my spine'. Craig had 'goose bumps' and Arlene gave it a triple A: 'Alesha, Absolutely Amazing'.

After her cha-cha-cha and jive to 'I Love To Boogie', Alesha was well ahead in the studio. Len had warmed up by now and paid Alesha an enormous compliment, 'Until now, when people have asked me who the best dancer was I've said Jill Halfpenny but now I'll say Alesha Dixon.'

Alesha had achieved something very special and unusual in *Strictly Come Dancing*: she had created an aura about herself that lifted her above the run-of-the-mill contestants trying to remember all their dance steps. It was Alesha's world. Kevin O'Sullivan observed, 'Something happened to her on the dance floor. She became a sort of goddess. I would argue that Jill Halfpenny was a better dancer technically but she didn't have the kind of heavenly presence that I think Alesha quite carefully created. She wore stunning, flowing garments, often in white, and looked ethereal. She made a point of looking ethereal.'

After the interval, both couples danced a Viennese waltz to the David Gray song 'This Year's Love' before ending with a freestyle show dance, which basically meant you could do any lifts and twirls that took your fancy. Alesha wore a glittering purple dress that was the best of both worlds: the back swept to the floor while the front revealed her legs.

They danced to one of Alesha's favourite songs, Bonnie Tyler's 'Holding Out For A Hero', which is something she has had to do most of her life. It was again a masterful, rousing performance that included being swung around and around like a dying swan – a move that revealed her complete trust in her partner. It was a tour de force, which prompted Bruno to say, 'This was more than a dance. It was a stunning, epic performance.'

The judges don't score the last two dances, so it was all up to the public vote, which was announced in the usual clif-hanging fashion. Bruce Forsyth began, 'And the winner of *Strictly Come Dancing 2007* is . . .' His co-host Tess Daly finished the sentence, 'It's Alesha and Matthew!' It was a moment of pure television delight.

All the other contestants, including Kelly Brook, rushed on to the stage to congratulate her, the judges stood to applaud, her mum slipped onstage to join the celebration and Bruce, who had taken a real shine to Alesha during the series, said, 'Alesha, you could become the biggest female star in the country.' Matthew was considerate in his appreciation of his partner: 'You are a star in the making. You've worked so hard. You are just like a professional dancer. You give 150 per cent. You are a sheer joy.'

Alesha probably thought she was already a star but the sentiment was sweet and heartfelt. They had gelled so well together. It was a small shame that Alesha never managed a full maximum of forty points from the judges, as many thought she deserved. But she was the highest scorer in eight out of thirteen dances. Her average of 36.5 per dance translated to a nine per judge for every single performance – no wonder Len said afterwards, 'She's probably the best there's been, absolutely a fantastic dancer.'

The most thoughtful post-final comments came from Craig:

'She's the most wonderful character, the most beautiful person back-stage and, onstage, she's a dream. To think that people can be treated so badly in their private lives is awful, but it offers hope to those in similar situations because she got herself out of it and has triumphed.'

CHAPTER FOURTEEN

Look But Don't Touch

Behind the scenes Alesha's manager, Malcolm Blair, was busy trying to maximize the commercial opportunities her triumph brought. She had a nice sparkly disco ball trophy to put on the mantelpiece at home. But the whole point of appearing on the show wasn't just to keep her grandmothers happy: she wanted to reignite her career, especially the musical part of it, because that was always most important to her.

As Kevin O'Sullivan observed, 'She effortlessly dominated the series.' Malcolm therefore was able to enter into negotiations from a position of strength. She wasn't only a victor; she was also a victim – twin attributes that can transform a celebrity into a fully-fledged star. Fiona McIntosh in her *Sunday Mirror* column echoed the thoughts of the watching viewer: 'No one deserved to get to that final more than the girl who's had such a poxy life not even Jimmy McGovern could make it up. . . In a world tragically short of young, female role models, we've got one at last. And if that wasn't worth voting for, then we did it for all the losers in Alesha's life, who must be watching this peach of a girl and cursing the day they ever let her down.'

If the 'losers' were watching, they were among a television audience of more than twelve million. The renowned publicity agent

Max Clifford thought Alesha could make as much as £5 million in the coming year, suggesting that she could be a Bond girl or, failing that, the new face of Marks and Spencer.

The initial reaction was favourable, with Malcolm's office fielding 150 calls and offers before lunchtime the morning after her victory was announced. There was talk of a role in the West End musical *Chicago* and a first movie part but this was little more than media speculation. The most intriguing suggestion was that she was being lined up to return to *Strictly Come Dancing*, not as a contestant nor as a judge but as a host replacing Tess Daly. Her priority, however, was always going to be her music, followed by more television exposure and the endorsements that would bring.

Before any important decisions were made, though, it was time for celebration at Kenza in Devonshire Square, where the guests included Matt and Flavia, now happy to be seen out as a couple. David Walliams was also there, prompting journalists, who had spotted him in the audience at the *Strictly* final, to link him with Alesha. Show business is a very small world but connections are always being made and you never knew who you might be working with in the future. They apparently shared a few dances but there was absolutely nothing to it. If Alesha could keep secret a two-year relationship with a member of a famous boy band, then she wasn't likely to flaunt a new romance at a party swarming with journalists and paparazzi.

Reports after the party suggested that Alesha had enjoyed one glass of champagne too many and had to be helped to her car. She was more likely to have needed a hand because her feet hurt. When she left the party, she had changed her stiletto heels in favour of a comfy pair of Ugg boots.

She was committed to a promotional trip to Japan, where her album *Fired Up* was due to be released in early 2008. She had chosen to do that rather than take part in the potentially less lucrative *Strictly Come Dancing* tour. She hoped to see her father in Thailand on her way to Japan. She had seen very little of Melvin since she'd left school but was due to spend four days with him. She told *The People*, 'There is nothing more important to me than my friends and family. My dad moved to Thailand, I didn't want him to but he loves the country so he left anyway and he has been there ever since. I hope that we get close.' In the end she had to cancel that leg of her trip because of Christmas commitments to *Strictly Come Dancing* and wait another year before she found the time for a ten-day break in Thailand.

Fired Up was eventually released in Japan on 20 February 2008. There was a moody new jacket photo of Alesha, a change in the running order, a new song called 'Voodoo' and remixes of 'Lipstick' and 'Knockdown'. Alesha made sure that the revamped version didn't include any soppy references to Harvey; he wouldn't be getting another mention on a record she was involved in. The album only reached number fifty-four in the Japanese chart but at least it had finally surfaced. Fans in the UK could buy the import at HMV.

The problem with trying to release *Fired Up* in the UK was that it was transparently an old album. The singles from it had been widely acclaimed but that was in 2006. Alesha had moved on – not just in terms of her music but also in the eyes of potential buyers. There was a multitude of *Strictly* fans who might appreciate the Girls Aloud, chart-friendly sounds of Xenomania more than the rockier feel of her first solo album. A number of record labels were keen to take her on but they would want fresh material.

At least her work commitments abroad ensured she had little time to pay attention to what was happening in Javine and Harvey's world. Javine had given another interview, this time to *New* magazine, in which she said, 'I don't want Alesha's forgiveness. She doesn't know me. I don't deserve anything from her.' Harvey was also in the papers, saying that he still watched the video of his wedding day and it made him sad. The couple finally had some news of their own in February, when their little girl, called Angel, was born following a water birth at The Birth Centre in Tooting, London. Alesha made no comment, although Harvey said she'd been told about it. She also did not make public news of her decree nisi, which had finally come through that month. It was granted in the High Court on the grounds that Harvey had committed adultery.

Alesha was back from the Far East in time to show up on the red carpet at the BRIT Awards wearing a bright red silk bodycon dress, which was brief enough to have been a Latin costume for *Strictly*. She was looking slimmer than usual – a sign that she had dropped a dress size thanks to the intense dance training. She needed to be noticed by the music industry again and the annual event at Earls Court was ideal. She signed autographs and chatted to the crowd before going in to watch, among others, Amy Winehouse perform her version of 'Valerie', a song she knew so well from her dancing triumph.

Afterwards she hosted a party at 50 Dover Street, which was in keeping with her improved status. She sang a duet with Leo Ihenacho, the acclaimed singer from The Streets – further evidence that she wanted to retain her musical credibility.

Her manager Malcolm, meanwhile, was busy developing Alesha as a brand. She was poised to sign a lucrative contract with a publisher for a frank and revealing autobiography and was one of a number of celebrities, including Gordon Ramsay, Barry Humphries and Jordan, who attended the British Book Awards, known in the publishing world as 'The Nibbies'.

She was chosen as the face or, more precisely, legs of the 'new, improved Veet collection' from the beauty company best known for their hair removal products. In a surprise move, she announced that her next television project would be a documentary for the BBC that would be 'a personal journey to explore what it meant to be beautiful in Britain today'. It was quite a jump from the cha-cha-cha but it was an indication that Alesha had a serious side to her. Danny Cohen, the controller of BBC Three, confirmed, 'This is a subject she feels strongly about.'

The documentary was filmed and ready for broadcast in July. It was called *Alesha: Look But Don't Touch* and was designed to show how our culture creates false images of beauty that ordinary girls can't live up to.

Alesha announced, 'I've set myself a mission in the age of digital retouching, to see if I can find a magazine brave enough to do an untouched photo of me on the cover.' That was just the peg for a revealing documentary in which, among the thought-provoking topics, was the example of a girl who had been given a £7,500 breast enlargement operation as her eighteenth birthday present.

Intriguingly, she also discovered that television was just as responsible as magazines for exerting the pressure on girls to be beautiful. The psychotherapist Susie Orbach, author of *Fat Is A Feminist Issue*, revealed that when television came to Fiji nearly twelve per cent of the island's girls became bulimic on account of the images of so-called perfection they watched on screen. It was depressing stuff.

Alesha was having no luck at all persuading a magazine to carry an untouched picture of her on the front cover. *Marie Claire* apparently didn't even answer her inquiry. The reaction seemed completely strange, because it was Alesha Dixon asking and she was acknowledged to be one of the most beautiful women in the country with or without retouching. Finally, *Celebs*, the magazine of the *Sunday Mirror*, agreed, although she said they were concerned about her 'strange armpits' for some reason.

The programme was generally well received as being something different. Brian Viner of the *Independent* thought Alesha was 'an engaging and eloquent presence'. Alesha, it was becoming apparent, was thoughtful about modern issues and had a social conscience that she hadn't had the opportunity to develop before. She also intended to set up her own film production company to tackle issues she thought were important.

At last a record deal was concluded and Alesha signed with Asylum, a division of Atlantic Records. The label had been founded in 1971 by the renowned producer David Geffen and sprang to prominence by signing superstar artists like Bob Dylan, Joni Mitchell and The Eagles. After some fallow years, it was relaunched as primarily an urban-based label in 2004.

Alesha was one of their first big signings and was given a four-album deal. Most of the songs had already been recorded with Brian Higgins, although Alesha wanted to make some alterations to reflect the changes in her life. The track that was earmarked to be the first single, 'The Boy Does Nothing', had started off as a jazzy sound, but Alesha wanted to create something with more of a feel-good atmosphere to reflect her mood after *Strictly* and also to put a smile on people's faces at a time when there was little good news in the world.

Alesha was delighted to get back to what she considered to be her real job. She told the *Observer*, 'At the end of the day it's not my job to turn up at premieres. I get quite embarrassed at those kind of things; they're not important to me. Some people worry when they're not in the tabloids but I'd rather just be seen when I'm doing something constructive. I don't have a desire to be seen all the time. If I've got an album, I'm doing *Strictly* . . . or I've got a documentary on TV, that's fine. The problem with young girls now is that they aspire to be famous, rather than to be well known for being good at something.'

Her remarks in this interview with journalist Peter Robinson gave one of the best insights into Alesha's character: she didn't want to be perceived as an empty-headed celebrity. She drew a distinct line between her private self and her public image. She would have hated being in the tabloid press when it became apparent she was dating the well-built Aston Villa footballer John Carew. She wouldn't have seen details of her love life as 'something constructive'.

The 6ft 5in striker was one of the leading black players in the country, although he was actually born and bred in Norway. His mother was Norwegian and his father was from Gambia. He made his international debut in 1998 and played ninety-one games for his country.

He and Alesha had much in common. Besides both being of mixed race, they shared a common social concern and were involved in promoting good causes and donating to charities. He was particularly active in giving to and raising money for organizations like MOT, a Norwegian initiative aimed at combating violence and drug use among young people. When he moved to England, he became involved in visiting sick children in hospitals around Birmingham. He was widely regarded as one of the game's nice guys.

Like Alesha's mother Beverley, he was a practising Christian. Just to make sure that he and Alesha had even more to talk about on dates, his sister, Elizabeth Carew, was an R & B singer who released her first solo record, a dance track called 'Destructive', in July 2008.

The *Sun* revealed they were going out in March after they were seen dining together in London. The newspaper quoted a friend saying, 'She deserves to be with someone nice after what she's been through. She's so lovely and lights up every room she walks into. It's great she's found someone who makes her smile. He's a gentle giant. He's a massive bloke, but a really nice guy.'

John was diplomatic when he was asked about Alesha by the *Daily Mirror*: 'We have been seeing each other – it's not like it's a secret. First of all we'll be friends and then we'll see what the future holds but we've spent some time with each other. I wouldn't say we're a couple because we are still getting to know each other but she's a fantastic person.' John, who is a year younger than Alesha, did confide that she had been helping with his footwork. It evidently paid off because he ended the season as Villa's top scorer with thirteen goals.

They didn't become a couple after all, so John was right to be cautious. Alesha was frantically busy and perhaps didn't have time to commit to anything serious. She was single again when she travelled to LA to spend more time on her new album. Her spokesperson confirmed that 'sadly it did not work out' with John. Instead, when she returned home, she could truthfully say that she was single and waiting to meet someone special, but had no idea how that was going to happen because she was working so hard every day. She remarked, 'I'm waiting to be swept away on a white horse.'

'The Boy Does Nothing' was an inspired choice to relaunch Alesha as a solo artist. The song was quite breathtakingly catchy and might have done even better as a summer hit. Instead, she was everywhere in the build-up to its autumn release. This included a guest spot on the next series of *Strictly Come Dancing* on 19 October, twelve days after she turned thirty.

The song had now been transformed into a tongue-in-cheek dance number. It had the jaunty feel of the classic 'Mambo Number 5'. Brian called it 'bottled happiness because it's just one of those songs that makes you want to dance and puts a smile on your face'.

It's not too cheesy to say that she really could have danced the jive to it as a competitor on *Strictly*, so it was fitting that she wore a very short ivory Latin dress when she sang it on the show. Bruce introduced her as the 'gorgeous' Alesha Dixon. The ethereal ballroom dancer of the previous year had been replaced by a sexy booty-shaking star. It was an exhilorating performance. The professional dancers took to the floor near the end and Alesha finished the song in the arms of Matthew, which was a neat touch. Tess Daly said she 'loved her to bits'. The fashion commentator Alison Jane Reid thought she looked 'voluptuous and very pretty'.

She looked even better in the video that was set in an underground club, which was actually Tottenham Town Hall. Alesha was wearing a very hot dress based on the boudoir underwear as outwear style, which was pioneered by the Italian lingerie house La Perla. Alison Jane observed, 'This is gloriously sexy. She often wears these short, sassy camisole dresses to devastating effect. She looks like a goddess here.'

Alesha sang and danced in an exuberant way that enhanced the feel-good quality of the song. It ended with various male dancers showing off their skills, while Alesha and the rest of the crowd sang a cappella, 'If the man can't dance, he gets no second chance.' There were so many catchy bits you didn't know what to sing along to next. The prospects for the single were promising.

Fraser McAlpine, in his BBC Chart Blog, thought the song was tailored to show off Alesha's dancing skills, which were particularly impressive in the video. But he liked the song: 'It's pretty hard to resist the urge to shimmy and kick your feet while listening, and Alesha's vocal is the cherry on the cake.'

That was a good point, because her vocals were showing signs of a greater maturity and composure now she had cast off the powerful rapping that had made her name. She thought her style had been too shouty and admitted, 'These days I only MC when I'm drunk.'

Not every critic liked it. The *Daily Record* said it was 'something Bob the Builder would sing along to . . . This is just truly awful.' The *Observer*, however, thought the song demonstrated that Alesha was going to be an even better pop star the second time around.

One thing the song didn't do was to stick the boot into her wandering ex-husband Harvey; it was more playful than anything else. He had problems of his own. At the beginning of August, the *Sun* reported he had been arrested after a furious row with Javine at their house in Dollis Hill. According to the report, he was angry after she threw his clothes out onto the street when he hadn't come home after a night out. A source told the newspaper that when he finally did return, 'Harvey went nuts and a huge row kicked off.'

Javine promtly called the police; Harvey was arrested on suspicion of threatening behaviour and spent a night in the cells. She withdrew her complaint, apparently regretting calling the police and not wanting Harvey to get into serious trouble.

She later claimed that the incident had been blown out of proportion. Alesha's new song was in the charts when Javine told *Now* magazine that Harvey hadn't been cautioned – the police, she said, had just let him go when he became calm. She also said a neighbour and not she had called them because of their loud arguement, and officers had done the right thing in seperating them 'to allow us to cool down'. To emphisize that all was well, the couple were photographed with their baby daughter on holiday in Puerto Banus in Spain.

'The Boy Does Nothing' was Alesha's first top ten hit and actually made the charts on downloads alone before climbing to number five. It proved to be just as popular around Europe, reaching number two in France and Spain and number one in Hungary and the Czech Republic. Further afield it was also in the top ten in Australia and ended 2008 in the UK at number forty-eight in the bestselling chart of the year.

The album, *The Alesha Show*, was released on 24 November, two weeks after the single. For the first time as a solo artist she used her full name, Alesha Dixon, on the album cover, which showed her sitting on a swing in a showgirl outfit. Eight songs were collaborations with Xenomania and there was the slight suspicion that the album could have been by Girls Aloud or Kylie Minogue. The *Belfast Telegraph* even suggested that Xenomania were the modern equivalent of Stock, Aitken and Waterman, who had been responsible for all the early Kylie sing-along hits.

The obvious commercial bias of the record may have been responsible for the more cutting reviews. David Benn in the *Mail on Sunday* thought it 'peppy and bouncy' but added, 'Each track is professional, bang up to date, entirely unmemorable and cornier than a family-size bag of nacho chips. And much less satisfying.' *Music OMH* online was more complimentary: '*The Alesha Show* contains at least five songs that could easily crack the top ten. . . She may have taken the obvious route back into the public eye, but for once a celebrity talent show has given someone deserving a second chance.'

With hindsight, the album is probably overproduced, sacrificing some of Alesha's individuality in favour of a chart-friendly sound. It was a far safer album than *Fired Up*. The strategy worked, however, because the album would eventually reach number eleven in the charts. The sales proved to be more steady than spectacular, but in 2009 *The Alesha Show* was certified as platinum, with sales of more than 300,000 – a huge result.

Building the Alesha brand throughout the year had been a big success. Fittingly, in the album's acknowledgements she paid tribute to Malcolm Blair for 'being there at a time no one else was!' He had negotiated so many deals she seemed to be everywhere, including at the Miss World pageant in Johannesburg, where she performed for a television audience estimated at two billion just before Christmas.

Her growing stature hadn't changed her attitude to protecting her privacy. She wasn't impressed when a reporter from the *Sunday Mercury* in Birmingham asked a fairly innocuous question about what she expected from a man. She responded, 'What do I expect from a man? Nothing.' And when he asked about John Carew, he was 'immediately drenched in diva venom'. She told him: 'This interview is all about men, is it? I'm really not going to sit here and do questions about men that I've dated.'

She wouldn't have enjoyed the stories that came out just before Christmas claiming that she was 'madly in love' with the boss of her record company, Ed Howard. They were apparently photographed 'passionately kissing' at Movida. They had also been out to dinner. The *Sunday Mirror* quoted a friend as saying, 'They make a great couple and the chemistry between them is obvious.'

The suspicion was that there was much less to this than met the eye. They were never pictured so close together again. Unsurprisingly, the increasingly private Alesha decided not to publish her autobiography. She was rich enough that the money wasn't her priority. Perhaps the exercise of telling her story to a ghost writer was the therapy she actually needed.

CHAPTER FIFTEEN

Sweet Charity

Alesha won her first-ever solo award towards the end of 2008. She had collected a MOBO with Mis-Teeq and the *Strictly Come Dancing* title with Matthew Cutler but she'd never won anything by herself. She was the recipient of the *Cosmopolitan* Ultimate Confidence Award. If it had come two years earlier, it might have been a sick joke. Then, she couldn't even get out of bed after her world – and her confidence – had been shattered by the break-up of her marriage and the loss of her recording contract.

In fact, Alesha had never been a confident person. This was the girl who hid her anxiety behind a cheerful smile and was almost too scared to ring up to find out more about the dance class that would change her life. Then she had even found the prospect of catching a train to London daunting.

Success and financial independence had helped to change all that for the better, although she told Sky Living television afterwards that, like any woman, she had 'good days and bad days'. She also said her top tips for being confident were to be comfortable in your own skin and not feel as though you had to be like anybody else.

Alesha was presented with her award at the Banqueting House, London, on 4 November – the same day Barack Obama won the presidential election in the US. Alesha was more excited by the events across the Atlantic. She said that words couldn't describe how she felt. She had watched the election unfolding on television and told the *Daily Mirror* that she'd sat on her bed, cried and clapped her hands when it was clear he had triumphed: 'It was incredible and it gives a message of hope to everyone.'

She was so inspired partly because the new President was also mixed race and could appreciate the difficulties in life that brought: 'We like to think we live in an equal society but a lot of the younger generation who are black and mixed race may still think that life will be a bit more challenging for them. Now, a lot of people will think there's nothing they can't achieve. What can be better than that?'

Alesha was certainly confident enough to reveal that politically she was a strong Labour supporter, a working-class girl with a keen social conscience. She had become friendly with the Prime Minister, Gordon Brown, and his wife Sarah, whom she'd met at a seminar about women in the media. She had subsequently been invited to breakfast at Downing Street and asked personally by Sarah to perform at a charity event in London.

She had sung the Dusty Springfield standard 'Son Of A Preacher Man' on Dermot O'Leary's radio show and her manager, Malcolm, suggested she sing it for the PM because he actually was a vicar's son. She dedicated the song to Gordon and then, in order to appear completely unbiased, she dedicated her second song, 'The Boy Does Nothing', to David Cameron, which made everyone laugh.

Gordon took a shine to Alesha, especially when she told him, 'I'm thinking of going into politics – so if you ever need me . . .' He was so impressed he called her a 'national treasure', which is about as nice a compliment as you can get, especially if you're only thirty.

She met Gordon again a couple of months later at a Downing Street reception to promote a celebrity walk to the peak of Mount Kilimanjaro in Africa, an expedition organized by Gary Barlow in aid of Comic Relief.

The charity was launched in 1985 by the scriptwriter Richard

Curtis and the comedian Lenny Henry. Originally it was intended to raise public awareness of famine in Ethiopia but it had expanded to benefit a huge raft of causes helping to combat poverty and injustice. Red Nose Day in March is one of the key fund-raising events of the year in the UK. Alesha was pictured outside Downing Street with her red nose, the familiar symbol of the event.

While the walk would be the highest-profile charitable event she'd done, Alesha had already quietly built a reputation as one of the biggest supporters of good causes in show business. She was usually on *Children In Need* and had been one of the presenters in 2008. The year before that, she had been the public face of Nickelodeon's See Something, Say Something campaign which, at the time, was the UK's biggest anti-bullying campaign. She said it was 'extremely close to my heart'. The idea was to encourage children to speak out against bullies and have the confidence to tell someone if they, or someone they knew, were being bullied.

She produced an original design in the shape of a circle as part of the Circle of Life awareness campaign, which was promoting blood donation. She explained, 'I give blood, because in the black and Asian community, there is only a one in a 100,000 chance of finding a match for a blood donor. By just sparing an hour of your time giving blood, you can save a life and I cannot stress that enough.'

Alesha supported the African Caribbean Leukaemia Trust (ALCT), a voluntary charity that sought to increase the number of black and mixed-race people on the UK Bone Marrow Register. She was a fixture at the charity's annual fund-raising ball.

In May 2008, she launched the Radio Lollipop station for the Evelina Children's Hospital, a specialist unit with 140 beds next to St Thomas' Hospital on the South Bank in Lambeth. This was hospital radio designed specifically for sick kids. She said, 'Music is a great way to lift the spirits and will really help to brighten the children's stay in hospital. It's never much fun being in hospital, but music can be very therapeutic and take their minds off their illnesses.'

The MOBOs have been good to Alesha and she has presented them on three occasions. In 2002, top left, with LL Cool J. Her co-host in 2010 was Reggie Yates and they were pictured either side of the awards' founder, Kanya King. In 2011 Alesha was joined by American singer-songwriter Jason Derülo.

Climbing Kilimanjaro for Comic Relief was no walk in the park. It was fun to start with.

But then Alesha suffered from altitude sickness and muscle pain, so it was a relief to reach the top.

And she still had to go to Number 10 afterwards to be congratulated by Prime Minister Gordon Brown.

2009 was a big year musically for Alesha. In a skirt made of badges, singing at T4 on the Beach, Weston-super-Mare, in July.

In pink and purple at the V Festival at Hylands Park, Chelmsford, in August. She gave her performance eight out of ten.

'Welcome To The Alesha Show' – Alesha gets into the swing of her first nationwide solo tour in October.

A woman in white at *Children In Need* in November. She opened the show with her most famous song, 'The Boy Does Nothing'.

The Red Carpet Parade. Alesha demonstrates the art of looking fresh every time: In a red bodycon dress for the BRITs 2008; a year later with a new fringe, matching pink lipstick and shoes; the golden girl at the BRITs 2010; and, for a change, keeping her legs covered but not much else in a black Stephane St Jaymes gown at the National Television Awards in January 2011. Her antique diamond drop earrings are worth £55,000.

Alesha loves nothing better than a night out clubbing – all sweetness and smiles setting out in a cab.

It's gonna be a great night!

Or not. . . are you sure we're not on the guest list?

Yes, it was a great night! Taxi home for Miss Dixon.

Strewth, it's cold. Alesha in the unglamorous setting of Battersea Park to shoot the video for 'To Love Again'.

This is more like it. On the beach in Miami, where she was filming the video of 'Every Little Part Of Me'.

Alesha has to dress well for work. She wore a sassy pink mini skirt, French Connection boyfriend jacket and embellished shirt by Marc Jacobs for the Blackpool auditions of *Britain's Got Talent*.

Posing for fans in Birmingham, she had changed to a £350 Mary Katrantzou for Topshop lampshade dress that sold out the same day.

Looking slightly overdressed in a cloud print Vivetta dress with her fellow judges at the *BGT* press launch. Oh really, Simon, is that the best you can do!

At the Leicester Square premiere of *Ill Manors* in May 2012 – simply sublime.

In July she hosted the first VQ Day, a national celebration held at the Royal Opera House to raise the profile of vocational qualifications. She had taken a sporting diploma herself to qualify her for a course at Loughborough. She said, 'I know how hard it is sometimes to follow your dream and choose the best option, but what vocational qualifications offer is a way of getting out there, getting stuck in, working hard, and making it happen.'

And there were more events – like the Bupa Great Capital Run, which she launched in Leicester Square – and ran – to raise money for Help a London Child. Alesha was a celebrity with a social conscience who was determined to give something back – not for the glory or the self-satisfaction it brought, but as a woman who understood her good fortune at changing her life around.

The climb of Kilimanjaro would turn out to be the most demanding charitable event she had ever done, but before she packed for East Africa Alesha was busy promoting the second single from *The Alesha Show*, a soulful ballad called 'Breathe Slow'. It's always tricky picking the right second song, especially if the first release has done well. Surprisingly perhaps, the track was one of the few on the album not written and produced with Brian Higgins. Instead, 'Breathe Slow' was a collaboration with the Danish duo Carsten Schack and Kenneth Karlin, who were better known as Soulshock and Karlin. They had been producing hits for nearly twenty years, including 'Thank You' and 'DJ' for Jamelia and 'Truth Is' for the 2004 *American Idol* winner Fantasia.

'Breathe Slow' had a very different feel to 'The Boy Does Nothing'. The *Glasgow Sunday Mail* called it 'a decent radio-friendly track': 'It's a gentle slice of upbeat R & B pop and the vocals stand out.' The *Birmingham Mail* called it a 'slick ballad', which was 'slightly Euro-pop in places'.

Fraser McAlpine, in his BBC Chart Blog, was disappointed. He had loved her previous record but called the new release 'utterly terrible'. To make up for his harsh opinion, he recalled what he claimed was Alesha's favourite joke – at least she'd said it was when he met her: 'Why is six scared of seven? Because seven ate nine!'

Everyone seemed to agree, however, that the video for 'Breathe Slow' was terrific. Even Fraser called it 'gorgeous'. It was filmed entirely in black and white on location in Las Vegas and opens with Alesha, her hair in a Spanish bun, entering a quiet café, where she contemplates the break-up of her marriage. She sips a cup of coffee before she takes off her raincoat to reveal a *Strictly* showgirl outfit in glittering silver. She symbolically leaves behind her wedding ring and then walks down the famous Vegas Strip. Gradually she recaptures her smile.

You can't tell from the immaculate production but the filming was hilariously disrupted by British boxing fans who had gathered in Nevada for the latest Ricky Hatton bout. Traffic came to a complete standstill when they recognized Alesha and swarmed around her to take pictures.

Alesha didn't look like a movie star in the video – she looked better than that. Alison Jane Reid loved 'her very sophisticated and grown-up look'. She was impressed by the parallel storyline, which saw Alesha working out: 'Never has anyone looked quite so hot in a pair of Adidas shorts and fitted scoop-neck sports top. She has a fabulous décolletage. I also like the fact she presents a healthy role model to young girls. She is healthily voluptuous and not skinny.'

Alison Jane wasn't the only one who admired Alesha in the video: her performance has received more than 11.5 million hits on YouTube. There's no doubt that it did wonders for sales and the song eventually reached number three, which was her highest-ever solo chart position. 'Breathe Slow' highlighted how much Alesha's voice had changed over the years. It was clear and sweet where it used to be deeper and raunchier.

Many took the story of the song to be about her break-up with Harvey and how she had battled to regain her composure after the shock of hearing what he had been up to. She still had to answer questions about him during most interviews, which must have been getting on her nerves after nearly two and a half years. But she told the *Daily Mail*, 'You can't be with somebody for six years and get over them just like that. It takes a while to flush them out of your system and that's why I've been single since, because I think it's really important to deal with a past relationship before you go into another one. I feel I've allowed myself to heal.'

She was in a good place, therefore, when she flew out with eight other celebrities to begin her Comic Relief climb of Mount Kilimanjaro in Tanzania. It had seemed such a good idea when Gary Barlow had first contacted her six months before to ask if she would be interested in taking part. It was a chance to see a beautiful part of Africa and raise money at the same time. Gary wanted a 'mountain of cash' to provide the people of the East African country with mosquito nets to help prevent the spread of malaria.

Kilimanjaro is a name that conjures up romance and spectacle. At 19,340 feet, it is the highest mountain in Africa. 'The Snows of Kilimanjaro' was an acclaimed short story published by the literary lion Ernest Hemingway in 1936. It told the story of a man remembering his life in Africa as he contemplated his death. The 1952 film based on the book starred Gregory Peck and Ava Gardner and was one of the great Hollywood movies of the time.

The romantic notion of the place didn't prepare would-be adventurers for the reality of reaching the top. You don't need to be a specialist climber to reach the summit but you do require a certain level of fitness and determination to combat the inevitable reaction to the altitude, the cold and the high winds. Shortness of breath, altitude sickness, headaches and hypothermia were just some of the joys Alesha could look forward to.

Her eight companions were Gary, who injured his back right at the beginning, which wasn't a good start, Radio 1 DJ Chris Moyles, television presenters Ben Shephard and Denise Van Outen, Boyzone singer Ronan Keating, Fearne Cotton and, from Girls Aloud, Kimberley Walsh and Cheryl Cole. The latter had just completed her first season as a judge on *The X Factor*. They weren't exactly going alone: they were accompanied by Jeremy Gane, whose firm Charity Challenge had organized the climb, as well as a team of 140 guides, porters, cooks and medics.

Looking at the celebrity list, you might have expected Chris Moyles, who was a bit overweight, to struggle most during the seven-day climb but that proved not to be the case. Three of the girls – Cheryl, Fearne and Alesha – had a terrible time.

Alesha had finally made it to Thailand to see her dad, but since returning to the UK she'd been too busy launching 'Breathe Slow' to train properly for the expedition. She told a radio interviewer, 'I'm visualizing myself walking up the mountain, and getting to the top. I have only had time to mentally prepare.'

Her 'visualizing' probably didn't include crawling up the mountain. She had been superfit for *Strictly* but that had been more than a year ago. She did manage a trip to the gym but told the *Sun*, 'I went on the treadmill the other day and when I came off my thighs were killing me.' She also joined the others at the National Olympic Centre in London, where they were tested for their ability to cope with altitude by exercising in a special chamber. It wasn't the real thing, but Chris Moyles came out on top, which was encouraging for him.

The whole adventure was going to be filmed for a television broadcast. With Ben Shephard, Alesha flew out ahead of the others to Arush, Tanzania, to record her emotions on seeing the peak for the first time. She told her video diary how daunting it seemed now that she had arrived, especially the idea of having to cope with snow higher up the mountain when it was so hot in the plains where the climb would begin: 'Looking at it, it's amazing to think we are going to do that. I seriously don't know how we're going to do that. But it's beautiful. To be that high up will be such a treat.'

It wasn't. Before she set off, she filmed a day with a local district nurse to illustrate the extent of the malaria problem in that part of Africa. She met a woman who had lost her husband to malaria and had the disease herself, as did her six children. Alesha said, 'I can't begin to imagine how this lady feels. They have no protection – none. It's the repetition of having it, treating it, then it coming back again... We complain about our NHS system and yes, it's not perfect, but it's far better than what they have here. We've got a cheek to complain, that's what I think. It's such a simple thing. We're not asking to change the world. It's just a net. Even walking the mountains we've got more luxuries than they've got here.'

That was particularly true before they set off. Then the team medic ordered them to ditch half their belongings, including some essential toiletries and spare clothes. Fearne was concerned that she was allowed to take only four pairs of socks.

The first couple of days were relatively easy. Alesha and Fearne strolled along at the back, chatting and eating sweets. The most dramatic event occurred when Alesha disturbed an ants' nest, which had her sprinting away, laughing, 'Have you ever seen anyone get up a mountain quicker?' She was troubled by a swollen foot but was finding it easier than Cheryl and Kimberley, who were cursing the high heels they always wore in Girls Aloud, because the shoes had given them problems with their feet.

Alesha had a scare on the second day when she tumbled ten feet down a steep ledge while having a discreet pee behind a bush. She was still mastering the Shewee, the portable gadget that consists of a plastic funnel to enable women to pee in private, when she slipped. She landed with a genuine thud on the ground. Everyone knew she was all right when they heard her distinctive laugh. She walked very gingerly for the rest of the day, which wasn't much fun as they were on the move for seven hours.

Despite everybody trying to remain cheerful, there were already signs that the altitude was beginning to have an effect, with some members of the group suffering from headaches and sickness when they were only halfway up. The next night Fearne collapsed outside the toilet tent. She had got up to use the loo but couldn't make it back to her bed. She was too weak to move and called out for help. She needed an anti-sickness injection to revive her but the following day there were real concerns that she wouldn't be able to carry on.

On day four Alesha began to struggle. She told the camera, 'I just felt really dizzy, so I've had to stop and I'm going to stay at the back because I don't want to slow anyone down. It feels like you're drunk, that's the only way to describe it – I feel like I need to go at Jamaican pace. When I was dizzy, and I had to be escorted over a rock, I felt like a wally because you don't want to be a drama queen.' In the end, she was spurred on by the sight of Fearne battling away.

The following morning it was Cheryl's turn to succumb. She needed an injection after being sick at breakfast time. She explained, graphically, 'I crawled out of my tent, and got a whiff of the food, and then it was projectile vomit. It was coming out of my mouth, out of my nose . . .'

The night before the climb to the top, known as the Uhuru Peak, Alesha was in better spirits and rashly said: 'My plan is to get to the top as quickly as we can and be out of breath when we get there.'

The final climb began by torchlight at midnight and was expected to take the group about six hours. It soon became apparent that Alesha was really troubled by sickness and severe muscle pain, and she dropped further and further behind the rest. One of the chief guides, Emmanuel Seka, dropped back to try to encourage her. He later revealed to the *Mail on Sunday* the extent of her agony and frustration.

He described how distraught she was that the others were so far ahead: 'She was saying, "Fuck, I do not want to go on any more." She was throwing her poles down and pushing me. She just said, "Shit, they've all left me and are going up without me." But I managed to persuade her that we were all in this together.

'She was swearing and crying. I told her to stop swearing. I told her it would be OK. She had two or three hours of pain. She was saying, "I do not feel myself, I cannot go on" and I just told her how close she was to the top.'

There is something refreshingly normal about Alesha exploding in a tantrum of frustration. Not everyone can be the stiff-upper-lipped hero of many a British war movie. Here was a woman doing her best not to let anyone down and being betrayed by her body – something she had no control over in the circumstances. She was literally being crippled by a lack of oxygen.

Emmanuel, who had accompanied more than 150 expeditions to the summit, was vastly experienced and managed to coax Alesha into carrying on by suggesting that she think of the sick children in the orphanage she visited before the climb. And he asked her to sing to him. After a while she started to sing and became less focused on the pain she was feeling.

And so, at the pace of a lame snail, they continued, flanked by eight guides who would themselves break into uplifting Swahili songs to urge her on. They talked about music and Emmanuel's favourites, Puff Daddy and Beyoncé – it seems there is no escape from that superstar for Alesha even at the top of a mountain in East Africa.

Meanwhile, the other celebrities had made it to the summit through gale-force winds. Fearne, Cheryl, Denise and Ben were the first to reach the top just as the sun came up. Their Comic Relief despatch said, 'At the summit, God knows how. A temperature of minus fifteen and air so thin your lungs positively burn with disappointment every time you take a breath means you can't stop long.'

Soon afterwards, Kimberley, Ronan and Gary arrived 'in agony'. A weary Gary exclaimed, 'It seemed like a hare-brained plan six months ago but somehow we're here. I can't believe it. Stretcher for Barlow!' Forty minutes later Chris Moyles trudged in and put his arms around the sign that proclaimed, 'CONGRATULATIONS.

YOU ARE NOW AT UHURU PEAK, TANZANIA, 5895 M, AFRICA'S HIGHEST MOUNTAIN, THE WORLD'S HIGHEST FREESTANDING MOUNTAIN.'

But where was Alesha? They started practising a Swahili song of celebration to sing to her when – or if – she made it. And then, two hours after the rest, she came into view. Jeremy Gane described it, 'She looked like the Queen of Sheba coming along with her entourage.'

When she reached the others, in a clearing above the rainforest, her celebrity companions broke into song and she even managed a little dance of appreciation before she collapsed on the ground with a giggle and said, 'Night.'

The way down was much easier – a five-hour stroll through the forest. Alesha apologized to Emmanuel for her behaviour. He recalled, 'She did not remember what she had done but she said sorry. I understand the emotions people go through and I told her it was OK.' Alesha took his address and said she would be back, but for a safari next time. Jeremy Gane observed, 'Alesha is outspoken and if she does not like anything she will say so. But Emmanuel has got presence and he's the kingpin. He's no pushover.'

Despite the level of support they had, it was still a commendable achievement that all nine celebrities made it to the top. This was a real challenge and not the made-for-TV hokum of *I'm A Celebrity . . . Get Me Out Of Here!* Afterwards Jeremy said, 'No one should under-estimate how gruelling this climb is. I have climbed the mountain twenty-one times and have never met a more spirited and humorous group who were determined to reach their goal from the outset.'

The best news was that the trek raised more than £3 million for Comic Relief and Gordon Brown pledged another £2 million of Government money to help combat malaria in the region. Alesha needed time to recover properly before she set out on a short UK tour supporting Enrique Iglesias.

She was asked about the experience as she prepared for the

concerts and admitted that it was probably the hardest thing she had ever undertaken and she had come back 'scarred and tired'. She told the *Warrington Guardian*, 'I think it's one of those things that if you did give up, you'd kick yourself for it later and regret it. I loved the experience but it took me a while to recover and it's definitely a once in a lifetime thing. I won't be doing it again!'

PART FOUR

National Treasure

CHAPTER SIXTEEN

A Strict Judgement

Everybody seemed to miss the point when Alesha replaced Arlene Phillips as a judge on *Strictly Come Dancing*. Media commentators were obsessed with an ageism row, pointing out that thirty-year-old Alesha was thirty-six years younger than the renowned choreographer. Others were outraged at her lack of expertise. But, for a while, nobody in the world of television could talk about anything else, which was, of course, exactly what the producers wanted. It was terrific news for the BBC even if it had to answer complaints from viewers.

The previous year, Sharon Osbourne, aged fifty-five, had stepped down as a judge on *Strictly*'s arch-rival, *The X Factor*, and her seat on the judging panel was taken by Cheryl Cole, aged twenty-five. Nobody suggested ageism then, because Sharon appeared to have left voluntarily, but it proved to be an effective move by the show and Cheryl quickly became the most popular figure on British television. *Strictly* needed to do something similar to shake things up.

Getting rid of poor Arlene was inspired, although it did take the more devoted viewers by surprise. What they hadn't realized was that *Strictly* wasn't merely a dancing programme: it was and remains principally a *television* show. It didn't actually matter if Alesha knew her tango from her fandango as long as it made good TV.

Kevin O'Sullivan observes, 'Did they really think it was about ballroom dancing? The day that Arlene was replaced by Alesha was the day I think it became clear to the great British public that this was just a telly show. In the same way, *The X Factor* isn't a competition to find the next big superstar, it's a four-month project in which ITV dominates the ratings and makes a load of money.

'*Strictly*'s constant problem is that it is too middle class and too old. No matter what they say, *Strictly Come Dancing* would never get on to ITV because the demographics are all wrong. Its audience is ancient. Sixteen to thirty-four-year-olds don't really watch it so, obviously, Alesha was attractive to them. She is also a great-looking girl, which helped.'

There's absolutely no doubt that when the producers offered the job to Alesha they were willing to sacrifice a great deal of expertise. It could be argued, however, that the three remaining judges, Craig, Bruno and Len, had as much experience, professionalism and mastery of the subtleties of dancing technique as any panel actually needed.

Craig was renowned as the hardest to please judge and the most reluctant to give a maximum ten, scrupulously marking down if there were any technical errors. He was born in the sleepy Australian town of Ballarat in Victoria but moved to Melbourne, the state capital, to pursue a career in dance. He gained experience in stage musicals, including *West Side Story*, *Me and My Girl* and *La Cage Aux Folles*, before arriving in the UK in his twenties. After further roles in *Cats*, *Jesus Christ Superstar* and *Miss Saigon*, among others, he turned to choreography and has twice been nominated for Olivier Awards for his work on the musicals *Spend, Spend, Spend* and *My One and Only*. On *Strictly Come Dancing* he proved a master of the catchphrase – even outdoing Bruce Forsyth with his 'Fab-u-*lous!*'

Bruno Tonioli is also from a small town, Ferrara in Northern Italy, which is best known for the nine kilometres of Renaissance walls that surround it. His parents wanted him to work in a bank but his life was changed when, aged seventeen, he watched the famous Liza Minnelli film *Cabaret*. He saw it eight times in a row. When he was old enough, he travelled to Rome to begin a dance career. He trained as a ballet dancer before moving to London and working as a free-lance dancer in stage shows and pop videos such as 'I'm Still Standing' with Elton John, before he too progressed into choreography. He specialized in videos for stars including Tina Turner, The Rolling Stones and Bananarama. His flamboyant television performances don't reflect the man who in real life is apparently much more reserved and serious.

Len Goodman, the head judge, was the one that brought a lifetime of ballroom dancing experience to the panel. He had been a champion ballroom dancer in the sixties, some forty years before he joined *Strictly Come Dancing*. He had been born towards the end of the World War Two in Bethnal Green and was brought up close to the station there in a two-up, two-down house. In his autobiography he tells some wonderful stories about his grandfather, who was a barrow boy from the East End, selling fruit and veg, and used the sort of memorable, down-to-earth phrases that Len would employ as a judge.

All three were heavyweights in the world of dance and Alesha couldn't rival their knowledge and experience. But, first and foremost, they were television personalities and that she *could* compete with. She also undeniably made the panel seem younger.

The BBC has a constant desire to lower the age of its audience. Kevin points out, tongue in cheek, 'It was getting good ratings, but the youngest person who watches it is probably about eighty-five. The presenter is an octogenarian and the kid of the panel is Craig Revel Horwood, who is in his mid-forties. They wanted to bring the age of the average viewer down, make the panel more beautiful and give it more street cred – although Alesha was already over thirty, remember.'

So why did Alesha choose to do it? Everything had been going so well, a complete contrast to the becalmed state of her career when she'd accepted the challenge of becoming a competitor in 2007. When she returned from Kilimanjaro it was to a world in which she was a top ten recording artist, a popular television personality and a fixture at every big event. She had chatted to Prince Charles at The Prince's Trust Celebrate Success Awards at the Odeon, Leicester Square. He asked her if she had grabbed a lift back down Kilimanjaro: 'I was, like, no, we had to walk!'

The third single from *The Alesha Show* was called 'Let's Get Excited' and demonstrated that her music was still in demand. It reached number thirteen in the charts in May 2009, a respectable effort considering that the album had been out for more than six months and had been selling well. More importantly, it rekindled interest in *The Alesha Show* and the album went back up to eleven, which was its highest chart position.

'Let's Get Excited' was an up-tempo dance track and one of the numbers that Alesha had recorded in Los Angeles the summer before, suggesting that Asylum didn't want her to sound too British. The producer, Kuk Harrell, is one of the biggest names in American R & B music and the man who co-wrote two of the most popular songs in recent musical history – 'Umbrella' by Rihanna and the thrilling 'Single Ladies (Put A Ring On It)', an American number one for Beyoncé that would win the Grammy Award for Song of the Year in 2010. It gave Alesha international kudos to work with him, although talk of an American breakthrough was premature.

The video wasn't as dramatic as the one for 'Breathe Slow'. The entire song was filmed in an East London nightclub and featured Alesha dancing energetically in two outfits, a black and white mini dress and skintight black leggings with gold shoes. It's fun and frisky but not particularly ground-breaking or imaginative. At the end, everybody gets showered by hoses for some reason.

'Let's Get Excited' may not have been 'Single Ladies', but at least it was different from the previous two singles. The chorus also contained the memorable line: 'I'm so excited, I'm a detective, I'm all over you.' The critics were divided in their opinions: they either liked it or hated it. The *South Wales Echo* congratulated her on making R & B 'without sounding like you're copying our American cousins'. The *Liverpool Echo*, on the other hand, included it in a list of the worst songs of the week. The *Beat Review* online was more enthusiastic, 'It's a party song, filled with electro-pop cuts, jittery beats and an absolutely stimulating message. It's another ace from Alesha.' Fraser McAlpine in his BBC Chart Blog was a big supporter of Alesha and thought the song was 'kinda bouncy and fun'. With hindsight, it was a shame she didn't release 'Italians Do It Better', which she wrote with Brian and Miranda, because most critics had identified that as one of the stand-out tracks on the album.

While Malcolm discreetly continued negotiations with the BBC, Alesha finished her tour with Enrique and started playing the circuit of outdoor concerts that come around every year and are now part of the English summer. There was time for her to be linked, dubiously, with singer Alex Vargas after being seen with him at a concert by The Script at the Shepherd's Bush Empire. They were all over each other apparently. Nobody bothered to point out that his band Vagabond were part of the Xenomania stable and were just about to release their first album. The group were also, coincidentally, supporting The Script on their UK tour.

By this time, in June, the press was aware of the possibility that Alesha would be replacing Arlene, although she refused to speculate about it during an interview with *Sky News*. When Eamonn Holmes asked her if she would bring the 'Cheryl Factor' to the show, she replied, 'If you say so.'

Alesha performed a rousing set at the Barclaycard Wireless Festival in Hyde Park on Sunday, 5 July. Three days later the BBC announced their autumn schedules and revealed formally what everybody already knew: Arlene was being shunted off *Strictly Come Dancing* in favour of Alesha Dixon. The change was revealed by the dynamic controller for BBC 1, Jay Hunt, who admitted that Arlene was 'disappointed'. Jay had to answer questions on the spot about ageism, suggesting that the story had been decided even before the press conference. She responded, 'Is it about ageism? Absolutely not, I'm committed to reaching out to the broadest possible audience.' Nobody seemed interested in the news that the famous ballet dancer Darcey Bussell would also be a judge and would be joining the series for the final three shows – it was all about Alesha.

Ms Hunt added that Arlene would be working on *The One Show* as their *Strictly Come Dancing* expert, which sounded like a pretty thin reward for her six years on the show. She also confirmed that Bruce Forsyth, who was eighty-one, had renewed his contract for another year.

More than 1,300 people initially complained about the change, prompting the BBC to issue a statement: 'Age or gender has absolutely nothing to do with the decision to replace Arlene on the judging panel.' Ms Hunt elaborated on her decision to remove Arlene: 'When I looked at the four people we had, Bruno is the joker, Craig is the Simon Cowell of the show and Len is the head judge. Arlene has elements of all of them, but when you look at it, Arlene was the obvious one to change.'

Esther Rantzen, then sixty-nine, who had been a contestant on the show in 2004, described the decision as an insult to the viewing public: 'We will no longer tolerate prejudice against age, particularly against ageing women.'

Thanks to the media debate, the matter was discussed by ministers during House of Commons questions. Labour's Deputy Leader, Harriet Harman, who was also Equalities Minister, said, 'I think it's absolutely shocking that Arlene Phillips is not going to be a judge on *Strictly Come Dancing*. As Equalities Minister, I am suspicious that there is age discrimination there. So I'd like to take the opportunity of asking the BBC: it is not too late, we want Arlene Phillips in the next edition of *Strictly Come Dancing*.'

It hadn't occurred to Ms Harman that the BBC would have to sack Alesha before she had even started her new job. Everybody, it seemed, had an opinion. Nick Ross, the former presenter of *Crimewatch*, suggested the appointment was actually 'lookist'. He made a fair point, because there were very few women in the country who could match the beauty of Cheryl Cole and Alesha was one of them. Amanda Platell, the columnist of the *Daily Mail*, was indignant that the 'hugely experienced' Arlene had been dumped for the 'novice' Alesha and predicted it would be a disaster.

The remaining judges seemed bewildered. Craig said he was shocked because he never thought they would change any of them and he would miss Arlene, who was a personal friend. He was apprehensive about Alesha: 'A celebrity contestant can never match someone who has been dancing their entire life, who has been competitive and in professional competitions.' Len said he would miss Arlene, whom he called probably the best choreographer in the world. He hoped the BBC weren't trying to introduce a younger audience – which was exactly what they were trying to do.

Arlene Phillips didn't speak out nor, for the time being, did Alesha. Instead, she flew to Los Angeles for more recording. It was like a Kilimanjaro reunion. Fearne Cotton arrived to start filming her documentary on Alesha. Fearne went to surprise her at the Anand Studios in Hollywood, where she was recording a new track with Gary Barlow. They had written a song together with John Shanks, who had won the Grammy Award for Best Producer of the Year in 2005 for his work with, among others, Kelly Clarkson and Alanis Morissette.

Fearne arrived just as she was laying down the vocal and was sent outside to wait by Gary until they were ready. She was let back in to hear Alesha sing 'To Love Again', a quite exquisite ballad that had the stamp of Gary Barlow all over it. Alesha's lyric about a girl who had been hurt in love but was now trying to find a way back to her heart struck a poignant note. Gary felt it was 'very real'. Fearne thought it 'very moving'. They wrote and recorded the song in a single day. Alesha found working with Gary and John a 'joy' and she clearly enjoyed the California sun. She loved her hotel, the Beverly Wilshire, and told the *Daily Telegraph* it was the best she had stayed in: 'The bed was humongous – extra, extra king size, you could easily have fitted six people in there. As I was always on my own, recording, it was nice to stay in a really sumptuous hotel to make it comforting.'

Fearne asked Alesha whether she had instantly said yes when she was asked to be a judge on *Strictly*. She replied that she hadn't, although she was excited by the possibility. The immediate controversy when the rumours about the job started made her think twice about accepting. She was down at the prospect. She explained, 'I was sat there thinking is it really worth it, do I really want to do this and, with each negative thing I was reading, it was actually firing me up to make me want to do it more.'

She astutely realized what was going on: 'Unfortunately, I am just the guinea pig in the middle of a bit of media hoo-ha. You put things into perspective, you shrug it off and, you know what, I am fine with it now and looking forward to it and just not bothered.'

She would turn out to be more bothered than she thought.

Alesha is sensible about business and her manager even more so. She may have been excited about joining the *Strictly Come Dancing* judging panel, but there were also practical reasons why it made good sense to accept. First, there was the money. She was already a very rich woman but a six-figure salary for working what was effectively a one-day week was too good to miss. Bruno and Len even managed to combine it with flying back and forth across the Atlantic to be judges on the US version, *Dancing With The Stars*. Secondly, she would be able to be a judge and still go on tour with *The Alesha Show* in the autumn. All the publicity from the series would do no harm at all to ticket sales. And thirdly, it gave her options for her future. She would soon be thirty-one and needed to make sure she remained in the public eye. She now had her own television production company and a new documentary on absent fathers would attract far more interest if she were a star on a top-rated show.

She warmed up for her debut as a judge by appearing at the V Festival in Chelmsford. She reminded the crowd that *Strictly* was about to start: 'Hope you're gonna show me support on Saturday night.' Big crowds love nostalgia and they revelled in her medley of Mis-Teeq hits but it was debatable how many of the cheering topless tattooed young men would be tuning in to watch the dancing at the weekend.

Her big first week of *Strictly* began with the newspapers revealing that her ex-husband and the mother of his child had split up. Harvey and Javine always seemed to be in the press when something big was happening in Alesha's life, but this was dramatic news. Javine's spokesman told the *Sun*, 'Javine has left Harvey and the family home for a myriad of reasons. The main crunch came when she found evidence of him being unfaithful. She now wants to be left alone to regroup, resettle and care for her daughter.'

Alesha's new job began on Friday, 18 September 2009. At least she was among friends. Bruce Forsyth had been a supporter since her time as a competitor and he seemed to be determined to give her a chance. Craig had been close to Arlene but he wasn't just a professional judge, he was a professional television personality, and it would do the show no good whatsoever if the judges were divided.

The backlash against Alesha began almost immediately, with complaints pouring in to the BBC that she wasn't as good as Arlene. There was a certain irony about the cries of ageism from the public because the voting viewers rarely backed the older competitors. The previous year, the actress Cherie Lunghi, then fifty-six, was widely acknowledged to be a wonderful dancer but she failed to make the final. In the first series Alesha judged, actress Lynda Bellingham, who was sixty-one, was the fourth one out, while Jo Wood, the 54-year-old ex-wife of Rolling Stone Ron Wood, lasted only two more weeks. And Esther Rantzen herself was voted off in week three when she competed. The oldest female winner to date is Natasha Kaplinsky, who was thirty-one when she collected the first trophy in 2004. Mark Ramprakash, thirty-seven in 2006, is the oldest-ever champion.

At the end of the first show, the producers gathered in Alesha's dressing room to congratulate her. They were all smiles and she left the studio relieved. That relief wouldn't last long once the press had had their say. Amanda Platell poked fun, calling her 'verbally challenged'. She identified Alesha's habit of repeating herself: 'She's even starting to rival the legendary ignorance of Jade Goody, with comments such as: "I have only one word for you – fierce, fierce".'

It was withering stuff. Amanda accused Alesha of doing 'unutterable damage to the marvellously joyful format that is *Strictly Come Dancing*'. She concluded, 'Now Alesha has proved she is a judge only a mother could love, it's about time SHE was voted off. And the sooner, the better.'

Amanda was not alone in savaging Alesha – it seemed to be a national pastime that first weekend. The *Sun* dramatically called her 'the most hated woman in Britain'. Jim Shelley, the *Daily Mirror*'s TV critic, said, 'The lynch-mob was such you'd have thought she had strangled a kitten.' Fortunately, the criticism motivated others to speak up in her defence. Craig Revel Horwood told *BBC Breakfast*, 'This backlash is just horrendous. I don't think she deserves it. Look at any of the recordings that Bruno, Len, myself and Arlene did early on – it has taken us a long time to get used to the format. To be able to form constructive criticism in ten seconds is not an easy thing to do. Alesha has a lot to say, she has been through it and won it. I am really passionate about this. We have got to give her a chance.'

Alesha appeared on the *Strictly* spin-off show *It Takes Two* to defend herself: 'I do know what I am talking about. People forget I had four months of solid training with the world champion, ten hours a day.'

By an ironic twist of fate, the world champion in question, Matthew Cutler, was the first voted off the show that weekend. He was partnering the former Wimbledon champion Martina Hingis, who didn't look a natural dancer. Alesha thought she needed to work on her arms more, which she described as a 'bit fly-away'. But she still loyally voted to save her in the dance-off against Rav Wilding, the *Crimewatch* presenter. Len, as chief judge, had the deciding vote, however, and chose Rav to stay.

This must have been a bitter pill for the producers to swallow because Martina was rumoured to have been paid £100,000 – the largest fee of any contestant that year. Matthew may or may not have been blamed for the disaster, but he left the show before the next series began, when he wasn't given a celebrity to partner and was demoted to be part of the professional dance troupe.

Alesha's own take on the reaction to her first show was that critics were, in fact, being ageist against young people and that there was an assumption that if you were under thirty you didn't really know what you were doing. She explained to Fearne, 'I really believe it's not about how old you are, it's your life experiences that form your character and therefore that is what is valid and what counts.'

The critics, both professional and armchair, had completely missed the position Alesha was expected to take on the panel. As Jay Hunt had explained, each of the other judges had a precise role except Arlene. None of them was the contestant's friend until now. Alesha wasn't expected to provide waspish comments, get into arguments with Craig and Len or joke around like Bruno. Those three were already doing more than enough of that. But none of them could say, as Alesha could and frequently did, that they knew how the contestants were feeling – because they didn't. One of the celebrities on that first show, Natalie Cassidy, who played Sonia Jackson in *EastEnders*, observed, 'To have her on the judging panel is a wonderful relief for us celebs as she knows exactly what we're going through.'

In time, the public would get used to her in that role but it's probably fair to say that in the UK the public always hates the replacement and gets all sentimental for the good old days. Chris Evans is a leading example of this. His Radio 2 show is an astonishing ratings success but there are still those who hanker for the time when Terry Wogan was in the morning chair. It seems to be part of being British.

Alesha might have hoped to be more articulate on the first shows. But this had little to do with her perceived lack of judging expertise. She wasn't yet a television veteran able to convey her thoughts to camera smoothly. Under pressure she tended to struggle and repeat herself as she searched for the right word. Being on television is an art that improves with practice. Alesha was a bright, hard-working and serious-minded woman. She didn't deserve to be sneered at because of her syntax.

CHAPTER SEVENTEEN

Old-Fashioned Entertainer

Just when Alesha might have thought things couldn't get any worse, Javine decided to tell the world how many times Harvey had cheated while he was married – with seven women, apparently, including her. She alleged in the *News of the World* that Harvey's infidelity had become worse after his wedding and also that the marriage to Alesha was a 'sham'.

She told the newspaper, 'Harvey is a serial womanizer with a big problem. He cheated on Alesha with A LOT of women. I did her a big favour by taking him off her hands – and after three horrible years, boy do I regret it.'

She claimed that he had told her that he would go out and find a girl to make him feel better whenever Alesha 'pissed him off'. She also alleged, 'He confided in me. He told me he'd slept with this well-known soap opera actress. He said he took Viagra and they had sex six times in a night. He told me he was always having sex with women on his shows.'

Harvey, she said, was 'seeing' a couple of girls in *Daddy Cool* before they got together, as well as meeting others after the show and at the pub. 'He justified it all by saying these girls meant nothing to him. That he was always really thinking of Alesha at home.'

Finally, she undermined the impression that they had been tortured by love when they were discovered together. She revealed that they started off as friends but over time it became obvious there was a strong sexual attraction between them: 'He finally swept me off my feet with all the attention he gave me. We fell in lust and in love.'

Javine's allegations have to be put into context: she was clearly angry about what had happened to her own relationship with Harvey and she paints a very unflattering portrait of the father of her young child – which was obviously the intention. He has never commented on her claims. Time would prove to be a great healer, however, and Javine and Harvey now have a much better relationship for the sake of their daughter. Harvey explained to *New* magazine, 'Once a child's involved you get things into perspective.' One can only imagine what Alesha thought as she scanned the Sunday papers for reports of her performance on *Strictly Come Dancing*. Yet again she was being made to look very foolish. It was bad enough knowing your husband had fallen in love with another woman without discovering that he'd been a serial shagger as well.

If that weren't bad enough for Alesha, when she opened her curtains in the morning, she was greeted by the sight of paparazzi hanging around the quiet street where she lived, hoping to snatch a picture of 'Britain's Most Hated Woman' because of the Arlene controversy. She could do without any further reasons for the papers to carry stories about her. But then her younger brother John was up in court on drugs charges.

He had been arrested earlier in the summer, just before Alesha was chosen as Arlene's replacement. He had been nabbed by police as he banged on a front door near to his mum's house. He appeared before magistrates in St Albans at the beginning of October and admitted possessing a small amount of cocaine and cannabis. He was fined £150 and ordered to pay £250 costs.

The People found a source who said it had been a nightmare time for Alesha: 'She's incredibly close to John. But she's always been staunchly against drugs. She was really worried for the future of her brother.

And she also hated the idea that her family would be tainted by his conviction for drugs.' Alesha made no comment, unsurprisingly, nor did John, although he did put a message on Facebook that said he had the best sister in the world.

She didn't look too downcast about life when she met up with Chris Moyles, another of her Kilimanjaro buddies, who invited her on his Radio 1 breakfast show. Chris and Alesha have a good rapport and he gave her a big bear hug when she arrived in silver leggings at the BBC studios in Great Portland Street. The interview wasn't taxing. She told him that she did care what people thought of her but was trying not to take the negative reports to heart: 'I'm not going to let it get me down.' She also said that she was single and there was no new love interest in her life, which was timely as the press were trying to link her with Peter Andre.

Harvey found his voice, not to talk about his split with Javine nor her allegations about his extramarital activities: he spoke to the *Sunday Mirror* exclusively about how upset Alesha was by the public reaction to her appointment as a judge on *Strictly Come Dancing*. He explained that he'd seen the negative comments in the newspapers and texted her to check that she was all right. 'She called me the next day and we had a chat. She wasn't her normal self at all. I knew she was down and I could tell she had been crying. She takes it personally.'

Harvey's remarks were well put, sympathetic to his ex-wife and perceptive about the situation she found herself in: 'I was really worried about her because she sounded bad, but to be honest I'd be more worried if she didn't care because I know it means so much to her. I said, "They're used to Arlene Phillips. When you've got a show as powerful as *Strictly Come Dancing* and you've got a formula, people don't take well to change."' He also compared Alesha to Mother Teresa because she was 'so nice', which may have been laying on the compliments a little too thickly. But his comments were gracious and showed him in a good light.

It appeared that Harvey and Alesha had been in touch since Javine's allegations but, looking closely at the dates, that wasn't the case. The conversation he described with Alesha took place before the revelations. It's impossible to know whether Alesha would have been so keen to ring him back if she had already read the *News of the World*.

Alesha was more nervous about the second week of *Strictly Come Dancing* than she had been about the first. She told Fearne Cotton that she did have a cry when she read the comments about her, especially the jibe that she was the most hated woman in Britain. She was a judge on a dancing competition not a prime minister squashing a miners' strike. Television, it seemed, was more important to the general public than real life.

Her interview with Fearne, as well as Harvey's insight, confirms an important facet of Alesha's character. She is a sensitive woman who keeps her emotions hidden from her public face. You never felt she had got out of bed on the wrong side or received some bad news in the post. She was always well presented, with the broadest smile on her face whatever she was feeling inside. She had been that way as a little girl and she hadn't changed.

Alesha admitted that she was a 'bit quiet' when she went in to the BBC for the second round of shows, unsure how to approach things. Bruce Forsyth did his best to back her by announcing on the show, 'What a week you've had. It's been so unfair, so unfair. You're a strong lady.'

The producers told her to try and put the criticism to the back of her mind and play to her strengths as a former competitor and winner. Kevin O'Sullivan explains, 'She was the contestant's friend. I am sure if you went back over the transcripts one of her main comments was "I know what you are going through."'

There were some positive sides to all the negative publicity. She celebrated her thirty-first birthday with a party that began at the Crazy Bear bar at the May Fair Hotel and finished up at Movida. She could at least toast the news that sales of *The Alesha Show* had more than doubled since she'd joined the panel of *Strictly*.

She was also chatted up by Prince Harry at Pangaea in Mayfair, although it's fair to say that Alesha did most of the talking. She was dancing with friends when a go-between tapped her on the shoulder and said, 'Prince Harry would like to meet you.' Alesha was very funny about it to the *Daily Mail*: 'I was like, "Wicked". I went straight over and was just being my chatty self. He was like, "Do you want a drink?" I said, "I'd love to stay and have one, but I've got my friends over there." So I just had a nice little chat and actually took a sip of his drink.'

She had to put the upset involving *Strictly* behind her and concentrate on rehearsals for her first major tour. She had been a recording artist for eight years but this would be the first time she had headlined her own series of concerts. She may not have been selling out Wembley Stadium, but there were twenty dates at major halls around the country arranged around her TV commitments. She ended up having to postpone three because of her other job.

She began at the Royal Concert Hall in Nottingham on 20 October 2009. She started, naturally, with 'Welcome To The Alesha Show', the opening salvo from the album. The curtain drew back to reveal a 'slender, sparkly showgirl perched on a swing', as the *Nottingham Post* described her. This first image suggested the light burlesque theme and cabaret influence that would follow.

The paper was slightly more impressed with her costume than her performance: 'We were constantly urged to stand up, dance around, wave our hands and sing along, in a manner that sometimes verged on the downright bossy, and there was a certain edge behind all that well-intentioned eagerness to please.' The *Daily Mirror* had turned up to her opening gig but described her tiny gold playsuit costume as Beyoncé-style, which was probably worse than calling her bossy.

The critics were much more positive as the tour progressed. A week later, the *Liverpool Echo* was dazzled by her performance at the Liverpool Philharmonic Hall: 'She sang brilliantly and she danced brilliantly – so she performed brilliantly.' Vicki Kellaway also said she was 'smart, fierce, gobby and outspoken about her love of pink', which suggested that Alesha was more comfortable in this musical environment than she was performing for the television cameras. Physically, the show was demanding. In Liverpool Alesha needed emergency treatment on her neck, which she had hurt on the opening night and wasn't getting better.

Most of the critics preferred her Mis-Teeq tribute to the newer, more mainstream numbers. She performed a medley of 'All I Want', 'B With Me', 'One Night Stand' and 'Why?' before giving 'Scandalous' the full treatment. She also demonstrated that she hadn't lost her ability for rapid-fire rapping and didn't need to be drunk to MC these days, as she had suggested previously.

Alesha's album and her show weren't especially cutting edge but at the same time they were current and full of zest and energy. Her audience was already showing a tendency to be middle of the road. She was perhaps selling tickets more because of her connection with *Strictly Come Dancing* than for her past as a member of an urban girl group. She was becoming safe, in that kids and grannies could sit beside each other in the same row as young men who fancied her. The latter would have particularly enjoyed the encore, a dynamic version of 'The Boy Does Nothing'.

The release of her single 'To Love Again' was timed to coincide with her only London show at the Shepherd's Bush Empire. Alesha and her manager Malcolm Blair were always acutely aware of commercial opportunities. During the show she introduced 'Lipstick' by announcing, 'This song is from my *Fired Up* album. They didn't release it in the UK.' This was a neat way of reminding the audience that they could buy the rare record at the gig: it was part of the merchandising. Alesha owned the rights, so any sales were a financial bonus.

Reviews of 'To Love Again' were disappointing. The *Scotsman* described it as from 'the beige end of Gary Barlow's songwriting spectrum'. The *Daily Mirror* said it was a 'groaning Gary Barlow ballad' that had a 'definite sub-Eurovision whiff'. Fraser McAlpine in his BBC Chart Blog thought it suffered 'but only very slightly – from a pre-existing genetic condition known as forgettabilititus'.

The song should have been one of Alesha's finest hours and deserved better but may have been affected by Gary spreading himself a little thinly since his revival with Take That. He has become a one-man songbook and perhaps, on this occasion, a little Gary fatigue had set in. The *Guardian* noticed the song's similarity to a Take That number, before adding weakly that 'it's quite good'.

The video was due to be filmed in Prague by bigtv, who had been responsible for one of Alesha's favourites, 'Doo Wop (That Thing)' by Lauryn Hill. But when she arrived with the crew, they discovered that Pope Benedict XVI was in town and the centre of the city was in chaos. To make matters worse, the beautiful and atmospheric Charles Bridge, which crosses the Vltava River and was meant to be the centrepoint of the poignant film, was covered in scaffolding.

So it was shot in a misty Battersea Park back in London. It was fairly predictable, featuring a sad yet beautiful Alesha walking among autumn leaves as she sang the emotional lyric. She looked like a supermodel in a short blue belted mini coat dress, bare legs and booted heels. Alison Jane Reid said, 'Given the autumnal scene, it looks like a very short coat! But it does show off her mile-high, supermodel legs. I love her hair here. Given the romantic theme of the song, her hairdresser has created a soft, sensual look with hair extensions and soft, gleaming curls.'

This was the first time she appeared to be channelling her feelings about Harvey into the public domain, but even something so personal and heartfelt failed to register with record buyers. The track peaked at number fifteen after its first week of release and was in the top forty for only one more week before disappearing completely. This was hugely disappointing considering the amount of publicity the song attracted.

Besides the tour, Alesha performed the song on *Children In Need*, which she co-hosted with Tess Daly and Terry Wogan. She sang it on *The Alan Titchmarsh Show* and at 7.45 in the morning on *GMTV* when she was introduced as the 'gorgeous Alesha Dixon' by Ben Shephard, yet another Kilimanjaro friend. Her pitch was perfect, and if she had been on *The X Factor* they would have said she 'nailed it', but still it refused to sell any better.

'To Love Again' was one of four new tracks added to the repackaged *The Alesha Show – Encore* album, another shrewd attempt to cash in on her relentless publicity bandwagon. 'The Light' was her final collaboration to date with Brian Higgins and Miranda Cooper. The irrepressible and infectious dance track 'Shake' was her first with Steve Booker, co-written by the acclaimed singer-songwriter Paloma Faith. Booker had just won the 2009 Ivor Novello Award for Most Performed Work for 'Mercy', which had been a number one for Duffy the previous year. The last track was 'All Out Of Tune' – which she wasn't – produced by a rising star of British hip-hop, Alexander Grant, better known as Alex Da Kid. He has the happy knack of writing and producing urban music with a commercial twist.

A former professional footballer with Bristol City, his work with Alesha was quite early on in his musical career. He would move on to collaborate with Nicky Minaj, Eminem and Rihanna. He co-wrote and produced 'Love The Way You Lie' for Eminem featuring Rihanna, which was the superstar rapper's biggest-ever hit; it sold more than nine million worldwide and was number one in the US *Billboard* chart for seven weeks. The song was about domestic violence, a subject close to Alesha's heart.

'All Out Of Tune' was a rousing and catchy big finale to the album and probably would have performed better commercially than 'To Love Again' but, at the time, Alex Da Kid was not in the same division as Gary Barlow. Surprisingly, neither this track nor the other two new ones featured in the stage show, so perhaps they were originally expected to be on her next album and not extras on a year-old one. They would have been better served on a new record, where they would have stood out more.

The serious newspapers were there for her London gig and they loved it. Matilda Egere-Cooper in the *Independent* found her stage presence 'almost blinding' and her voice 'extremely accomplished live' for a pop vocalist: 'It's her girl power that makes her so captivating, whether she's headbanging her way through "Lipstick", paying a sensational tribute to Mis-Teeq or forcing middle-aged men to gleefully question whether they wash up (and indeed clean up) during the show's closer "The Boy Does Nothing". She's fabulous.'

Caroline Sullivan in the *Guardian* confirmed that Alesha was now more show business than street, saying she incorporated the show-girl elements of Kylie Minogue and the 'sassy oomph' of Beyoncé: 'There was a whiff of the *Royal Variety Performance* about things.' Caroline concluded by saying it was premature to call Alesha a national treasure, 'but she makes the case that "old-fashioned entertainer" can be a title worth having.' It remained to be seen whether that label suited Alesha's own ambitions for her future career.

The single, the album, the TV appearances and the tour were all part of a drive to put the negativity of joining *Strictly* behind her. Alesha was everywhere. She launched her own range of jewellery called, unoriginally, Alesha, which included a microphone-shaped necklace that was her favourite piece: 'Its pink, it's bling and it's me.' She joined forces with singers Pixie Lott and Kelly Rowland to back some exclusively designed T-dresses, which would be on sale at River Island, the High Street chain. All the profits were going to The Prince's Trust for the benefit of young people.

Commercially, however, her biggest news of the year came when she signed a four-year deal to be brand ambassador for LA Fitness. Her contract was performance-related and was rumoured to be worth more than a million pounds a year if the company did well. Alesha was chosen because she was not a fitness specialist but someone who could bridge the gap between the company and ordinary people. The idea was that she would make the whole business of keeping fit more approachable. The company's managing director, Martin Long, said, 'She's very fit, she's got bags of energy and a great smile.' Alesha was in danger of becoming a money-making machine.

Her fame wasn't enough, however, to get her and her entourage in to Funky Buddha in London. Apparently she arrived with twelve men and just one girl, expecting to be let in to the VIP area, but was turned away because the club's policy wouldn't allow so many men. Usually only black American stars go clubbing with such a huge entourage, so it was a rare insight into Alesha's secret nightlife. She mostly avoids the paparazzi except on rare occasions like this, when she was caught looking on foolishly as a woman checked the guest list.

Meanwhile, Alesha's interview with Fearne Cotton had finally been shown on ITV2 in November and she came across well. There were no shots of her dancing or judging in *Strictly* mode, which was a good idea.

By the time she was fully focused on the closing rounds of that year's *Strictly*, much of the controversy had died down. The viewers were more interested in who was going to win, which turned out to be Chris Hollins, a BBC sports journalist.

On the show Alesha was becoming more confident and forceful in her views. She told actor Craig Kelly, 'I don't believe I had to endure that. You are not as good as you think you are. It was like you were tiptoeing over hot coals. You cha-cha is very feminine. Last week there was a glimmer of hope; this week, dad's back.'

A sign that Alesha was now more established on the panel came when she joined Bruce Forsyth for his traditional performance during finals night in Blackpool. They sang a duet together of 'Something's Gotta Give', the classic Frank Sinatra and Ella Fitzgerald song. The Brucie and Alesha version was hardly in that league, but it was good-natured family entertainment, and she looked sensational in a white ballgown slit to the thigh, which was perfect for a twirl with Bruce. The *Guardian* would certainly have called it old-fashioned entertainment.

CHAPTER EIGHTEEN

Creative Differences

Alesha's next serious venture in television was a documentary called *Who's Your Daddy?*, which focused on the problems faced by children who don't know their fathers. It had been her own idea, reflecting one of her biggest concerns in life: 'Every child has the right to know who and where they come from and if they've got any brothers and sisters out there.'

The programme wasn't Alesha's own story, although in a brief introduction she explained that her parents had split when she was four. She said she was lucky because she knew who and where her father was, even though he wasn't living with her. Her confidence was knocked by the situation but at least she had a relationship with him, even if it wasn't the one she might have wished for. This was a documentary for and about those who weren't so lucky.

The statistics were grim and upsetting: 50,000 babies a year are registered with only their mother's name on the birth certificate – a figure that Alesha said was 'scary'. The National Council for One Parent Families, now Gingerbread, reported that three million children today have experienced the trauma of their parents separating, and a million of them never see one of their parents again.

She pointed out some of the drawbacks of the situation: 'Just imagine – your father has a disease running through his side of the family but you don't know him, so you don't know anything about it. If you did, you might actually be able to do something about it.

'Likewise, if you don't know who your father is, you won't know if he's gone on to have other kids so you could end up bumping into a half-brother or sister down the local pub or club without knowing it. One thing could lead to another and, well, it's a pretty scary thought.'

Alesha met one girl called Amy, who had never met her father and disclosed that if she met a man on a night out, the first thing she would ask him was 'What's your surname?' in case it matched her dad's. The programme found her father and watched, from a distance, while they had an emotional reunion.

Alesha also confronted a man dubbed the 'Sunderland Shagger' by the media; he had fathered eight children with eight different women. His excuse was: 'I just don't like condoms'. From the horrified expression on Alesha's face, she was an inch away from bashing him.

She also discussed the problem with some friends back in Welwyn Garden City. One told her, 'I felt on my own all the time. I sought out relationships with older men.' Another said, 'The guys don't get punished for walking away from their children.' Alesha herself observed wryly, 'Girls will sleep with idiots if they don't have a great role model.'

Strictly Come Dancing, with all its sequins, sparkle and popularity, was allowing Alesha to explore avenues that were more important to her. She was already thinking of making a programme about domestic violence. *Strictly* was the means to progress her career and was never an all-consuming occupation. She remained far more interested in her music.

After the successful tour, she had the added bonus of her first solo BRIT nomination. She was a contender for Best British Single for 'Breathe Slow' in a category dominated by artists connected with *The X Factor*, including JLS, Alexandra Burke and Cheryl Cole, among others. It was her turn to be interviewed on the red carpet outside Earls Court. She told Caroline Flack she didn't think she would win but she felt really lucky to have been nominated. She also told her she would be attending two parties afterwards and expected to get drunk.

She was right about her prospects. JLS won for their number one hit 'Beat Again'. The award was voted for by UK commercial radio listeners. The public tend to vote for the most popular act. Alesha was arguable unlucky not to be nominated for Best British Female, but none of the other TV stars of the time, including Cheryl and Alexandra, were either. Instead, more critic-friendly acts like Bat For Lashes and Florence + The Machine were favoured.

The after-show party at Merah wasn't as good as she'd hoped. She left early amid claims that the atmosphere in the club had become aggressive and unfriendly. The *Daily Star* reported that white people were 'banned' from an area roped off for the superstar Jay-Z, who didn't have a clue what was going on.

Oritsé Williams of JLS was quoted as saying, 'This place is doing my head in so I need to get in my car and go home. I've had enough of everyone getting in our faces, the vibe is not cool.' According to the newspaper, Alesha said, 'My friends have been getting knocked about and no-one seems to care. I need to get out of here. I'd rather be at my local kebab shop, Elsie's, right now than back inside with all that aggro. What a horrible end to the night. I was having a blast at my record label party and now the mood is soured. I wish I'd never come.'

Alesha never made a secret that music was her 'first love', so she was keen to resume writing and recording her next album. The next part of her strategy for her career after the success of *The Alesha Show* was breaking into the US. It hadn't worked for Mis-Teeq, even though they'd made good initial headway with 'Scandalous'. Nobody talks negatively in advance of trying to crack America. Instead the air is full of optimism. Unfortunately, if it doesn't happen, it can have a bad knock-on effect on a recording career.

The most noticeable change for the next album, which was provisionally called *Unleashed*, was that Xenomania weren't involved. They were responsible for hit after hit for Girls Aloud but their connection with Alesha came to an abrupt halt. They weren't renowned for producing American hits, so that may have been a factor. They were also keen to improve their own Xenomania stable of stars and that business plan may not have suited what Alesha had in mind.

Instead, the notable American producer Jim Beanz flew into London and announced that he was looking forward to working with Alesha, who he was sure could 'crack the States'. He had produced for Britney Spears, Rihanna and Nelly Furtado, and remixed 'I Just Wanna Know' for Taio Cruz, one of the few British urban artists to have done well in the US. He said of Alesha: 'She sings, she dances, she's got a great sense of humour – and she's beautiful.' In the end, Jim didn't feature on the album at all.

The papers reported that the first single would be a big ballad called 'Love In A Box' but nothing by that name featured in the final track listing on an album that was now called *The Entertainer*. It was all rather confusing.

Alesha decided to drop her surname for the album. She wanted to appear current and therefore picked fresh, up-and-coming collaborators. She told the *Daily Mirror*, 'The music scene has changed so I was trying to pick producers that can keep up with what was going on. I wanted to make an upbeat record that was really bold. *The Alesha Show* was a transition. With this album, I'm in the zone, I'm in the place I want to be.'

The lead single was eventually announced as 'Drummer Boy', which she had recorded in Los Angeles with the Haitian-American producer Shama Joseph, aka Sak Pase or ShamRock. He had achieved prominence as part of a musical partnership with songwriter Verse Simmonds called The Juggernauts. For this particular track he worked with Nate Walka, a young writer who had already won a Grammy for 'Blame It', a number one for Jamie Foxx featuring T-Pain.

Alesha loved the song the moment she joined them in the studio. She explained to Pete Lewis in *Blues & Soul* magazine that she instantly knew she had to have it: 'I'm always looking for something that's just full of life, that's different, quirky and can't be put in a box.'

She felt that 'Drummer Boy' fitted her personality. 'I loved the TOUGHNESS of it! I particularly loved the fact that it is female-empowering, but not in a feminist-trying-to-wave-the-flag-and-be-rude-about-men kind of way. Instead it's more about me just being a female in a strong position – which just hits exactly where I AM in my life right now!'

The song began with Alesha shouting the line that she needed a better drummer boy and was quite rude about men in a sexual kind of way, with the invitation to pick up 'your stick' and hit her with 'your best shot'. Alesha explained, 'It's a metaphor for wanting a better lover, really.'

But it was also bonkers, beat heavy and brilliant – and definitely not the work of an 'old-fashioned entertainer'. It was catchy but not like 'The Boy Does Nothing', which put a smile on your face.

The video too was arguably Alesha's finest – a mesmerizing three minutes full of pace and dazzling colour. She teamed up with the acclaimed Norwegian-born film-maker Reinert K. Olsen, who worked under the name of Ray Kay and was based in Los Angeles. He had been responsible for the memorable videos for Lady Gaga's 'Poker Face' and 'Fight For This Love', the debut number one for Cheryl Cole.

Alesha flew to Los Angeles to shoot the video in one 21-hour session. She told her website, aleshadixon.net, 'Couldn't feel my feet after!' She also said she'd had the 'best time' on the shoot, which incorporated seven costume changes, ten dancers and twenty drummers. Not everything went smoothly, however. She accidentally walloped a female dancer in the head with a large ring she was wearing: 'She just fell back and didn't move. She was lying there, really trying to fight back the tears. I started crying because I felt so bad! She had a massive bump on her head immediately. But she was back up by the end of the video because she's a professional. But it was horrible!'

The *Daily Mail* thought the video reaffirmed Alesha as one of the UK's leading performing talents. It was nominated as Best Video at the 2010 MOBO Awards. *Unreality Shout* online said, 'It's like watching a carnival parade super-charged with testosterone and thigh.' The site was also impressed with the song itself and Alesha's performance of a 'fierce, dominant-sounding alpha female giving a vocal performance with more attitude than a hormonal teenager'.

'Drummer Boy' is one of those songs that improve with listening. Fraser McAlpine in his BBC Chart Blog called it 'fantastic'. Everything was surely set for Alesha's first number one. But it never happened, despite all the publicity and the positive press coverage. The single was a flop when it was finally released on 23 August 2010. It peaked at a hugely disappointing fifteen in the charts.

Perhaps the diverse audience that had made *The Alesha Show* such a success wasn't ready for a radical change of image. They probably wanted something similar to the sing-along 'The Boy Does Nothing'. 'Drummer Boy' was a record to play very loud in a club and not to sing on the karaoke down the local pub on a Friday night.

It was time for Alesha to go back to *Strictly Come Dancing* amid rumours that she wouldn't have returned if 'Drummer Boy' had been the success she'd been hoping for. She was reported to have signed her contract only two weeks before the start of the show. She told Andy Welch of the *Belfast Telegraph* that she did have to think about it before deciding to return, 'My label were resistant for me to do it, as they have no vested interest in the show, and there's no evidence that being on there sells them more records. Let's be real, they've invested a lot more in my career than *Strictly* has, but it's my life and career, and I enjoy it.' Alesha was also outspoken about how she had been treated in the media the previous year: 'I was just an easy target for a lot of older female journalists who were, quite frankly, just being bitchy.'

She told the *News of the World* that *Strictly* was only one day a week and one hundred per cent of her energy had gone in to making her new record and not *Strictly*: 'We're dealing with dancing and we're dealing with entertainment, so it's not really to be taken too seriously.'

The general feeling in the media was that Alesha was doing the show only to keep her name in the spotlight. The *Sunday Mirror* found a source who said, 'Len is very unhappy. He likes Alesha – but he knows she's not doing the show because of her love of dance.'

Musically, it might have been smart to regroup and try to find a number like 'Breathe Slow' to release next. Instead Alesha continued to pursue the youthful audience who had so enjoyed the Mis-Teeq days. She was the guest vocalist on 'Take Control', a new song by the Roll Deep collective, which had been formed by the influential urban producer Wiley. The band, which had up to a dozen members, at various times featured both Tinchy Stryder and Dizzee Rascal and had been largely responsible for bringing the sound of grime to a wider audience. Wiley is often referred to as the 'Godfather of Grime'.

The current line-up decided Alesha would be the perfect choice as guest vocalist and sent her the song. She jumped at the chance, unsurprisingly, because the group were having a stellar year with two number ones, 'Good Times' and 'Green Light'. Unfortunately for Alesha, they seemed to have peaked before her collaboration with them.

The video took seven hours to shoot on a rainy night in Peckham. Alesha spent most of her time dancing round a car park. It wasn't glamorous. The boys raced about on quad bikes and she sang her catchy chorus, but it fell far short of the excitement generated by the

'Drummer Boy' video. The public never really warmed to the song, which only reached number twenty-nine. It was another disappointment.

Alesha sang her next single, 'Radio', on *Strictly Come Dancing* on 14 November, the first time she had performed on the show since her dynamic performance of 'The Boy Does Nothing' two years before. Maybe that would improve sales.

The song had been written by a young mixed-race Scottish singer called Emeli Sandé, who had given up studying medicine at Glasgow University in her fourth year to pursue a career in music. The producer Shahid Khan, aka Naughty Boy, was another rising star of the music scene. He and Emeli had teamed up before on Wiley's hit 'Never Be Your Woman'. Working with Naughty Boy and Emeli was part of Alesha's policy of using bright new talent for *The Entertainer*. Ironically, within fourteen months it would be Emeli who was celebrating a number one album with *Our Version of Events*.

'Radio', it seemed, was a last, almost desperate attempt to generate interest in *The Entertainer*, which was due for release at the end of the month. Its anthemic quality was certainly more mainstream than her two previous singles – you couldn't imagine Bruce enjoying 'Drummer Boy' or 'Take Control'. The track only reached number forty-six so, from a recording point of view, things were getting steadily worse.

The video was filmed in a trailer park near Los Angeles and featured a couple rowing in the unit next to where Alesha is singing the song. The argument gets worse and they start fighting, prompting another neighbour to call the police. The man is arrested. It wasn't exactly a portrayal of domestic abuse, but it did prove an interesting contrast with Alesha's next documentary, *Don't Hit My Mum*.

This was the real thing, in which Alesha spoke of the violence her mother had faced. It was brave but also unsentimental, revealing that 75,000 children in the UK are thought to witness abuse in the home each year. Brian Viner of the *Independent* thought Alesha did 'an admirable job of drawing attention to this blight on a civilized society'. The media mainly focused on the more sensational aspects of Alesha's own story, namely watching her mum being beaten.

But the documentary moved on from that to look at the broader picture and the effect domestic violence had on children's lives as a whole. Camila Batmanghelidjh, the founder and director of the charity Kids Company, told Alesha, 'The one thing that happens to children of domestic violence, either being a witness to it or being exposed to it, is that they are constantly frightened. Even when the horrible things are not happening, the child is wondering when is it going to happen, what is going to happen – constantly wondering.'

Alesha pulled no punches in putting forward her very strong views on the subject of children caught in the trap of violence at home. 'A lot of the development in these children has stopped at a young age because they have not been able to develop parts of their brain or they have not been able to grow up carefree like most children should be – at school having the time of their lives, looking forward to going home and seeing mum and dad. They aren't. They are in hell and they are going home to hell and it's taking away the innocence of a child.' It was a powerful message, spoken from the heart.

Alesha also revealed that she felt 'fearless' in her life now, at the age of thirty-one: 'But I spent the majority of my life being scared of many things and very insecure and not particularly confident. But I feel I have worked through that now.'

That fearlessness was reflected in her album *The Entertainer* and why she originally wanted to call it *Unleashed*. She told the *Daily Mirror*, 'When women listen to my music, I want them to feel empowered. I'm not as anxious as I was in my twenties. It's about women not being afraid to be ballsy, I guess. Once you've been through tough times you can only become stronger.'

She went back to MCing and made sure there was no room for anything slow on the album: 'It's up-tempo club music. I'm trying to avoid slushy ballads. Even though it's honest and talks about real subjects, it's driven by hard beats.'

Some critics loved it. Michael Ashton on *musicOHM* online said, '*The Entertainer* is an album of diverse dance floor tracks that emulates some of pop's recent omnipresent female chart toppers such as Rihanna, Cheryl Cole and Lady Gaga.' *Funky* online called it 'a brilliant assertive, widescreen pop album'.

The problem for Alesha was that she was caught between two stools. Devotees of *Strictly Come Dancing* found the album too modern and unapproachable, while fans of urban music couldn't get past her association with sequins and sambas. She was pleasing nobody and on release the album reached number eighty-four, which was embarrassing.

Alesha had seen *The Alesha Show* as a transitional album but, in hindsight, it was exactly right for pleasing both worlds. Alesha was already thirty-one, not twenty-one, and it was going to be very tricky to appeal to teenagers who preferred *The X Factor* to *Strictly*.

She applauded enthusiastically when the *EastEnders* actress Kara Tointon won the 2010 series of *Strictly*. Alesha had awarded her the first maximum ten of the series for her paso doble.

Alesha's reward for surviving the series was a trip to hospital for an operation on her feet. She needed bone correction surgery to put right some of the work she'd had done several years before. Considering the problem, the amount of dancing in unsuitable high heels she had endured is extraordinary. She wasn't allowed to walk immediately afterwards. At least she wasn't at home by herself any more. A cousin, Emmaline, was now sharing the house in Welwyn. She was the youngest daughter of Beverley's brother Lee. She was company, as well as someone to walk the dogs. Alesha had given a second rescue dog a home the summer before when she visited the Southridge RSPCA Animal Centre in Potters Bar. She 'fell in love' with Daisy, a Jack Russell and pointer crossbreed, the moment she saw her. The little dog had been taken there when her previous owner had lost his job and could no longer afford to keep her.

As soon as she could put weight on her feet, Alesha needed a holiday and she and Emmaline took a nine-day cruise along the coast of Mexico. Her nan Clem loved this sort of break, so Alesha had always thought cruises were best suited to grandmothers, but it turned out to be an ideal rest for her. It was an idyllic break, long days of chilling out, eating steak and the local specialities like chilli chicken, sipping cold drinks and lazing by the pool. She had always wanted to swim with dolphins but experienced the next best thing when she saw a school of them playing in the water off Cabo San Lucas.

The last throw of the dice for *The Entertainer* was the release of a fourth single, 'Every Little Part Of Me', featuring Jay Sean, one of the few British urban artists to do well in America. His 2007 release 'Down' was a US number one, eventually selling more than four million copies there and six million worldwide. Not even his presence could change Alesha's fortunes.

They filmed the video before Christmas in Miami and the newspapers carried some rare shots of Alesha dressed for the beach. The video, however, was set in a car park, where she and Jay rendezvous after committing a robbery, but the police are waiting to arrest them.

Alesha has seldom looked sexier, wearing a lime-green, ultra-tight mini-dress. Alison Jane Reid commented, 'It's a very alluring dress, which looks as sheer as a spider's web. It really shows off that gorgeous, athletic body.'

The song itself is a classic modern dance track. If it had been Rihanna featuring Jay Sean, it would have been number one. Instead it was number seventy-eight.

In the acknowledgments to *The Entertainer*, Alesha chose not to make any personal thanks. She didn't even mention her mother and certainly no men. Instead she reserves the biggest appreciation for Asylum, her 'wonderful label', for 'fighting for me'. After the album's dismal performance, it came as no surprise that she parted company from her 'wonderful label' little more than six months after she wrote these words.

The news came at the beginning of June 2011, when it was announced that there would be no third album. It's always a grey area as to who parts company with whom in these circumstances. Malcolm Blair issued a statement that it was his client's decision: 'Alesha would like to announce that after discussions with her record label, Asylum/Atlantic, we have decided not to extend her recording contract.

'It became clear during our discussions that both Alesha and her label had some creative differences, which we were unable to resolve, and it was mutually agreed that the best course of action for both parties was to part company on good terms.

'Alesha would like to thank Asylum Records for their support and hard work over the past two albums and wish them all the best going forward.

'We are currently in discussions with other labels and look forward to a new record in 2012.

'Alesha is proud to have been Asylum Records' first platinum-selling artist and to have delivered them their first international success with "The Boy Does Nothing", which has now sold almost one million copies worldwide and was a top ten hit in twenty countries.'

The creative differences were never spelled out but it's not hard to imagine that the record company wanted a return to the music of *The Alesha Show*.

CHAPTER NINETEEN

Cowell's Umbrella

Alesha needed to shake things up in her life. She was again talking up her hopes for taking her music to America and was looking for a management team over there. But, as of June 2011, she was on a snake rather than a ladder. The situation was nothing like as serious as the time she was dropped by Polydor in 2006. Then she really did have no options. At least now she had an extremely well-paid job and many endorsements. It also helped that she was a millionaire.

She said, perhaps not entirely seriously, that she was thinking of branching out into acting and fancied a cameo role in *Desperate Housewives* or playing the 'tart' in a soap: 'I could be the new barmaid in the Queen Vic on *EastEnders*, and I wouldn't take any rubbish from anyone.'

Of far more significance, however, were the rumours that she might be leaving *Strictly Come Dancing* to join *The X Factor*. The departure of Cheryl Cole had left a vacancy on the show and, according to reports, Alesha was keen to fill it. She was asked as early as February 2011, when she was still trying to plug 'Every Little Part Of Me', what she would do if Simon Cowell approached her. She told *Metro*, 'I'd have to say no because I am a loyal person and I committed to *Strictly Come Dancing* and obviously they're on at the same time.

'If *Strictly Come Dancing* doesn't want me back, then so be it, but

I am committed to *Strictly*, I love *Strictly*. I have had a fantastic time the last season that has just gone and I am a loyal person.'

Her response in a magazine interview a couple of months later was slightly different. She said she couldn't possibly comment, but was more enthusiastic about the rival show. 'I do think it's great that the judges get to mentor. It's much more creative. We don't do that on *Strictly*, we just comment and give our opinion.

'I'm into anything that enables me to use my creativity. I'm not scared of hard work or a challenge.'

The media interpreted this as posting Simon Cowell her CV. She fanned the rumour flames when she tweeted, 'Off to Syco now for a meeting! Loving the sun!' Anyone who follows Alesha's Twitter feed will know that she seldom wastes time on harmless chat about what she is having for dinner or conducting private rows in public. She's not like Tulisa, whose whole life is spelled out daily in a stream of thirty-character posts.

Instead, Alesha uses Twitter as a business tool to promote her professional diary or her commercial interests like LA Fitness. She doesn't give anything away, so the news that she was meeting Simon Cowell's company didn't slip out by accident. The *Sunday Mirror* reported that talks had been going on for weeks. They found a source who said, 'She'd be sad to turn her back on *Strictly*, but *X Factor* is in a completely different league.'

There was actually very little difference between the two in terms of ratings, but *The X Factor* presented a huge opportunity for recording success. It was also in a greater state of change than people realized. Simon Cowell was understandably focused on the launch of the American version, but he was also fretting about the future of the British show. While the 2010 series, won by Matt Cardle, had been a ratings success, he realized the show was in danger of losing touch with a younger audience. As far as ITV is concerned, the sixteen to twenty-four age group is the one that it wants to attract because they bring in the money from advertising.

Alesha, aged thirty-two and a judge on the middle-class, middle-aged BBC flagship programme, was hardly going to reach out to teenagers. Even Cheryl Cole wasn't exactly cutting edge. She looked great on the cover of *heat* magazine and was an aspirational figure for young girls, but her glamorous image had taken the edge off her street credibility. Cheryl may have been only twenty-seven, but in the UK Simon needed someone younger. Tulisa Contostavlos from N-Dubz was, at twenty-three, nearly ten years younger than Alesha and a member of one of the most popular live bands in the country. Kevin O'Sullivan observed, 'Tulisa was always his first choice and remained that.'

While Alesha might not have been the right replacement for Cheryl, she would have made a perfect substitute for Dannii Minogue. But by the time that position on the panel became vacant a few weeks later, Alesha had already signed up for another series of *Strictly Come Dancing*. Understandably, the producers were anxious to secure her because of the media gossip, which probably enabled Malcolm to increase her salary. The rumours were that for her third series Alesha would be the best-paid judge.

In the end, Simon Cowell chose Kelly Rowland of Destiny's Child to be Dannii's replacement. Again, the American group was casting a shadow over Alesha's career. As a solo artist of a similar age, whose records had done progressively less well since she'd left the group, Kelly's credentials were very similar. If the cards had fallen differently, then Alesha probably would have been a better choice than Dannii from the beginning, but that was in 2007, when Alesha was in show business limbo.

Soon after returning to *Strictly*, there was the chance to look fabulous as the presenter of the 2011 MOBOs at the SECC, Glasgow, in October. This time her co-host was the young American R & B star Jason Derülo and the two of them built up a good rapport. The MOBOs were still a huge event and an ideal one for bringing Alesha back into the spotlight after a quiet summer.

The new series of *Strictly Come Dancing* was arguably its most successful ever, regularly beating *The X Factor* in the ratings, much to Simon Cowell's irritation. A great deal of that was due to the hilarious escapades of the astrologer Russell Grant, who breathed new life into the show, especially when he was fired out of a cannon. You never knew when a contestant was going to click with an audience – John Sergeant had, so had Ann Widdecombe, and now it was the turn of the portly stargazer.

Alesha, too, was at her best throughout the series. Kevin O'Sullivan observed, 'When she started on *Strictly*, I think she was pretty awful partly because of her speech. It was grating. She was also trying to be too street for the sort of show it was. But by the third series, it was seamless really. You didn't think about it. It was just Alesha on *Strictly Come Dancing*. She is clearly very bright and picks things up. I think she is very smart.'

Some behind-the-scenes gossip that she was reaping the benefit of some private elocution lessons was never aired in public. She did produce arguably the most controversial moment of the series, when she commented on the dancing of Nancy Dell'Olio, the former partner of ex-England football manager Sven-Göran Eriksson. She was not a fan, and when Nancy emerged from a coffin for her Halloween dance, Alesha commented, 'Nancy, I think you are a sexy woman and you know how to work it, but I have to be honest – you are a walking disaster. Your legs are so far apart and that's not very feminine. You both should have stayed in the coffin.'

Her remarks may have contributed to Nancy being voted off that week. The fiery Italian sent an email to producers demanding a public apology from Alesha and stating that she was taking legal advice about the matter. There was clearly ill feeling when the Christmas special was filmed a few weeks later and the two were kept well away from each other to avoid a confrontation. Alesha explained to Graham Norton, 'My criticism wasn't personal. It was funny.'

Alesha also noticed the winning dancer at an early stage: she praised Harry Judd, the drummer with the group McFly, and awarded him two consecutive tens. Fellow contestant Holly Valance reportedly joked, 'What is it with Alesha and Harry? Are they having it off? A ten is something the rest of us can barely dream of.' They weren't having it off, of course; she had simply identified Harry as the best dancer in the competition, and was vindicated when he was victorious.

Alesha was showing a happy knack of generating controversy – something that always attracts the attention of Simon Cowell. He loves stirring things up on his shows, because it gets people talking about them in the office on a Monday morning. She had to apologize on Twitter for appearing a little tipsy alongside Craig and Bruno on *Alan Carr: Chatty Man*.

She made the show, glugging wine from a bottle and then referring to the Duchess of Cornwall, who had visited the set, as 'a bit of a *Strictly* stalker'. Apparently Alesha had also met the Duchess when she was invited to Highgrove in connection with The Prince's Trust and had taken her nan Clem along. The Duchess came over and said she recognized her from sitting in the audience of *Strictly*.

Better still, when Alan asked if any of the male contestants ever became aroused by some of the more risqué costumes, she replied, 'Everyone is really frisky on the show, everybody is horny. The year I was a contestant, everyone was just really gagging for it.' Needless to say, her remarks made headlines in the popular press the next day. Simon Cowell would have loved the publicity if *Strictly* had been one of his shows.

Behind the scenes, when the show ended, Alesha's manager was in talks with Simon, who was far from pleased at the recent success of *Strictly* against *The X Factor*. He was also known to have been very disappointed at the previous series of *Britain's Got Talent*, which produced an unmemorable winner, Scottish singer Jai McDowall.

Cowell is primarily a businessman not a television personality. He may well have thought of Alesha for *Britain's Got Talent* rather than *The X Factor* all along. The biggest success of a relatively lacklustre series had been Tulisa, who had made a connection with the audience. Maybe Alesha could do the same for the talent contest.

Simon Cowell admires ambition and appreciated Alesha's drive. Like her, he was a native of Hertfordshire but grew up in the genteel surroundings of Elstree, a world away from Alesha's humble origins fifteen miles away. As a boy he would watch famous people arrive next door, where a film studio boss lived. He witnessed Elizabeth Taylor, Bette Davis and Gregory Peck arriving for parties. It made a huge impression on him: 'I thought, "This is very glamorous. I'd love to live in a house like that and have a party like that."' He has fulfilled that ambition totally.

He left school at sixteen with a very modest academic record and is an entirely self-made man. He began his path to success as a runner at Elstree Studios, where his main job was making the tea. His father Eric was able to pull a few strings and young Simon moved to a job in the post room at EMI. He stood out because of his enthusiasm and his determination, but there was an extra ingredient that placed him above the crowd – he would take a risk.

His first big gamble came when he borrowed £5,000 to back the debut single of a bubbly, black American dancer called Sinitta, whom he happened to be dating at the time. The song, 'So Macho', became a camp disco classic and sold nearly a million copies, reaching number two in the charts in the summer of 1986, when Alesha was seven.

His next famous coup came when he signed the actors Robson and Jerome to the Sony BMG label. Robson Green and Jerome Flynn were two of the stars of *Soldier Soldier* and had sung a tepid version of the classic 'Unchained Melody' in one episode with no intention of becoming pop stars. Simon recognized a potential gold mine and persuaded them to release the track on S Records, which would later become his more famous Syco brand. It was number one for seven weeks, sold more than one million copies and was the biggest-selling record of 1995. More importantly, it was the first example of Simon recognizing the power of television – something Alesha was now well aware of herself.

When *Pop Idol* began in 2001, one of the arrangements Simon put in place was that the winning song would be released on his S Records label. He was keen to protect that investment and was persuaded to become a judge. By the end of the first series he was well on his way to becoming an institution. But his new stardom was only a bonus as he set about securing a television empire.

Kevin O'Sullivan confirms, 'I don't think it's too controversial to say that Cowell doesn't do anything unless it's to his own financial advantage. The *Got Talent* brand around the world makes a lot of money. Both the talent and the judges were poor last year. Cowell knew that if he didn't do something in 2012, then *Britain's Got Talent* would die. It's a mistake to think that *BGT* is a sideshow for him, it's not.'

Only Amanda Holden was left from the previous panel of three judges. The comedian Michael McIntyre had looked uneasy on the show and didn't want to come back. The American actor David Hasselhoff, known as The Hoff, hadn't made a connection with the audience.

Cowell's first decision was to rejoin the panel himself. His second was inspired, if expensive. He signed up the comedian David Walliams from *Little Britain* for a reputed salary of £800,000. Walliams was very different from McIntyre in that he was a funny man who was more an actor than someone who simply told jokes. That would prove the case when the new series began, as he cleverly built up the humour with a series of running gags that left you waiting for the next instalment. The intriguing thing is that he didn't jump at the chance first of all. A programme source reveals that he was 'scared stiff that it was a terrible career move'.

Simon then decided to bring in an additional woman to the panel.

It had worked well with *The X Factor*. Originally Sharon Osbourne was the lone female between Simon and Louis Walsh. But when Dannii Minogue joined, it brought an extra dimension, as the two clearly didn't get on. The same was true with Tulisa and Kelly Rowland, who had a genuine feud during the 2011 series of *The X Factor*. Alesha Dixon would be perfect – someone to stir things up with Amanda and, even more importantly, signing her would put one over on *Strictly Come Dancing*.

Cowell is not cavalier in making such appointments. He may get them wrong – the brief stay of Kelly Brook on *Britain's Got Talent* was a case in point – but he is fastidious about working out who would be best. Quite simply, Simon Cowell wanted to hurt *Strictly Come Dancing*. He made no bones about it. The show was doing too well.

For Alesha, it wasn't a difficult decision to make. For starters, it was reported that her salary would increase from a basic £100,000 for *Strictly* to £350,000 for *Britain's Got Talent*. She may have been a rich woman but this was a huge amount of money for a few months' work. That wasn't the point though. Kevin O'Sullivan explains, 'To be quite frank, the point was her progression to a higher plane of showbiz. She was now in the orbit of Simon Cowell, which is a far sight better than a fairly parochial BBC One show.'

Alesha would be under the Cowell umbrella and, providing she did well, could expect a boost to her music career as well as the possibility of promotion within the empire. She might have wanted *The X Factor* but this was a welcome alternative.

Her defection was officially confirmed on 2 January 2012. Everybody was very polite and civilized about it. The BBC said, 'We wish her all the best. She has done three very successful series with us and we look forward to announcing our new line-up in due course.' Alesha commented on her website, 'After three incredible years on the *Strictly Come Dancing* judging panel, I have decided that it is time to move on. *Strictly Come Dancing* will always hold a special place in my heart, as it has been such an amazing experience, both as a winning competitor and as a judge.

'I would like to say a big thank you to everyone involved in the show, the production team, my fellow judges, and a very special thank you to the fans for their support.'

Simon Cowell said he 'loved' Alesha: 'She is feisty, opinionated and knows what it's like to be both a competitor and judge on a hugely popular TV show. This is going to be a brand-new experience for her and I think she is going to bring a lot to the table.'

Len Goodman said on Radio 5 Live that he was 'disappointed' if Cowell's motivation for poaching Alesha had been just to hurt *Strictly*. He told the host, Richard Bacon, 'I would never knock the opposition and I think it is spiteful and mean if that is the case that Simon said, "I just want to be spiteful towards *Strictly*".

'Because why would you want to do that? Why would you want to spoil millions of people's pleasures? It's not the right way to behave, so if that is the case – shame on you, Simon.'

Much of the media comment suggested that Alesha had made the move for the money, but she told Mark Jefferies of the *Daily Mirror* it wasn't the reason and she would have left *Strictly Come Dancing* in any case: 'I feel three years was a respectable amount of time. It was time for new things. I genuinely make decisions on what feels right, what's comfortable and what excites me. You worry about the money after.

'You only get one life, it's not a rehearsal, so you have to go for it.'

Alesha clearly owed *Strictly Come Dancing* a great deal. Her association with the programme, both as a contestant and as a judge, had made her a household name. But she had also given the programme beauty, glamour and unstuffy normality. Her replacement would be the ballerina Darcey Bussell, an appointment that would generate no controversy.

The most gracious and wise remarks about her defection came from the 83-year-old host Bruce Forsyth, who had always had a soft spot for Alesha: 'We're going to miss her tremendously, but I think she will be great on that show. She'll get more exposure and be heard more. She'll have a chance to show off her great sense of humour. I think she will do marvellously.'

Refreshingly, Sir Bruce didn't feel at all let down by her leaving: 'It may be called show business, but I'm not sure people realize that it has always been more "business" than "show".'

CHAPTER TWENTY

The Talented Miss Dixon

Three weeks after the announcement that she would be joining *Britain's Got Talent*, Alesha put on a bright canary-coloured dress slit to the thigh and beyond, and braved the freezing January temperatures for the first set of auditions in Manchester. She would have to become used to everyone focusing on what she was wearing just as much as on what she said. Her stylist, Katie Greengrass, revealed that they had chosen the Acne dress because they wanted something bold for the opening day: 'It was terrible rainy weather, but Alesha still went for it and looked amazing.'

Alesha was relishing the chance to come out from behind a desk and be more experimental in her style. During her ten years in the public eye she has never been particularly adventurous or extreme. Alison Jane Reid observes, 'She is incredibly pretty. When she first burst on the scene with Mis-Teeq, her look was sporty and sassy, yet still with some interesting sweet and feminine flourishes, all designed to show off her lovely curves and gazelle-like athletic body.

'She would wear a camisole or cute embroidered top or dress that looked like underwear as outerwear and team it with shimmering eye make-up, hoop earrings and quirky jewellery. It was all very twenty-something. I think the difference now is that her make-up is flawless and more subtle, and she has gone from High Street clothes that didn't quite fit – and sometimes looked a bit cheap and garish – to some serious British and international designers.

'She's now wearing some exciting couture gowns and ritzy day-wear from designers like Alexander McQueen, Mary Katrantzou, Diane von Furstenberg, Marios Schwab, Peter Pilotto and Gucci.'

One of the most striking characteristics of Alesha's fashion journey through the years is that she has never sported much of an urban look. Even when she was one of the first ladies of garage, she was more Welwyn Garden City than Camden Town. Alison Jane confirms, 'She was more Home Counties than ghetto fabulous.' Only occasionally did she lapse into chavtastic pink tracksuits, preferring in the main outfits that showed off her best feature, her legs.

Alesha will be thirty-four on her next birthday and, in fashion terms, she has grown up. Alison Jane says, 'In the beginning, Alesha went for clothes that were very casual and just seemed too "summer holiday" for a public appearance. Now she has fun with her fashion, teaming maybe a colour block mini with a sharp jacket. She has grown-up allure. This isn't "black" style; her look is international now.

'The same is true of her accessories and make-up. She has matured. These days she doesn't seem to wear much make-up or bling. Alesha has gone from the ubiquitous oversized cheap gold earrings to hardly any jewellery, and when she does wear accessories, they are mostly very understated and expensive, such as a beautiful pair of pearl clips. She has banished the shimmer and ice cream-coloured lips of old and now she always looks flawless and film star beautiful with a "no make-up make-up" look that requires the expertise of a talented make-up artist.'

When she was a little girl, Alesha had a large afro mop of hair. That look has gone and in 2010 the press even suggested it was thinning. She needs to pay particular attention to her hair because it's a key part of her image. She likes to wear it long and flowing in soft waves or pulled back to show off her stunning bone structure. Top session hairdresser Heather Manson comments, 'When Alesha wears her hair long, this isn't all her own hair. She is wearing very expensive hair extensions to achieve that glossy, swishy, celebrity, head-turning mane of luxuriant waves.'

Alesha may be a remarkably beautiful woman but she has to spend a lot of time and money to look as if it is all completely effortless. Her personal trainer, Janet Malinowska, a former professional ballroom dancer, puts her through a rigorous routine every other day. Alesha told *Health & Fitness* magazine, 'Sometimes she nearly reduces me to tears because it's that painful! But having somebody to push you always helps.'

Janet added, 'I'm quite demanding on Alesha, but she has hectic work demands so we have to work with those and her needs. If there's no pain, there's no gain, so our sessions are pretty hardcore!'

Alesha admits that she is similar to many women and worries about certain areas like her tummy and thighs but she is basically happy with her body: 'There are areas that are not perfect, and that's OK. My favourite part of my body is my legs. They're long and shapely and I love showing them off! But I would love a bigger bottom.'

She told *Closer* magazine that she envied the voluptuous bottoms of Beyoncé and Jennifer Lopez: 'I think they look like a woman should, so I like to give my bum a bit more special attention. My personal trainer thinks I'm weird as I'm the first person she's ever met who wants a bigger bum, but I don't care about having bigger boobs or a flat stomach. I just say, "Give me an ass!"'

Janet finds Alesha's attitude refreshing in that she doesn't want to be superskinny. Instead she's happy to work with what she's got: 'What's good about Alesha is that she has solid goals – like wanting a firmer, higher bottom.'

Alesha needs to look good not just for *Britain's Got Talent* but also for her ongoing contract with LA Fitness. She designed a special workout called Alesha's Dance Fusion, based on her sessions with

Janet, for women who wanted a figure like hers. So there was no sneaking a quick burger into her dressing room during breaks.

That was even more the case when she was signed up by WeightWatchers to front their £15 million campaign to attract members after the New Year, traditionally a time when many people resolve to lose the Christmas pounds. The size ten Alesha said before its launch: 'One of my best friends – a girl I grew up with – suffered with weight issues and it affected every aspect of her life. It was very hard to watch. She was angry and unhappy. She had such low self-esteem she turned to drink and because she didn't feel worthy of love, that affected the partners she chose and she picked people who weren't good for her.'

Alesha sang 'Do It Our Way (Play)', a song that had been specially composed for the promotion. The track was available as a digital download – Alesha's first new record for nearly a year. It featured in an advert in which 180 WeightWatchers' members, who had lost a total of 422 stone between them, mimed to Alesha's voice. The song was very catchy and probably could have found a spot on *The Alesha Show* album. Alesha joins in at the very end of the ad, leading the slimmers down a London street in jubilation. It was strangely uplifting.

But, as some disgruntled members pointed out on Twitter, Alesha had clearly never been near a meeting. One tweeted, 'How can you have the balls to front a campaign when you have NEVER had a weight problem? You have NO idea what it's like.'

Alesha responded, 'Hey, I wrote the song for the advert hun, to empower people 2 feel good in their own skin. I'm not a WeightWatchers ambassador. It's not about "Me", it's about the people in the advert, I wrote the song so they could tell their story, they were amazing!'

A spokeswoman for the slimming club confirmed, 'We are well aware that Alesha does not need to lose weight and that she hasn't got a big weight loss story but it wasn't about that.

'To be clear, Alesha is not the new face of WeightWatchers and we have never positioned her as that so that's where people have made that assumption. She has just worked with us for this song and the TV advert.'

If Alesha had gone to a meeting and had to reveal what she kept in her fridge, it would have been lots of cheese, avocados, salmon and eggs. She preferred herbal tea to coffee but did have a weakness for milk bottle sweets, which she had on permanent order from her local corner shop.

Alesha seems ordinary in her choices and – just as other stars of Cowell's shows like Cheryl and Tulisa have done – she has always said she is a High Street kind of girl happiest in stores such as Topshop and Zara, as well as her 'absolute favourite', Arrogant Cat. But the demands of being under constant scrutiny for what you wear inevitably changes that.

Now she mixes head-turning designer pieces with well-chosen clever finds from the High Street. Alison Jane Reid explains, 'This is a huge trend and a sign of recessionary dressing. The Duchess of Cambridge does this and the impact is incredible, with a dress selling out in a matter of hours because it is accessible to everyone.

'The same happened to Alesha with a quirky day dress she wore to one of the auditions. It was a colourful mismatch print by Mary Katrantzou for Topshop that cost £350. It sold out in a day.'

Newspapers and magazines were naturally hoping that Alesha would be competing with Amanda Holden in the fashion stakes. The strategy had worked for *The X Factor* when fashion commentators filled many pages comparing the outfits of Cheryl and Dannii Minogue or Tulisa and Kelly Rowland. It wasn't going to work on this occasion. At the very first audition, Amanda exclaimed, 'I won't stand for any bastard saying we're in a fashion war. I'm forty and up the duff.'

Amanda had taken the new girl aside over breakfast and warned her that everybody would try to pit them against one another. They had decided not to go down that road. The actress is not above being catty when she wants to be, however. When she was asked why Alesha might do better than Kelly Brook, who was ditched in 2009 after just two shows, she responded, 'She's probably got something else – a brain.'

Alesha and Amanda did genuinely become friends as the series progressed, however, often popping into each other's dressing rooms. They still had to put up with the 'women at war' sort of story but it wasn't true. A show insider revealed, 'You only have to see them together to see that they are friends. Simon chats with David while Amanda talks to Alesha all the time during retakes and breaks. They pop into each other's dressing rooms and it's all "Hiya, darling, how are you?" They love each other. No star goes to another's dressing room if they don't get on. It doesn't happen.'

They didn't have much time to get acquainted at first. Amanda gave birth to a baby girl called Hollie just three days later. But then the new mother was on the critical list for a further three days after experiencing a 'huge loss of blood' during the delivery.

Amanda had suffered two miscarriages in the previous two years and had revealed after the birth of her elder daughter Lexi that she had a condition called placenta previa, in which a low-lying placenta blocks the birth canal and can lead to severe bleeding. She needed an emergency blood transfusion to save her life.

Deprived of the chance to exaggerate ill feeling between Alesha and Amanda, there were some half-hearted attempts to suggest a row between her and Simon Cowell. One newspaper even suggested it was 'war'. Simon had apparently said on air, 'What a silly comment to make. That's a silly thing to say, Alesha.' He also joked drily, 'Sorry, who are you, anyway?' It was pantomime stuff and was duly booed by the audience in Birmingham.

Alesha didn't take it to heart nor did she storm off to her dressing room as one paper suggested. That was 'rubbish'. She was annoyed, however, with the boys constantly winding her up over being single. She told *Celebs on Sunday* magazine, 'Oh my God, they have annoyed me. I'm the bait – every man that auditioned whether he was eight or eighty, David was like "I think he'd be good for you, Alesha". I let it get to me – it actually wound me up and I ended up telling them both to shut up.'

The atmosphere on the judging panel was completely relaxed and full of laughter, mainly thanks to David Walliams, who revealed himself to be a master of the format. He poked fun at Simon, who more often than not dissolved into a fit of the giggles in a very unCowell-like manner. When the panel was discussing whether the Queen would like one of their acts, David chipped in, 'Don't worry, they're not talking about you, Simon.' He saved his best joke for his opening remarks in the final: 'When I woke up this morning, I turned to my Simon and I said ... this is the big one.'

Alesha couldn't compete with that but then she didn't need to – as long as she laughed her famous laugh, which one critic wrote sounded like a donkey with asthma. Instead she was feisty and compassionate. She wasn't standing any nonsense from a contestant who told her she didn't know what freestyle dancing was because all she had done was ballroom. She responded, 'I don't play the drums, but I still know what a drum kit is!'

But when, at the London audition, a nine-year-old boy called Malakai Paul was overcome and stopped singing, Alesha rushed on stage to comfort the sobbing child. She soothed, 'Are you all right, sweetheart? You did so good. You tell me if you want to sing or not.' He pulled himself together, carried on his performance of 'Listen' by Beyoncé and won through to the live finals.

By this time, Amanda had returned to the show and she and Alesha were able to continue their friendship. Alesha even sent her the link to watch the now notorious Tulisa sex tape. They also had to join together to respond to the many stories about Simon Cowell's sex life after a new biography alleged he had conducted a brief affair with Dannii Minogue and lusted after Cheryl Cole. 'We would never sleep with Simon' ran the headlines. Amanda said, 'I'd never be another notch on his bedpost. I'd very much rather be his friend because friendship lasts longer.' Alesha told the *Sunday Mirror*: 'No amount of money in the world would make me sleep with Simon. I've told him a million times that there are some things money can't buy and that's love. Look, I will not be in one of his books as the new judge he fancies in the future. Trust me.'

It was all great publicity for *Britain's Got Talent*, which after a shaky start against the *The Voice* completely trounced its BBC rival. The final was watched by an average of 11.9 million viewers while only 5.6 million were tuning in to the singing contest. The peak audience figure during the show was 14.5 million. It was a resounding vindication of Cowell's revamp of the panel and the introduction of a £500,000 first prize.

Normally Alesha spends three hours a week going through her outfits with her stylist. But the preparation needed to be much more intensive for six consecutive nights of live television. Some times she was more successful than at others. The best were probably a Mary Katrantzou digital print dress and a Marios Schwab design described by Alison Jane Reid as a Barbarella goddess gown. The former was colourful and elegant. Alison Jane observes, 'It created the effect of a modern showgirl and managed to be extrovert and colourful while still being wonderfully sexy.'

Alesha was prepared to take fashion risks during the series and, while she was perhaps better suited to the daytime dresses she wore at auditions, she was never less than striking. Alison Jane was impressed, 'Alesha has the body of a Bond girl and the charisma, grace and beauty to carry it off to dazzling effect. She is becoming a fashion icon not just for black or mixed-race women but for all women.'

The icon was suitably pleased when Ashleigh and Pudsey won. She gave the impression that she might have voted for the urban boy group, The Mend, if she had been at home, but she also has a genuine love of dogs, something she shares with Simon Cowell.

After Pudsey's amazing routine, she told Ashleigh, 'For anyone out there in this country who treats animal cruelly, what you're doing is showing them how special dogs are and what you can do and achieve with the right owner and love.' It was the best possible result for the show's future and, therefore, indirectly for Alesha's.

After a final celebration at the Dorchester Hotel, Alesha dropped out of the spotlight again, as she prefers to do when she isn't actively promoting her career. She is secretive about her life and prefers to live as much as possible without the constant attention of the paparazzi. Only occasionally do they infiltrate her life, as in August 2010, when she was pictured having a serious row in the street outside Movida.

She enjoys going out clubbing but can rely on a small posse of loyal friends to watch her back and keep her name out of the newspapers. She would have hated the story that there was a new man in her life, which appeared during the *Britain's Got Talent* series. The *Daily Mirror* carried a story saying that she was in a romance with a model and former backing dancer called Azuka Ononye.

They had been photographed together on the balcony of a room at a five-star yoga retreat, Shanti-Som near Marbella on the Costa Del Sol. According to the article, they had known each other for six years. It was impossible to know from the picture whether they were really together or just holidaying with a group of friends.

The paper quoted a friend: 'Everyone's really excited that Alesha has found love again. They get on brilliantly and Alesha likes the fact Az isn't a celebrity and is just a normal, down-to-earth guy.'

Az may be the new love of her life, a good friend or just someone she fancies. He is her type, however. MC Harvey was a well-built, fit young black man. So were Noel Simpson and two less serious boyfriends, John Carew and James Chandler, as well as various men she has been linked to over the years.

Her former husband, Harvey, has had a difficult time. He told *New*! Magazine, 'The past three years have been the toughest in terms of my personal life, and professionally I actually felt like I was blacklisted by the industry. It felt like I'd murdered someone!' He is still recording and released a single with ex-football Leon McKenzie called 'Finally' earlier in the year. He is also acting and appeared in the *The Big I am*, a British gangster film that starred Michael Madsen.

Harvey is no longer in touch with Alesha but sees Javine regularly when he calls to pick up his daughter Angel who he dotes on. He is still gracious about his ex-wife in interviews, praising her work ethic and wishing her all the best in her new television career with Simon Cowell. Javine continues to pop up on reality shows and came second in *Celebrity Come Dine With Me* in 2010.

Alesha is still friends with Noel and announced Damage's summer concert at the Jazz Café in Camden Town on her Twitter page. Damage had decided to reform in 2009 after meeting up regularly for dinner. One day they were sitting around Noel's kitchen table and started talking about a reunion. They made their comeback in July 2010, first performing in Dagenham, supporting Stacey Solomon, and then at Leeds Party in the Park.

Noel is now happy in a steady relationship and is enjoying being the father of a little boy. He still cares passionately about his new career managing a youth centre and helping young people.

His old girlfriend Alesha Dixon is also a person who cares passionately about the important things in her life. She is Avon's Beauty and Empowerment Ambassador, supporting the company's domestic violence initiatives. One in four women in this country alone is being abused. She declared, 'It's an issue that needs more attention. It's horrific and it's heartbreaking.'

Her mother Beverley has completely turned her life around and is now a happy and content woman who has been in a relationship for more than ten years. She has become a very talented painter and is still always available to walk her daughter's beloved dogs.

Alesha had added a third to the gang, a cocker spaniel called Rosy. She remains passionate about animal welfare. She supports the vet's charity PDSA and, as part of a £6 million Pet Hospital Appeal, modelled specially designed T-shirts starring the children's characters Roobarb and Custard.

She also backed an organization called PetRetreat, which arranges fostering for pets trapped in a house where domestic abuse is taking place. She explained, 'Animals are the silent and often forgotten victims of abuse. Not only do they have to live in the same household, but they can live in fear of what could happen to them should the abuser lash out at them as well. As around half of households in the UK own a pet, it's not surprising that many families seeking refuge from domestic abuse have animals that need taking care of while they get settled.'

Alesha says she's single and prefers the company of her dogs. She appears very self-sufficient and you wouldn't blame her if she ran a mile from any commitment to a serious relationship in the future. She remains closest to her mother.

Like all single women in show business, she has to put up with lots of stories speculating about children. Usually they say she's getting broody, although her funniest response was when she was speaking to Fearne Cotton: 'I don't want to have them before I have kind of done the things I want to do but I also don't want to leave it too late. So it's kind of striking that balance, plus I need to find someone to donate me some sperm. Ha ha!'

Her most poignant remarks about it were made during the documentary *Don't Hit My Mum* in which she said, 'Our responsibility as adults is to put children first. That is probably why I don't have them yet, because I believe the day I have them is the day I have to become a selfless person and their needs come before mine.'

For the moment Alesha clearly has unfulfilled ambitions. Her television career is thriving. As well as her *Britain's Got Talent* duties, she presents a BBC programme called *Alesha's Street Dance Stars* that aims to find the best young dance crew, aged eleven to sixteen, in the UK. She spent part of the summer of 2012 attending auditions around the country for the second series. Quietly, and without much publicity, the show has become very popular. She seems to have been desperately unlucky in her music career to date and deserves to be more successful. Perhaps the new music she is working on will change that. She may pop up as a judge on *The X Factor* or, in the future, Simon Cowell could introduce her to an American audience on *The X Factor USA*. Americans would respond well to her great beauty and elegance and, unlike Cheryl's Geordie speech, her accent tends to be one easily understood there. But would she ever want to leave her friends and family for a long period of time? She will undoubtedly continue to show her serious side in documentaries and, in a perfect world, would end up as the new Oprah Winfrey, a dream she has said she would love to achieve.

Alesha is already a star, of course, arguably the biggest black or mixed-race female personality on British television. But you never think of the colour of her skin. She's just Alesha really, the beautiful girl from Welwyn Garden City with a great laugh and a dazzling smile. Her ability to bounce back from the worst of situations, both personally and professionally, has earned her a special place in the hearts of the people. A national treasure? Yes, she is.

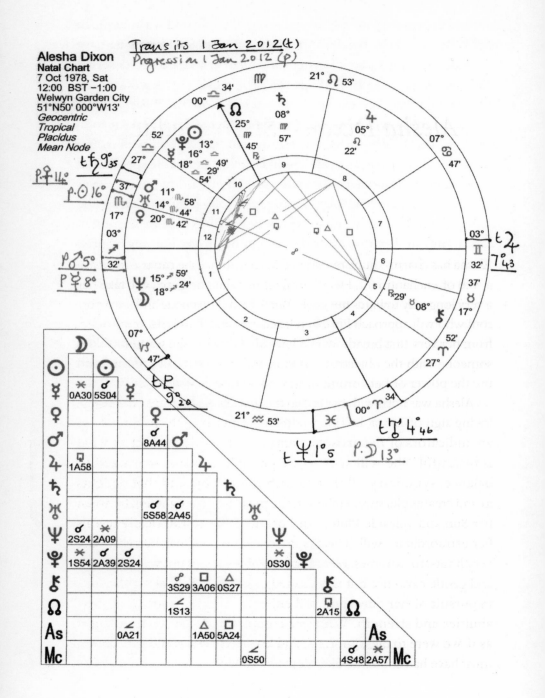

Alesha Dixon
Natal Chart
7 Oct 1978, Sat
12:00 BST −1:00
Welwyn Garden City
51°N50' 000°W13'
Geocentric
Tropical
Placidus
Mean Node

Transits 1 Jan 2012 (t)
Progression 1 Jan 2012 (p)

Alesha Dixon – Steely Goddess

Alesha has charm – huge reserves of it; charm that she can use to weave a web of enchantment. Her natural refinement and grace will take her a very long way towards her goals. But Alesha is no gentle and unearthly soul who will approach life in a relaxed manner. This is someone who, from her very first breath, would have known what she wanted. This is someone with the objectivity, passion and instinct to set priorities and use the power of her communicative skills to reach her goals.

Alesha was born with her Sun in the sociable, cooperative, harmony-loving sign of Libra, linking to dreamy, fantasizing Neptune. These are indicators of her artistic talents and ability to appreciate what is beautiful. She will seek to weigh up situations, sensitized to balance, symmetry, all that contributes to flow and that delights in and creates pleasure. However, the presence of a tight link between her Sun and volcanic Pluto, Lord of the Underworld, clearly reveals her extraordinary will. This is someone who will push herself to the very limits, to extremes. Here is someone who does not want a passive and gentle existence but is dedicated to walking right along the edge in pursuit of her quest and will enjoy the thrill of each test of her abilities and strength. Whoever commanded that we should live as if we were to die tomorrow, and learn as if we would live forever, must have had someone like Alesha in mind.

Those with Pluto dominant at birth invariably enter a world that seems challenging. Their overriding perception of existence is that it is serious and, while it might be fun on occasion, it generally involves power-play and struggles. Alesha's Sun and Moon, the planets associated with parental figures, are both linked to this planet of trials and her early years would have been witness to those closest to her undergoing experiences that involved destruction and regeneration. Pluto's story is that of a God, who is given rulership of the regions beneath the earth, where souls were sent after death. For company, Pluto abducted the maiden Persephone, who became his wife. Thus issues that involve abuse of power, matters that are taboo or shameful, things that people try to keep hidden, are associated with the planetary energy.

Alesha would doubtless have experienced the intense discomfort and sadness that came from the difficulties of the parental union and other home circumstances. One lesson would clearly have involved the need to make space for herself so that she did not feel constantly invaded or assailed by others' problems. Establishing this self-protective survival skill, an early privacy policy, means she will be an expert in handling communication – letting in only what is constructive and letting out even less, filtering instinctively. It will be very hard indeed for anyone to get to know the real Alesha and a serious partner would need to acknowledge this might be a lifetime task. On a more day-to-day level, this has obvious advantages for someone who has the talent and character to rise to the top of her chosen career. Alesha has a defensiveness, which will play out in not showing her hand until she is ready, steeliness and great sensitivity to anyone with a hidden agenda – she will spot this a mile off.

Another early issue might have involved actually getting herself heard. It is evident that in her home life this would be a challenge. Either she would have allowed circumstances to annihilate her sense of individuality or she would develop a powerful voice and make sure her interests became the interests of everyone else.

The Pluto link also inclines a person to impatience. Such souls do not suffer fools gladly and are quite able to sabotage those above them in authority if they are perceived as a threat in some way.

Alesha's Moon, the planet associated with the mother, was in the adventurous sign of Sagittarius at birth, suggesting a parent who is naturally philosophical and positive; for the most part, seeking lessons in the classroom of life. A certain restlessness may have been an ingredient of her outgoing and generous personality. A link to the planet Neptune, Lord of Compassion, suggests a person whose natural kindness, empathy and tolerance left her unable to establish self-protective boundaries. Alesha will have learned from her mother's experiences that having too much understanding and forgiveness is a huge disadvantage when confronted by undesirable or exploitative behaviour.

The link between the Moon and Neptune will manifest in Alesha as a yearning for something inspirational, something that will take her beyond the familiar and allow her to explore her creativity and spirituality. Here is a soul that wants to grow and soar. Alesha would have recognized early on that everyday situations, which would have provided security and satisfaction for some, would prove too ordinary and confining for her. Although she may not recognize this in youth, with maturity she will appreciate she has inherited this rejection of the ordinary from her mother. Emotional chaos, unfortunately, was the downside; wisdom, emotional intelligence, the positive.

Alesha's father provided a counterbalance. If her mother, at some level, could be impulsive, her father exhibited a more logical approach to life. Both planets that symbolize father in the chart, Sun and Saturn, are linked to Mercury, Lord of Connections and Travel. Her father would have wanted what he said to be taken seriously and his opinions to be respected. He may have had to deal with a paternal legacy of never feeling quite good enough. His way of dealing with this, of building self-worth through being of service in his work, useful in a precise, practical way, will resonate with Alesha, providing a bond of respect. She would have tried hard to please this charismatic, sensitive man, who was capable of being quite critical both of himself and those close to him. His influence in her early years would have been significant. Even if physically his presence was short-lived, his voice would become internalized in Alesha, pushing her to do better, to succeed and thus to heal the pain of abandonment.

Alesha grew up with people prepared to take emotional risks. A Moon–Jupiter signature evokes a mother who had faith in life, and a tendency to bite off more than she could chew; the links between the Sun, Uranus and Pluto suggest a father who felt or became redundant to the family. Of equal importance to both parents was a need for space, both literally and in their personal lives. Alesha's childhood would have been one with few rules and much freedom. However, despite the tribulations that disengaged parenting doubt-less brought, Alesha's birth chart supports the idea that overall she benefited from these conditions. This open, highly unpredictable background was perfect for developing her creative talents. While many aspects of her unconventional circumstances would have brought discomfort, Alesha will have learned – and quite quickly too – a positive message: that inner conflict and outer trials are not only acceptable but are indeed the source of growth and creativity.

Alesha's own need for challenge and autonomy are clear from these links between the Sun, Moon and heavyweights Neptune and Pluto. Reinforcing the message is a grouping of the planets Venus and Mars, symbols of male and female energy and relationships, placed either side of rebellious, wilful Uranus. Here is someone who simply isn't programmed to deal easily with long-term day-to-day commitment, including the conventional marriage scenario. What will inspire her will be intense, exciting liaisons, passionate associ-ations often with built-in meltdown. This will be the case with both romantic attachments and personal or working friendships. Alesha may have relationships that go on for decades, but such links will be the exception rather than the rule and the need for each individual to have space will need to be acknowledged and met from the start.

This is partly because Alesha can prioritize and will draw upon this strength to identify those people who can best help her attain her goals. She is enormously hard-working, often obsessive about detail. She has been gifted with skills and talents and will feel a strong obligation to develop these and then use them to be of service to others. Often her life is about learning and she will welcome those people who can provide the chance to cover new ground, whether exploring emotional territory or otherwise.

The Venus–Uranus–Mars planetary grouping emphasizes her enormous energy and passion for beautiful movement. Sometimes this will come and go but her dynamism is an essential part of her character. She is resourceful, can make quick decisions and easily get herself out of tight corners, and will bring originality to her art. Her honesty and willingness to go against convention will earn her popularity. On the negative side, Alesha can be tactless, stubborn and wilful. She will act instinctively in a crisis and jettison baggage in lightning fashion, like the professional survivor she has been from the word 'go'. For her life is about continual reinvention – death and rebirth – urgent creativity and, ultimately, service to others.

Over half the planets in Alesha's chart are in signs associated with relationships. Specifically, these are civilized, bridge-building Libra, and possessive, intimacy-loving Scorpio, which hint at the great importance of her emotional world and friendships, whether social or more intimate. What is clear is that this may often be something of a combat zone, albeit one with an increasing gloss of refinement as she matures.

Fortunately for a public now expectant but saddened by bright comets that flash by with their trail of debris, Alesha has a rock-solid foundation. This is revealed by great Saturn, Lord of Time, High

Standards and Quality Assurance. Where Saturn resides in the chart is where we find fear. Placed in Virgo, in Alesha's chart, it is clear that she will have worried hugely about her talent, her self-deprecation driving her on to avoid mediocrity. Virgo embodies a certain self-sufficiency and Alesha will always derive great comfort from very practical objectives linked to generous visions that she can work on in her own time and space. Perfectionism can be a problem, grandiosity also, but her self-esteem will come increasingly from knowing she is a useful person whose efforts will pay off in helping others. Quite simply, this sense of purpose will ground her time and again when relationships become turbulent.

There is an exact and positive link between Saturn and Chiron, the planetoid known as the Wounded Healer, which reminds us of Alesha's troubled early years. She will use her own difficult experiences to heal and do so with the thoroughness and meticulousness one expects from Saturn in Virgo. This passionate, vibrant, creative person has a humanitarian mission and she will come at it with the originality that blows apart years without change instantly.

Alesha has a productive, highly successful year ahead of her. Three major planets, Pluto, Uranus and Jupiter, form very supportive links to important points in her birth chart, with key months being January, April, July and November 2013. The Uranus–Jupiter link that Alesha will experience most exactly at the beginning of April is often classified as genuinely lucky, bringing unexpected opportunity, as well as a sense of freedom, born of the confidence to take on anything new that life offers. It will present a chance to broaden herself in a way that will make her life more interesting and rewarding.

This year and 2014 will also be a period when the link between transiting Pluto and Alesha's Saturn, the planet that has so much to do with her ability to work hard at mastering her skills, will enable her to make slower but very profound changes. She will achieve greater recognition as an authority in her chosen field, hence gaining more power to progress in areas of particular interest. It is very important for those with tight Sun–Pluto links to be able to use their power legitimately, to be able to lead, and these beneficial aspects will take her further towards the goal of being of such acknowledged status in her chosen field that she can work more autonomously and call the shots.

There follows a more trying period in 2015. This is when the transiting Pluto forms a tense link, first to the Sun and secondly to its own natal position at the time of her birth. This latter aspect is one associated with those times of frustration and often forced transition commonly termed the mid-life crisis. Although she will only be thirty-six years old in January 2015, this is when she will encounter tests in terms of her integrity, values and health. It is likely that Alesha will hit her stride in terms of ambition but any excess of wilfulness or ruthlessness is likely to create opposition. It could be that expecting too much of her body will result in a period when she has to stop and rebuild herself. This is by no means a wholly negative time but one during which she will need to be more accommodating than she is normally comfortable with. Circumstances will demand a great deal of her over the course of this year and the next; relationships, whether personal or professional, may end if they constitute a barrier to her future growth. Steering a course through the challenges will ultimately be positive, providing she does not disregard practicality and remembers, as in all consideration she is very likely to, that her gifts are given to help others as well as herself.

Madeleine Moore
June 2012

Life and Times

7 Oct 1978 Alesha Anjanette Dixon is born in Queen Elizabeth II Hospital, Welwyn Garden City. Her Jamaican father, Melvin Dixon, is a refrigeration engineer and her mother, Beverley Harris, is a hairdresser. Alesha's first home is a council house in Sewells, a small street in Welwyn Garden City.

Sept 1982 Begins education at the Harwood Hill JMI and Nursery School, two minutes' walk from her house and described by a contemporary as a very 'right-on, sweet school'. Alesha's mother and father split when she was four.

Sept 1989 Starts at Monk's Walk School, where she excels in sports, representing Hertfordshire in the 200 metres and 4 x 100 metres relay. She also choreographs her own dances for school plays.

Oct 1996 Turns eighteen, expecting to become a PE teacher, but her life is changed when she is spotted at a London dance class by production company boss Louise Porter, who believes she can turn the teenager into a star.

July 1997 Boy band Damage release first album *Forever* and Alesha receives a special mention from Junior, the nickname of her boyfriend, Noel Simpson.

Oct 2000 Features in the video of the Damage song 'Rumours' after Noel presses for her to be involved.

Jan 2001 Mis-Teeq, featuring Alesha, Sabrina Washington, Zena McNally and Su-Elise Nash, release their first single, 'Why?', on Telstar Records.

April 2001 The remix of 'Why?' becomes their first hit, reaching number eight in the charts. Alesha heard the news at her mum's house in Welwyn Garden City with her family gathered round. She recalled that she started crying. Zena decides to leave the group and the other three make their first appearance on *Top of the Pops*.

June 2001 As a threesome, Alesha, Sabrina and Su-Elise release their second Mis-Teeq single, 'All I Want', and just miss out on number one, beaten by Shaggy featuring Rayvon with 'Angel'.

Sept 2001 Mis-Teeq are nominated as Best UK Act and Best Newcomer at the 2001 MOBOs. They perform their upcoming single 'One Night Stand', taking to the stage on Ducati motorcycles. Alesha is tenth in a one-off *Smash Hits* poll entitled the '100 Sexiest', which was won by Rachel Stevens of S Club 7.

Oct 2001 'One Night Stand' becomes Mis-Teeq's third consecutive top ten hit, reaching number five in the charts. Their debut album, *Lickin' On Both Sides*, is released and makes number three. Alesha dedicates the album to her mother but also thanks her boyfriend, MC Harvey, for bringing so much joy into her life.

Feb 2002 Alesha says they would love to win the BRITs after the group are nominated in the Best Newcomer category, but they miss out to boy band Blue. They support Shaggy on a nationwide tour.

March 2002 A fourth single from the album, 'B With Me', reaches number five in the charts. Announces her engagement to MC Harvey.

June 2002 Mis-Teeq perform the old Supremes hit 'Stop! In The Name Of Love' at The Queen's Golden Jubilee concert at Buckingham Palace.

Alesha says, 'It is the best gig I have ever played at.' Yet another single from the album, 'Roll On/This Is How We Do It', peaks at number seven. They perform in the Dance Tent at the Glastonbury Festival.

Sept 2002 Alongside veteran rapper LL Cool J, Alesha hosts the MOBO Awards for the first time at the London Arena. Mis-Teeq are shortlisted for Best Garage Act, which they win, and UK Act of the Year but they are pipped by Ms Dynamite.

March 2003 Mis-Teeq's best-known track, 'Scandalous', is released and reaches number two. Their second album, *Eye Candy*, comes out two weeks later and also makes the top ten at number six. The group are part of a £5 million ad campaign by Coca-Cola.

April 2003 Alesha tells *FHM* magazine that she has had sex in the toilets at a posh London club and has also tried it with handcuffs.

July 2003 'Can't Get It Back' is Mis-Teeq's seventh and last top ten hit.

Sept 2003 Mis-Teeq begin their first headlining tour at the Liverpool Royal Court. They support a new campaign for Cancer Research when they perform in Wolverhampton. They sign a £100,000 sponsorship deal with Reebok.

Oct 2003 Alesha and Harvey buy their first house together in an exclusive area of Welwyn for £317,000. They are engaged but have yet to set a date for their wedding.

Jan 2004 Alesha is invited by Pharrell Williams to star in the video for his band N.E.R.D's new record, 'She Wants To Move'. She gets on a plane to Los Angeles the next day.

Feb 2004 Mis-Teeq are nominated as Best Urban Act at the BRITs. 'Scandalous' is shortlisted as Best British Single.

April 2004 Telstar Records goes into administration with debts of £8.5 million.

June 2004 'Scandalous' is released in the US and reaches number thirty-five in the *Billboard* Hot 100.

July 2004 A compilation of the best bits from their first two albums, called *Mis-Teeq*, comes out in the US but fails to make an impact, peaking at number 125 in the charts. The Halle Berry movie *Catwoman* features 'Scandalous' on its soundtrack but fails to improve album sales.

Jan 2005 Mis-Teeq announce they are splitting up to 'explore other opportunities'. MC Harvey is arrested following a confrontation with a policeman in Welwyn Garden City. CS gas is used to subdue him.

March 2005 The last track Mis-Teeq recorded, 'Shoo Shoo Baby', appears on the soundtrack of *Valiant*, a Disney cartoon about an heroic wood pigeon in World War Two.

April 2005 A greatest hits album is the group's last hurrah and makes number twenty-eight in the UK.

June 2005 MC Harvey is sentenced to 150 hours' community service after being found guilty of assault and using threatening behaviour. Alesha becomes Mrs Harvey in a small, private ceremony at the idyllic St John's Church in Lemsford, on the edge of the famous Brocket Hall Estate. They honeymoon in Hawaii and Las Vegas.

July 2006 Appears on the last-ever edition of *Top of the Pops*, singing her first solo single, 'Lipstick'. Despite positive reviews, the song peaks at number fourteen when it comes out the following month.

Sept 2006 Loses out to Corinne Bailey Rae in the Best UK Female category at the MOBOs. Attends the first night of her husband's new musical, *Daddy Cool*, and afterwards, at the premiere party, is pictured with singer Javine Hylton, one of his co-stars.

Oct 2006 A second solo single, 'Knockdown', produced by hit factory Xenomania, reaches a disappointing forty-five in the charts, her lowest position to date.

Nov 2006. Parts company with Polydor. Her first solo album, *Fired Up*, never makes it to the shelves of UK record stores. Splits from Harvey after he admits he is having an affair with Javine.

Feb 2007 Lists her wedding dress for sale on eBay with a reserve price of £2,000. She accepts a bid of £7,500, with the proceeds going to charity, but it turns out to be a hoax. Co-presents *The BRITs Red Carpet* at Earls Court.

Sept 2007 Is announced as one of the contestants on the fifth series of BBC flagship programme *Strictly Come Dancing*. She is eighth in the early betting, behind Gethin Jones, the *Blue Peter* presenter. She only needs to take part in a group dance for the first programme.

Oct 2007 Dances the rumba with her professional partner, Matthew Cutler, and is placed third by the judges. Bruno Tonioli tells her, 'You have the seducing powers of Salome.'

Nov 2007 Scores two maximum ten points for her waltz, the first of eighteen she would score in the competition – a record. Supports Nickelodeon's See Something, Say Something anti-bullying campaign.

Dec 2007 Nightclub doorman James Chandler tells the *Sunday Mirror* Alesha is giving him private dances at home. Her brother, Mark Harris, reveals to the *News of the World* that they had an impoverished childhood and their mother was a victim of domestic abuse. As a result, Alesha cuts him out of her life. Wins *Strictly Come Dancing*, beating Matt Di Angelo from *EastEnders* in the final.

Feb 2008 Is granted a decree nisi in the High Court on the grounds of MC Harvey's adultery. Poses in a bath full of condoms as part of a safe sex campaign called Condom Essential Wear.

March 2008 Is dating the Norwegian-born striker John Carew, who plays for Aston Villa. Their relationship lasts two months.

May 2008 Launches the Radio Lollipop station for the Evelina Children's Hospital in London. She says that music can help sick children by taking their minds off their illness.

July 2008 Her first documentary for television is broadcast on BBC Three. Called *Alesha: Look But Don't Touch*, it reveals how our culture creates false images of beauty that ordinary girls can't live up to. She is unveiled as the new face – and legs – of Veet, the famous hair removal brand. Fronts VQ Day, the first national celebration of vocational achievement, at the Royal Opera House in London.

Oct 2008 Performs her new single, 'The Boy Does Nothing', on *Strictly Come Dancing*. The song would become her best-known solo hit the following month, making number five in the UK charts. Celebrates her thirtieth birthday.

Nov 2008 *The Alesha Show*, her first solo album in the UK, is released on the Asylum label nearly four years after the demise of Mis-Teeq. The album just fails to make the top ten but eventually goes platinum. Wins Ultimate Confidence Queen at the 2008 *Cosmopolitan* Ultimate Women of the Year Awards.

Dec 2008 Wins a poll for the sexiest legs in Britain run by bodywash company Skinbliss, beating Cheryl Cole into second place.

Feb 2009 'Breathe Slow', the second single from *The Alesha Show,* achieves her highest chart position to date at number three. The video has achieved more than 11.5 million hits on YouTube.

March 2009 Is one of nine celebrities, led by Gary Barlow, who climb Mount Kilimanjaro for Comic Relief. Alesha is the last to arrive at the summit, having struggled with altitude sickness and muscle pain.

May 2009 'Let's Get Excited', the third single from *The Alesha Show*, reaches number thirteen in the charts. Begins European tour supporting Enrique Iglesias.

July 2009 Is announced as the new judge on *Strictly Come Dancing*, replacing Arlene Phillips. Equalities Minister Harriet Harman suspects age discrimination and tells the House of Commons the decision is absolutely shocking; she calls for Arlene to be reinstated.

Aug 2009 Appears at the V Festival in Chelmsford and asks the crowd to support her on Saturday nights, when *Strictly*'s next series begins.

Sept 2009 Begins her new job as a judge on *Strictly Come Dancing* and faces some harsh criticism in the media. The *Sun* calls her the 'most hated woman in Britain'. Her ex-husband Harvey splits from Javine, the mother of his young daughter.

Oct 2009 Her younger brother John is fined £150 by St Albans magistrates for possessing a small amount of cocaine and cannabis. Her first solo nationwide tour, *The Alesha Show*, begins at the Royal Concert Hall in Nottingham. She hurts her neck on the opening night.

Nov 2009 Releases 'To Love Again', a song she wrote and recorded in a day in Los Angeles with Take That producer John Shanks. They order sushi to celebrate their achievement. Performs the song on *Children In Need*, which she co-hosts with Terry Wogan and Tess Daly. It reaches number fifteen in the charts.

Dec 2009 Lands a lucrative deal, potentially worth more than a million pounds a year, to be a brand ambassador for LA Fitness. Sings the classic 'Something's Gotta Give' with Bruce Forsyth at the *Strictly* finals in Blackpool.

Feb 2010 Receives her first solo BRIT nomination when 'Breathe Slow' is up for Best British Single but loses out to 'Beat Again' by JLS.

March 2010 Presents *Who's Your Daddy?*, a documentary for the BBC that focuses on the problems faced by children who don't know their fathers.

Sept 2010 'Drummer Boy' is the first release from Alesha's next album, *The Entertainer*, and represents a change in musical direction. The commercial reaction is disappointing and the single peaks at number fifteen. Sings track when she opens the Help For Heroes concert at Twickenham.

Oct 2010 Co-presents the MOBOs at the Echo Arena in Liverpool with Reggie Yates. 'Drummer Boy' receives a nomination for Best Video. Features as guest vocalist on 'Take Control' by Roll Deep.

Nov 2010 Performs new single 'Radio' on *Strictly Come Dancing* but, despite being written by Emeli Sandé, it only reaches number forty-six in the charts. Presents *Don't Hit My Mum*, her third BBC documentary, in which she portrays the problem of domestic abuse in the UK and describes the violence her mother had faced at home. *The Entertainer* flops, only making number eighty-four in the album charts.

Dec 2010 Flies to Miami to film video for new single and is pictured on the beach two days before *Strictly* finals. Has corrective bone surgery on her right foot.

Feb 2011 Teams up with Jay Sean for 'Every Little Part Of Me', the fourth and final single from *The Entertainer*. It fails to improve things and reaches a lowly number seventy-eight in the charts.

April 2011 Is one of eight celebrities who write an open letter to the *Guardian* calling for the public to boycott the Grand National, saying it is cruel. Alesha is supporting a campaign by the League Against Cruel Sports for a safer race.

June 2011 Parts company with record label Asylum. Her manager, Malcolm Blair, cites creative differences.

Aug 2011 Hosts *Alesha's Street Dance Stars*, a nationwide competition to find Britain's best young dance crew, on CBBC.

Sept 2011 Begins third series as a judge on *Strictly Come Dancing*, despite rumours linking her with a move to *The X Factor*.

Oct 2011 Presents the MOBOs for the third time. Her co-host at the SECC in Glasgow is young American R & B star Jason Derülo.

Dec 2011 Appears tipsy on *Alan Carr: Chatty Man* and apologizes on Twitter.

Jan 2012 It's official: Alesha confirms she is leaving *Strictly Come Dancing* to join the judging panel on *Britain's Got Talent*. Her new salary is a reported £350,000, compared with the £100,000 she was said to earn on the BBC show. Her song for the new Weight-Watchers campaign, 'Do It Our Way (Play)', is released on digital download. Attends first *BGT* auditions in Manchester wearing a bright yellow Acne dress.

May 2012 Announces, 'I can't cope. This moment is too much', after watching eventual winners Ashleigh and Pudsey perform during the final of *Britain's Got Talent*.

June 2012 Begins filming the second series of *Alesha's Street Dance Stars* in Manchester. Is working on her fourth solo album.

Acknowledgements

I had never been to Welwyn Garden City before. It's a pretty town, especially the centre, where it has a feeling of space and cleanliness. I was sitting outside a café in the main square when I started chatting to a couple of elderly gentlemen at the next table. They had lived there all their lives and knew lots about Alesha Dixon, the town's most famous daughter. They knew the pub where her dad used to play football and the theatre where her grandmother took an active role.

It was typical of a place where there was a strong sense of community. The pub they mentioned, the Hollybush, was a very friendly local full of people happy to chat about Alesha, who is clearly a very popular figure thereabouts. Everyone I chatted to wished her well and felt protective towards her, perhaps a quiet acknowledgement of the tough times she has faced. Thanks to everyone who spoke to me on my travels and helped me with this book.

I wanted to say a special thank you to Noel Simpson of Damage for his courtesy and help. I wish him and the rest of the boys good luck with their ongoing comeback. I would like to mention the brilliant producer Karl 'K-Gee' Gordon and Louise Porter, who was an enormous influence in Alesha's early professional life.

Thank you to everyone at my publishers, Simon & Schuster, for their continued support: my publisher Carly Cook, who has been so enthusiastic about this project, and her brilliant team – Jo Whitford, Briony Gowlett and Emily Husain; Jo Edgecombe for overseeing production; Lizzie Gardner for my new jacket design; Emma Harrow for publicity; and Rumana Haider and Gill Richardson for looking after the all-important sales.

Thanks to my agent, Gordon Wise, who continues to guide my career with great skill, and his assistant at Curtis Brown, John Parton. I am grateful to my superb researchers – Esther Boateng, Catherine Marcus, Julia Mannfolk, Alison Sims, Emily Jane Swanson and Patricia Westaway. Thanks also to Jen Westaway for transcribing my interviews and to copy-editor Arianne Burnette for her sterling work on the manuscript. We have come a long way since our first book together on Justin Timberlake.

My old friend Kevin O'Sullivan provided great insight into the world of *Strictly Come Dancing* and *Britain's Got Talent*. Alison Jane Reid is one of the UK's leading fashion commentators. She is currently a contributing feature and fashion writer to *The Lady* magazine as well as a regular writer for *Country Life*, *Coast* and Illustrated London News Group. When not interviewing famous people, she has her own 'English eccentric' magazine online: www.ethical-hedonist.com. There are some superb online music sites these days and I urge you to check out HitQuarters particularly if you have ambitions in the record business.

Madeleine Moore has again produced a fascinating birth chart. I strongly recommend you read what she says about Alesha's stars. You can also read more about my books at www.seansmithceleb.com.

Finally, thank you to Jo Westaway for her patience, good humour and research – and coming down the pub with me to discuss it.

Sean Smith is the UK's leading celebrity biographer and the author of the number one bestseller *Cheryl*, the definitive biography of Cheryl Cole, as well as bestselling books about Robbie Williams, Tulisa Contostavlos and Kate Middleton. His books about the most famous people of our times have been translated throughout the world. His subjects include Kylie Minogue, Justin Timberlake, Britney Spears, Victoria Beckham, Jennifer Aniston and J. K. Rowling. The film *Magic Beyond Words: The J. K. Rowling Story* was based on his biography of the Harry Potter author. Described by the *Independent* as a 'fearless chronicler', he specializes in meticulous research, going 'on the road' to find the real person behind the star image.

PICTURE CREDITS

© Getty: 1, 2, 11, 12, 16, 17, 21, 22, 23, 24, 30, 32, 33, 34, 39
© Rex Features: 3, 4, 6, 8, 10, 13, 15, 18, 20, 25, 27, 37, 40, 42, 43
© PA Images: 7, 9, 14, 19, 26, 29, 31, 41
© Big Pictures: 28, 35, 38
© Exposure: 36

Index

Index

Index

Index